Literary and Cultural Representations of the Hinterlands

This interdisciplinary collection explores the diverse relationships between the frequently ignored and inherently ambiguous hinterlands and their manifestations in literature and culture. Moving away from perspectives that emphasize the marginality of hinterlands and present them as devoid of agency and "cultural currency", this collection assembles a series of original essays using various modes of engagement to reconceptualize hinterlands and highlight their semiotic complexity. Apart from providing a reassessment of hinterlands in terms of their geocultural significance, this book also explores hinterlands through such concepts as nostalgia, heterotopia, identity formation, habitation, and cognitive mapping, with reference to a wide geographical field. Literary and filmic revisions of familiar hinterlands, such as the Australian outback, Alberta prairie, and Arizona desert, are juxtaposed in this volume with representations of such little-known European hinterlands as Lower Silesia and Ukraine, and the complicated political dimension of First World War internment camps is investigated with regard to Kapuskasing (Ontario). Rural China and the Sussex Downs are examined here as writers' retreats. Inner-city hinterlands in Haiti, India, Morocco, and urban New Jersey take on new meaning when contrasted with the vast hinterlands of megacities like Johannesburg and Los Angeles. The spectrum of diverse approaches to hinterlands helps to reinforce their multilayered and multivocal nature as spaces that defy clear categorization.

Ewa Kębłowska-Ławniczak is a Full Professor of English Literature and Comparative Studies at the University of Wrocław, Poland, where she teaches English literature and cultural and adaptation studies. Much of her research has focused on visuality and the nexus of space and literature. She is the author of *Shakespeare and the Controversy Over Baroque* (Wrocław UP); *Visual Seen and Unseen: Insights into Tom Stoppard's Art* (Wrocław UP); and *From Concept-City to City Experience* (Atut 2013). She co-edited several collections of essays including the latest (with Eva C. Karpinski)

Adaptation and Beyond: Hybrid Transtextualities (Routledge 2023), she guest co-edited for the *Journal of Adaptation in Film and Performance*, and has been editor-in-chief of *Anglica Wratislaviensia* (Poland) since 2013.

Dominika Ferens is an associate professor of American literature at the University of Wrocław, Poland. Much of her research has focused on affect, race, gender, and sexuality in American literature. In *Edith and Winnifred Eaton: Chinatown Missions and Japanese Romances* (2002), she examined the paradoxes of Orientalism in the writings of two sisters of Chinese-English-Canadian descent. Her book *Ways of Knowing Small Places: Intersections of American Literature and Ethnography since the 1960s* (2011) looked at literature's quarrels and affinities with ethnography. Since 2006, she has co-edited the open-access *InterAlia: A Journal of Queer Studies*.

Katarzyna Nowak-McNeice is an associate professor of American literature and culture at the University of Wrocław, Poland, where she teaches American literature. She is the author of *California and the Melancholic American Identity in Joan Didion's Novels: Exiled from Eden* (2019; paperback edition 2020) and *Melancholic Travelers: Autonomy, Hybridity and the Maternal* (2007). She co-edited three volumes, *Representations and Images of Frontiers and Borders: On the Edge* (2022), *A Dark California: Essays on Dystopian Depictions in Popular Culture* (2017), and *Interiors: Interiority/Exteriority in Literary and Cultural Discourse* (2010). Her scholarly interests include critical posthumanism and global literatures in English.

Marcin Tereszewski is an assistant professor at the University of Wrocław, Poland, where he specializes in modern British fiction and literary theory. He is the author of *The Aesthetics of Failure: Inexpressibility in Samuel Beckett's Fiction* (Cambridge Scholars Press, 2013). His current research interests include an examination of psychogeographical and architectural aspects of dystopian fiction, particularly in relation to J. G. Ballard's fiction.

Literary Criticism and Cultural Theory

For more information about this series, please visit: https://www.routledge.
com/Literary-Criticism-and-Cultural-Theory/book-series/LITCRITANDCULT

Literary and Cultural Representations of the Hinterlands

Edited by
Ewa Kębłowska-Ławniczak,
Dominika Ferens,
Katarzyna Nowak-McNeice, and
Marcin Tereszewski

Routledge
Taylor & Francis Group

NEW YORK AND LONDON

First published 2024
by Routledge
605 Third Avenue, New York, NY 10158

and by Routledge
4 Park Square, Milton Park, Abingdon, Oxon, OX14 4RN

Routledge is an imprint of the Taylor & Francis Group, an informa business

Library of Congress Cataloging-in-Publication Data
Names: Kębłowska-Ławniczak, Ewa, editor. | Ferens, Dominika, 1964- editor. | Nowak-McNeice, Katarzyna, 1977- editor. | Tereszewski, Marcin, editor.
Title: Literary and cultural representations of the hinterlands / edited by Ewa Kębłowska-Ławniczak, Dominika Ferens, Katarzyna Nowak-McNeice, and Marcin Tereszewski.
Description: New York : Routledge, 2024. | Series: Literary criticism and cultural theory | Includes bibliographical references and index.
Identifiers: LCCN 2023037350 (print) | LCCN 2023037351 (ebook) | ISBN 9781032617718 (hardback) | ISBN 9781032617756 (paperback) | ISBN 9781032617732 (ebook)
Subjects: LCSH: Hinterlands in literature. | Hinterlands in popular culture.
Classification: LCC PN56.H535 L58 2024 (print) | LCC PN56.H535 (ebook) | DDC 809/.9332--dc23/eng/20230914
LC record available at https://lccn.loc.gov/2023037350
LC ebook record available at https://lccn.loc.gov/2023037351

ISBN: 978-1-032-61771-8 (hbk)
ISBN: 978-1-032-61775-6 (pbk)
ISBN: 978-1-032-61773-2 (ebk)

DOI: 10.4324/9781032617732

Typeset in Sabon
by MPS Limited, Dehradun

Contents

Contributors

Mona Becker is a postdoctoral researcher and teacher at the Department of English and American Studies at the Martin-Luther-University in Halle, Germany. She was awarded a PhD in playwriting in 2019 from the University of Essex. Her current research focuses on postmemorial narratives of National Socialist and colonial violence in anglophone fiction.

Dominika Ferens is an associate professor of American literature at the University of Wrocław, Poland. Much of her research has focused on affect, race, gender, and sexuality in American literature. In *Edith and Winnifred Eaton: Chinatown Missions and Japanese Romances* (2002), she examined the paradoxes of Orientalism in the writings of two sisters of Chinese-English-Canadian descent. Her book *Ways of Knowing Small Places: Intersections of American Literature and Ethnography since the 1960s* (2011) looked at literature's quarrels and affinities with ethnography. Since 2006, she has co-edited the open-access *InterAlia: A Journal of Queer Studies*.

Ewa Kębłowska-Ławniczak is a Full Professor of English Literature and Comparative Studies at the University of Wrocław, Poland, where she teaches English literature and cultural and adaptation studies. Much of her research has focused on visuality and the nexus of space and literature. She is the author of *Shakespeare and the Controversy Over Baroque* (Wrocław UP); *Visual Seen and Unseen: Insights into Tom Stoppard's Art* (Wrocław UP); and *From Concept-City to City Experience* (Atut 2013). She co-edited several collections of essays including the latest (with Eva C. Karpinski) *Adaptation and Beyond: Hybrid Transtextualities* (Routledge 2023), she guest co-edited for the *Journal of Adaptation in Film and Performance*, and has been editor-in-chief of *Anglica Wratislaviensia* (Poland) since 2013.

Barbara Klonowska works in the English Department at the John Paul II Catholic University of Lublin, Poland. She teaches courses on British literature and has published on contemporary British fiction and film. Her book-length studies include *Contaminations: Magic Realism in Contemporary British Fiction* (2006) and *Longing for Romance: British Historical Romances 1990-2010* (2014). With Zofia Kolbuszewska and Grzegorz Maziarczyk, she co-edited volumes of essays on utopia/ dystopia: *Echoes of Utopia* (2012), *(Im)perfection Subverted, Reloaded and Networked: Utopian Discourse across Media* (2015), and *Brave New Human in (Trans/Post)Humanist Utopias*. Her research focuses on contemporary literature, literary theory, and utopian studies.

Zofia Kolbuszewska is an associate professor of American literature at the University of Wrocław, Poland. Her research has focused on American postmodern literature and cinema, utopia, and forensic imagination. She has published *The Poetics of Chronotope in the Novels of Thomas Pynchon* (2000) and *The Purloined Child: American Identity and Representations of Childhood in American Literature 1851-2000* (2007); edited a collection of essays *Thomas Pynchon and the (De) vices of Global (Post)modernity* (2012); and co-edited *Echoes of Utopia: Notions, Rhetoric, Poetics* (2012), *(Im)perfection Subverted, Reloaded and Networked: Utopian Discourse Across Media* (2015), and *Borderlands: Art, Literature, Culture* (2016).

Marta Komsta is an assistant professor of English literature at Maria Curie-Skłodowska University in Lublin, Poland. Her research interests include representations of utopia and dystopia in film and literature, cultural semiotics, and ecocriticism. She has published in the journals *Critique: Studies in American Fiction* (with Emrah Atasoy), *Studies in American Fiction*, and *Utopian Studies*, among others. She is the author of *Welcome to the Chemical Theatre: The Urban Chronotope in Peter Ackroyd's Fiction* (Peter Lang, 2015) and the co-editor (with Justyna Galant) of *Strange Vistas: Perspectives on the Utopian* (Peter Lang, 2019).

S. U. Kriegel is a PhD candidate at the Department of English Studies at Freie Universität Berlin (Germany). She has taught a variety of classes on British and South African culture, media, and the history of the British Empire, and she has published on mobility in South African fiction. Her PhD dissertation focuses on mobility and space in South African literature and film in relation to questions of power. Other research interests include terrorism in a transatlantic context, gendered spaces, and the use of new media.

S. M. Mithuna is currently enroled as a PhD research scholar at the Department of Humanities and Social Sciences, Birla Institute of Technology and Sciences, Pilani (Hyderabad Campus). She completed her post-graduate studies in English language and literature at the

Institute of English, University of Kerala. Her research interests include criminology, film studies, and gender studies. Her ongoing research looks into the cinematic representation of gendered subjectivities in Malayalam Cinema through criminological perspectives.

Katarzyna Nowak-McNeice is an associate professor of American literature and culture at the University of Wrocław, Poland, where she teaches American literature. She is the author of *California and the Melancholic American Identity in Joan Didion's Novels: Exiled from Eden* (2019; paperback edition 2020) and *Melancholic Travelers: Autonomy, Hybridity and the Maternal* (2007). She co-edited three volumes, *Representations and Images of Frontiers and Borders: On the Edge* (2022), *A Dark California: Essays on Dystopian Depictions in Popular Culture* (2017), and *Interiors: Interiority/Exteriority in Literary and Cultural Discourse* (2010). Her scholarly interests include critical posthumanism and global literatures in English.

Paulina Pająk (PhD) works at the Institute of English Studies, University of Wrocław, Poland. Her research has focused on modernist literature and interwar print culture, memory in Virginia Woolf's works, the Bloomsbury Group, transnational publishing networks, and modernist legacies in culture. Recent publications arising from this research include articles and chapters in *Virginia Woolf and Heritage*, *Woolf Studies Annual, Anglica Wratislaviensia, Virginia Woolf and the World of Books, Politeja, Women's History Review*, and *Modernism/ modernity*. She has co-edited *The Edinburgh Companion to Virginia Woolf and Contemporary Global Literature*.

Izabela Poręba is a PhD candidate in literary studies at the University of Wrocław, Poland. She holds an MA in Polish philology and digital and network publishing. Her current research focuses on postcolonial theory and contemporary world literature, and her dissertation project explores the postcolonial strategy of re-writing. An affiliate editor of the open-access journal *Praktyka Teoretyczna*, she is also a member of the Olga Tokarczuk Ex-Center. In 2023, she edited a special issue of *Czasopismo Zakładu Narodowego im. Ossolińskich* on the postcolonial mapping of Polish literature. Her articles have appeared in *The Polish Journal of the Arts and Culture, Academic Journal of Modern Philology*, and *Śląskie Studia Polonistyczne*.

Sascha Pöhlmann is a professor of American literature and culture at TU Dortmund University in Germany. He taught at the universities of Bayreuth, Munich, Konstanz, and Innsbruck, and at Weber State University in Odgen, Utah. He is the author of four monographs on Thomas Pynchon and postnationalism, future-founding poetry from

Whitman to the present, the city and the road in American literature, and assassination in American fiction. He (co-)edited essay collections on Thomas Pynchon, Mark Z. Danielewski, foundational sites in modernity, electoral cultures, unpopular culture, American music, video games and American studies, and most recently flyover fictions.

Mateusz Świetlicki is an assistant professor at the University of Wrocław's Institute of English Studies and the director of the Center for Young People's Literature and Culture. His scholarship focuses on North American and Ukrainian children's and YA literature and culture, memory, gender, and queer studies, as well as popular culture and film. His latest book is *Next-Generation Memory and Ukrainian Canadian Children's Historical Fiction: The Seeds of Memory* (Routledge, 2023). He has published in English, Ukrainian, Polish, and Croatian.

Marcin Tereszewski is an assistant professor at the University of Wrocław, Poland, where he specializes in modern British fiction and literary theory. He is the author of *The Aesthetics of Failure: Inexpressibility in Samuel Beckett's Fiction* (Cambridge Scholars Press, 2013). His current research interests include an examination of psychogeographical and architectural aspects of dystopian fiction, particularly in relation to J. G. Ballard's fiction.

Maya Vinai is an assistant professor at the Department of Humanities and Social Sciences, Birla Institute of Technology and Sciences, Pilani (Hyderabad Campus). Her current research includes literary representation of the cosmopolitanism of port cities, spice-politics, territorialization of the seas, and battle of "outliers" in the Indian Ocean. Her publications are situated in such areas of research as literary interventions of the Gulf diaspora, as well as caste, gender, and identity in contemporary Indian English fiction. Her works have appeared in several journals of repute, including *Asiatic: IIUM Journal of English Language and Literature*, *South Asian Review*, and *Writers in Conversation*.

Raffael Weger studied sinology and comparative literature at the University of Vienna and Peking University. His paper "Magical Realism, Mythorealism and the Re-presentation of History in the Works of Yan Lianke" has been published in the *Routledge Companion to Yan Lianke*. Raffael Weger is a member of the LiBeratur Award jury and working as an independent reviewer for Litprom's translation funding initiative. His areas of research include contemporary Chinese fiction, magical realism, mythorealism, and climate fiction.

Editors' introduction

Hinterlands: A return of the outside

Ewa Kębłowska-Ławniczak, Marcin Tereszewski,
Dominika Ferens, and Katarzyna Nowak-McNeice

The countryside, suburbs, peripheries, edgelands, wilderness, heartlands, and hinterlands are not new to literary, cultural, or interdisciplinary studies of literary texts and film. Space, place, location, landscape, territory, distinct geographical regions (such as Canada's heartlands, Australia's outback, or the Eastern European Recovered Territories), as well as the long-established concept of literary setting and filmic location, define pertinent spatial relations, forms of organization, and geographical features essential for understanding literary works and audio-visual productions. Islands, mountains, deserts, groves, and other diverse imaginary and specific locations, sometimes supplemented with paper or digital maps, can be perceived as crucial distinctive features of such genres as traditional travel writing, life writing, regional fiction, pastoral poetry, and urban drama, as well as experimental city novels, mapping patterns of communication, and augmented cityscapes (Michel 153). The essays collected in this volume converge around the notion of hinterlands, a setting and a spatial concept which has been considerably underrepresented in literary studies. As will be shown in the following chapters, hinterlands represent a particularly potent type of space, both transgressive and heterotopic, a space that allows for the co-existence of otherwise contradictory social orders. The multifarious ways in which hinterlands operate within and between established locations present a challenge to any study of this topic; however, given the oftentimes marginalized status of these spaces, such a study also presents an opportunity to lay bare processes – economical, social, and psychological – that govern our perception and understanding of spaces that have remained outside mainstream interest.

The relatively recent eruption of interest in the otherwise neglected "outside" derives partly from the spreading popularity of Nordic noir, a mobile and adaptable genre which has exerted a significant influence on proliferating audiovisual and literary forms translated to sell successfully in Denmark, Germany, Poland, the United Kingdom, and the United States of America (Hedling 198). In line with the policy of the popular

DOI: 10.4324/9781032617732-1

Shakespeare Hogarth Project, a Nordic noir author of crime fiction, Jo Nesbø, was invited to write an adaptation of *Macbeth* (2018) in the noir style and produced a thriller located in a multilayered urban hinterland. Reaching far outside the geographical confines of the Scandinavian region, the style impacted popular serial drama production, notably in Denmark and in the United Kingdom, contributing to a new form of miniseries (Hansen 275). The list of productions which bring together the "bleak and the beautiful", revealing hinterlands both far and near, is long and, to name but a few, includes *Y Gwyll/Hinterlands* (S4C 2013–2016), *Broadchurch* (ITV 2013–2017), the Czech HBO Europe drama *Pustina/ Wasteland* (2016), the German Netflix series *Dark* (2017–), and the Polish *Rojst/The Mire* (Showmax 2018, Netflix 2019). This globally spreading style turned out to be so flexible and adaptable that it did not diminish the local colour of the specific locations. *Hinterland*, made twice by the same filmmakers, has a local Welsh and an English language version so that the linguistic complexity of the region has been preserved. Moreover, as reviewers observe, "the county of Ceredigion feels like an actual member of the cast" (Frost), not just a spectacular backdrop or location but a multimodal landscape partly revealed and partly concealed to provoke further investigation. The otherwise marginalized language (Welsh) and the often invisible or obscure, fuzzy locations of the hinterlands come to the fore. These rediscovered hidden, underrepresented areas, displaying their surprising epistemological potential, can be viewed through the lens of a "spatial turn" (Tally 2017, 3–4; Tally 2013, 11–42) or, more specifically, a "spatial anthropology" (Roberts 364).

Physical hinterlands: Geography, history, politics

Before the cultural currency and agency of hinterlands were rediscovered and acknowledged, most notably in popular culture, the "Hinterland Theory" or "Hinterland Doctrine", whose beginnings can be traced back to early twentieth-century historical and geographical concepts, would marginalize hinterlands as unexplored regions or *terra nullus* located "at the edge of places where history takes place, the port cities, oceans, or empires that integrate the hinterland into bigger historical narratives" so that consequently their inhabitants would be perceived as "recipients of change" and "without agency to create their own histories" (Unangst 499). Interestingly, the motif of cultural domination and regained agency pervades review comments written in response to both *Hidden/Craith* (2018 TV series) and *Hinterlands*. The originally geographical term introduced by George Chisholm in his 1903 edition of the *Handbook of Commercial Geography* described hinterlands in terms of physical and economic conditions whose spatial relationships took on political meaning somewhat later, involving definite cultural and historical implications. Eventually, the notion of the *hinterland* "behind a seaboard" (Chisholm 54) would pervade imperialist discourse, support colonialism and justify numerous expansion projects launched in the 1880s, the twentieth century (Unangst 508; Patel 74), and later. Although the geographical vocabulary could be altered (Walter Christaller referred to primitive regions in need of deterritorialization and reterritorialization), the aim was political and economic expansion. Ultimately, the tangible physical hinterland as the outlying area would dissolve into other terms denoting control over territories both distant and near that came into the sphere of diverse political and economic "interests" of the agent or centre.

In the *Encyclopaedia of Urban and Regional Studies* (2019), Evy Mehzabeen argues that the once definable hinterland has become "one of the most fluid of spaces" (5). Though the entry provides a list of tentative definitions resting on a relationship between a "core" and some "peripheral space" called hinterland, the divide is no longer easily definable because their borders overlap. Though we still refer to cities, the city can be traced everywhere (Amin and Thrift 1), so the traditional divide between the city and the country, used both in human geography and in literary studies as the heritage of Raymond Williams' *The Country and the City*, cannot be easily maintained. On the contrary, Amin and Thrift emphasize the permeability of urban borders and social heterogeneity (5), which replace the former stability and homogeneity of the urban centre with urban processes, functions, and mobility. Phil A. Neal's *Hinterland: America's New Landscape of Class and Conflict* (2018) concentrates on this new mobility and urbicide resulting from a sudden inflow of the variously excluded hinterland population into cities, which "leads to an overloading of [their] metabolism ... , and therefore the beginning of politics proper" (12). Distinguishing between "far" and "near" hinterlands, Neal points to their "distinct political dynamics" (17). Though the "far" hinterlands are largely deindustrialized and more distant areas – which are sometimes called "rural" and include "urban zones of collapse" (18) – they are no longer to be considered peripheries. The "near" hinterlands surround cities with towering blocks and, as Neal argues, take the form of suburban slum areas (18) not to be mistaken for suburban middle-class prosperity.

From spatially bounded concept cities to planetary urbanism

For hinterlands to (re)gain their heterotopic and fluid state, and thereby reassert themselves in relation to other more visible spaces, the stable definition of the "traditional city" had to be disrupted (Amin and Thrift; Henri Lefebvre). Understood as containing the three tropes of city-country opposition, the city as a self-contained system, and the city as an ideal type (Wachsmuth 359), the traditional city in the twentieth century, and especially in the 1960s, saw a large-scale epistemological shift in determining the urban in opposition to the idea of the rural. With massive industrialization and suburbanization, as well as significant demographic and socioeconomic shifts within these regions, such clear-cut distinctions no longer hold any currency, requiring urban theoreticians and cultural geographers to re-evaluate how to fruitfully approach the structural and social definitions of the urban.

In the 1990s, the concept of the "spatially bounded city" was further questioned by, among others, William Cronon (*Nature's Metropolis*, 1991) and later on by Matthew Gandy (*Concrete and Clay: Reworking Nature in New York City*, 2002). The cities emerging from their books both define and are defined by their hinterlands, and the line of demarcation between the two spaces becomes fuzzy. By invoking current understandings of the hinterland, we hope to avoid the no longer sustainable demarcation between urban and non-urban naturalized by such writings as Raymond Williams's *The Country and the City*.

Henri Lefebvre's concept of planetary urbanization was an important catalyst for much of the thinking that would dominate urban studies in the decades to come. The realization that the process of urbanization is not limited to the city rendered obsolete the traditional rural/urban distinction in how we think about the city, thus inaugurating the possibility of thinking about "other" sociospatial arrangements that do not conform to stable epistemological patterns. This line of inquiry was further bolstered by the so-called spatial turn in literary and cultural studies, which asked to conceptualize spaces no longer as absolute but as relative (Henri Lefebvre in *The Urban Revolution* and Gaston Bachelard in *The Production of Space*).

Predicting the complete urbanization of society, Lefebvre posited a distinction between the city (as a form) and urbanization (as a process), the former being only one of the many possible manifestations of the latter. One can draw borders on a map for administrative purposes, but these artificial lines fail to adequately delimit these new forms of socio-spacial organization: "The inner boundedness of the traditional city and of our traditional notion of the city form was prised open by the advent of the industrial city" (Merrifield 167). New modes of transport, bringing about what David Harvey terms "the time/space compression" (201–26), together with new technologies and infrastructure created new spatial organizations requiring not so much a new vocabulary but new underlying assumptions. The concept of planetary urbanization inaugurated an epistemological shift towards an analysis of a process rather than a defined structure, a process that takes care to acknowledge its constitutive network of relations. The implications and challenges of this shift are far-reaching not only in the field of cultural geography, but also for literary research. The needs are to rearticulate long-held assumptions, to redefine staid perspectives, and to rethink the urban requires jettisoning traditional concepts of industrial growth; this need accounts for the futuristic rhetorical imagery present in the works of science fiction and speculative fiction which grapple with the emerging patterns of planetary urbanization in a way that is not bound by geographical determinants.

Within the paradigm of planetary urbanism, localities which had previously been relegated to "outside/hinterland" status – whether manmade (motorway networks, industrialized zones, ports, tourist enclaves) or natural (deserts, jungles, mountain ranges, the wilderness) – are now seen as taking part in a globalized urban structure. Hinterlands are thus just one of the many marginalized spatial entities which have now reasserted themselves as spaces with agency and meaning. Neil Brenner and Christian Schmid develop the idea of the "disintegration of the 'hinterland'", that is, of previously invisible areas which are now being repurposed to serve functions directly tied to urbanization – otherwise, empty spaces are now used for "back office and warehousing locations, global sweatshops, agro-industrial land-use systems, recreational zones, energy generation grids, resource extraction areas, fuel depots, waste disposal areas or corridors of connectivity" (161). A similar fate has befallen the concept of "wilderness", which in a like manner is undergoing a transformation by "unfettered worldwide urbanization" (162).

By destabilizing the definition of the traditional city, along with its tropes of self-containment and rural-urban dualism, "new urban morphologies" (Wachsmuth 354) have asserted themselves, challenging the privileged spaces of centrality. These possibilities have appeared as a result of the city being no longer treated as a tangible social object but rather as a city concept, a "sociological object"; that is, as an ideology "which partially helps obscure and reproduce relations of power and domination that critical spatial theory seeks to expose and confront" (Wachsmuth 354). The idea proposed by Lefebvre, amongst others, is to look beyond the city as a physical entity and treat it more like a concept "that mediates our everyday experience of urbanization processes that are too complex for us to directly perceive" (Wachsmuth 358). Because urban space cannot be experienced in its totality and thus exceeds analytical comprehension, it can be rendered intelligible only by way of ideological representation.

Cognitive mapping

Considering the complexity of the topic, this collection of essays must represent a spectrum of multiform, hybrid critical practices inspired by spatial humanities, philosophy, literary geography, sociology, critical urban theory, literary and cultural studies, assuming that creatives in the field of literature and film engage in literary geography and literary cartography, in their "representations" (Wachsmuth 354) or "figurations" (Jameson 348) of real and imagined spaces, including the increasingly enigmatic hinterlands. The new hinterlands, a problem rather than a concept or doctrine, escape clear-cut definitions and expand dynamically, blurring the borders between the "far" and the "near"; the visibility of everyday experience; and the invisibility of the flyover, the subterranean, uncanny and unhomely spaces and places. The ordering, "transparent abstraction of concept city" is either contested, replaced, or melts into what James Donald formulates as a "densely textured urban imaginary which produces an 'anthropological', poetic and mythic experience of space" (325) that is no longer geographically or scientifically mappable. The optimistic and influential phenomenology of cityness put forward by Kevin Lynch in *The Image of the City* (1960), where the hinterlands are mentioned only once, dissipates and subverts hitherto proposed concepts of habitation. In line with these subversions, one of the mottos in Ivan Vladislavić's *Portrait with Keys* (2006) recognizes haunted places or the uncanny as the only liveable ones. The South African writer and editor invokes Michel de Certeau's comments on the overwhelming loss of control over space, thus admitting to the massive "re-emergence of the elements that the urbanistic project excluded" (de Certeau 95) to comment further on the futility of scientific maps as unhelpful and generally unreliable cognitive devices. In the new post-apartheid and post-panoptic reality, experience teaches the narrator and "a host of [other] writers" that "getting lost" and "misdirecting" brings one closer to the truth than do landmarks (*vide* Lynch 101) and maps that paradoxically "prevent [us] from thinking too deeply" (Vladislavić 17). In search of new maps including the "far", remote, and poorly populated regions of the hinterlands, Neil Brenner observes that they are never "included in the conventional cognitive map of the urban age" but are treated as "an empty void" and "a massive blank space" (229), a new *terra nullus* or the otherwise invisible. Instead of regular city maps, Vladislavić proposes using book directories as cognitive maps providing some guidelines in cases where even maps of nighttime lights fail to visualize the non-city invisible zones (Brenner and Ibanez 229).

Spatial methodologies involving scientific maps and grids, ideologies, representations, or figurations encounter difficulties in addressing the experience of individuals and social change. While Neil Brenner and Martin Arboleda propose that the "spatial turn" should be superseded by a "relational" one involving a "myriad of spaces and actors ... thousands of kilometres away" (282), Hazel Andrews suggests, in broadly cultural terms, that mapping must proceed in conjunction with the "cognitive and mental" maps created by groups and individuals to include "different levels of practice and performance" (229). Therefore, seemingly banal but enigmatic places like hinterlands are not only entangled in networks of globally and horizontally expanding relations, but should be considered multimodal palimpsests or semantic constellations involving memory, affects, languages, "visual images, nonverbal communication, and the infrastructure of the surrounding environment" (Wee and Goh 1). Taking a more metaphorical route, and following perhaps Fredric Jameson's use of "cognitive mapping" – an aesthetic and pedagogical category, and a master-trope (347) – it is necessary to postulate a dynamic conjunction between the efforts to chart space and to unearth the "realm of meaning" embedded in the space (Hazel 325). It is affective meaning as well as histories and traumatic experience which enable us to gauge individual locatedness and the ways it "affects our collective identities" (Cevasco 84). In times of crisis when the marginal comes to the fore, Michael Titelstad argues, literature is exceptionally "well placed to mediate between analytic maps and particular pathways of meaning" (679); hence, the effort of the creatives to retrieve the lost, invisible, and hidden from oblivion. In a recent interview with Maria Elisa Cevasco, Jameson argues that the recovery of the "outside", that is of the margins, and the assumption of their perspective has an "epistemological advantage" over the blindness of the centre (87–88), though it definitely lacks either homogeneity or the reassuring sense of completeness.

Taking the perspective of the complex and "unmapabble" hinterland – hidden, marginal, disorienting, alienating, and overlaid with conspiracy plots (Jameson 351) – writers and film producers respond by pursuing suitable means of expression, film, and literary conventions. The gothic, eco-gothic, eco-criticism, Nordic noir, horror, crime fiction, and thrillers have reappeared globally, for instance in Australian fiction (Doolan 188) and European film (Hansen 275). Multimodal palimpsest landscapes of the hinterlands match multilayered storylines to uncover the underbelly of contemporary societies, their recent past overlaid with homogenizing narratives incapable of containing the complex relations between land, landscape, territory (Ingold 190), and setting. Instead, they stage absence and unspeakable or unrepresentable loss (Wilson 8). Hinterlands, unconfined by any specific representational idea of landscape (Roberts 368), admit the bland, the bleak, and the beautiful, offering a surplus of images on the one hand and, on the other, a deficit of landscape in terms of a place of habitation as defined by Tim Ingold, and a frame for the setting. The aesthetically rather than theologically governed landscape becomes autonomous (Martin Lefebvre 24). The return of the outside in the guise of hinterlands allows for an ex-centric perspective, which transforms the subservient frame and region into an autonomous location and *ergon*.

Though our treatment of hinterlands can be roughly divided into three categories, the collection presents a wide spectrum of critical practice where some approaches blend with others and clear demarcations seem impossible. Firstly, hinterlands are defined in relation to the extensions of agglomeration centres into what has historically been defined as peripheries, fringes, or fuzzy edges. Secondly, hinterlands are represented as far-away lands, territories, and heartlands – non-city spaces that Neil Brenner (2020) calls "operational landscapes", tied to urban cores and transformed into high-intensity infrastructures. Thirdly, they are metaphorical and real territories, sometimes located close to the heart of urban cores, invested with special qualities, notably their complex semantic constellation, which makes their assessment, representation, or figuration all the more difficult. In this way, the book deals with real, culturally specific hinterlands (American, Australian, Belorussian, Canadian, Chinese, English, German, Indian, Moroccan, Polish, Slovenian, South African, and Ukrainian) as well as with imaginary and metaphorical locations. The 16 selected essays are distributed among four distinct parts – "Hinterlands as Movement and Transit", "Heterotopic Hinterlands", "Regenerative and Nostalgic Hinterlands", "Hinterlands Revisited and Reimagined" – a tentative division or scaffolding we found helpful, though its value is by no means heuristic. Framing the volume are two essays about Los Angeles, one of the megacities that set the trends in planetary urbanism. While the first essay concerns Los Angeles' distant hinterlands, the last examines its internal hinterlands, offering theoretical insights for future research that further complicate our understanding of this term.

Part I: Hinterlands as movement and transit

The novels and films discussed under the heading "Hinterlands as Movement and Transit" map postcolonial, neocolonial, and post-industrial hinterlands by following displaced characters on the move. The uninhabitable or barely habitable hinterlands in question range from pockets of urban decay in New Jersey, villages within the economic orbit of Johannesburg, and the transnational hinterlands of megacities, to the Arizona desert, claimed as a temporary refuge by the unhoused, underemployed, and mostly elderly people sidelined by the late-capitalist economy. Each of the works takes stock of the material and psychological waste left in the wake of global urbanization, while thematizing human adaptability and resilience. Fragile coalitions form. Alternative values, both ethical and aesthetic, are shown to emerge on the move, as characters change vantage points and, forced to slow down, learn to pay more attention to each other and their surroundings. Whereas in some works the urban centre features prominently as the destination or precarious home of migrants from the hinterland, it is conspicuously absent from others. It becomes clear from the texts in this section that, due to globalization, hinterlands need to be measured on a sliding scale: some are internal or adjacent to megacities, others are far-flung and only recognizable as such when we follow the trails left by people, natural resources, money, and goods across enormous distances.

The asymmetrical relation between the metropolis and its distant hinterlands is thematized in Karen Tei Yamashita's novel *Tropic of Orange*, analyzed by **Dominika Ferens** in Chapter 1. While Los Angeles in *Tropic* has no apparent near hinterlands, it is fused with distant regions that are not immediately recognizable as hinterlands "because they are separated from the city by a border (Mexico) and an ocean (East Asia)", Ferens observes. "Economic growth in Los Angeles triggers crises in Mexico and across the Pacific, which then reverberate back in the city". Not only do processions of displaced people traverse the space of this novel, but the landscape itself is set in motion when the Tropic of Cancer becomes detached from the grid and drags the entire Mexican hinterland northward, deforming the physical space of Los Angeles. This upheaval, according to Ferens, serves as a vivid trope for the economic processes endemic to late capitalism, one that would otherwise be difficult to render in literary prose.

South Africa's legacy of banishing black bodies to the hinterland is the subject of **Sophie Kriegel's** Chapter 2 on Phaswane Mpe's novel *Welcome to Our Hillbrow*. "Mobility is not a good that is equally accessible to everybody", writes Kriegel. "It reflects power differences that privilege mobility over stasis and associate it with the more powerful. Hinterlands are often seen as remote, unimportant places of stasis, when in fact the centre depends on the resources that can be mobilized in the hinterlands". As the novel's protagonists shuttle between their ancestral village and the city after the fall of apartheid, they make obsolete the conventional distinction between the two spaces, Kriegel argues, for individual memory suggests endless positive and negative analogies. Based on these analogies, one protagonist builds a fragile new national identity for himself before committing suicide, while the other claims as her rightful place Oxford University, the educational hub of the metropolis for which South Africa was once a distant hinterland.

Ethical and aesthetic value shifts triggered by global socioeconomic upheavals are emphasized in **Zofia Kolbuszewska's** provocative juxtaposition of two films: Chloe Zhao's *Nomadland* and Jim Jarmusch's *Paterson* in Chapter 3. The protagonists of *Nomadland* roam the United States in their camper vans in search of temporary employment, periodically returning to a campground in Arizona to meet their community on wheels. Meanwhile, the protagonist of *Paterson* drives along the same daily route through the backwaters of a megacity, his bus providing a communal space for the passengers getting on and off. Forced to rely on each other because the postindustrial economy has stripped them of the illusion of self-reliance, the protagonists of these films use their limited agency for "community-building ... self-care, fixing and repairing, respectful handling of instruments, utensils, tools and equipment, as well as recycling and ecological proactivity". While Kolbuszewska asks us to contemplate the slow-cinema form of *Paterson*, its protagonist's aesthetic vision, and, more generally, "the power of poetry as a strategy of resisting the late-capitalist reduction of reality to economically assessed utility", she is far from claiming poetry as a shield against the "process of physical and social dereliction in the wake of havoc wreaked" by urban growth on the hinterland.

Part II: Heterotopic hinterlands

The chapters in this section address the interplay between the two titular concepts of hinterlands and heterotopias in their literary expressions. Michel Foucault's somewhat ambiguous concept of heterotopia, first introduced in a lecture for architects in 1967 and later developed in his essay "Of Other Spaces", has equipped critics with a potent theoretical instrument to describe places marked by alternative social ordering. By injecting alterity into the commonplace, heterotopias manifest themselves in opposition to ordinary everyday space, which allows them to function as counter-hegemonic sites of resistance. These are "counter-sites" where the "real" sites beyond the enclosed heterotopias can be represented and/or contested; in these places, the social order is suspended, reordered, or reconstructed, thereby offering a critical perspective on the established hegemonic social order.

The section begins with **Marta Komsta's** Chapter 4, "Spaces of Identity in Morocco: Maureen F. McHugh's Nekropolis", which investigates the heterotopian aspects of hinterlands in their geographical and psychological contexts. Komsta places the focus on the semiotic ambiguity resulting from the liminal nature of hinterlands, which in *Nekropolis* is presented by the interpretive ambivalence of the cemetery itself, resulting from the dual role it occupies; it is situated within the city wall, while at the same time being a periphery. The necropolis is also shown to have a subversive function, as it is a safe haven from the jurisdiction of a repressive religious state, becoming in effect a kind of utopia for its residents, a home to the outcast community who as such are invisible to the rest of the society. Not only places but also bodies are seen to function as heterotopias, both being positioned in opposition to hegemonic religious discourse, and it is precisely in this semiotic link between the representation of hinterlands as spaces of repression and at the same time as spaces of resistance that the Other can reclaim itself independently of hegemonic interpretation. Both the hinterlands and the protagonists' selfhood remain beyond comprehension and thus unknowable to one another, thereby asserting the impossibility of appropriating the Other.

A more explicitly postcolonial perspective is offered by **Izabela Poręba** in Chapter 5, "Unraveling the Haitian Hinterland as a Twofold Space: Dany Laferrière and Yanick Lahens", where she explores Haiti's topography by way of two novels: *Pays sans chapeau* by Dany Laferrière (1996) and *Douces déroutes* by Yanick Lahens (2018). Both novels investigate the Haitian capital, Port-au-Prince, in relation to the concept of hinterland, defined as the "spatialized other" of the imperial centre, a place necessary for the maintenance of the empire, but – much like the necropolis in Komsta's chapter – rendered invisible by the official narrative. Komsta draws attention to the fact that hinterlands are much more than spatial/topographical phenomena, as they are determined to a great extent by a discursive process, one which takes place within specific ideological determinants. The issue of how such hinterlands are formed is one of the prevailing themes of Poręba's chapter. Other themes taken up by Poręba revolve around alienation and exploitation which are seen to define the centre/margin relationship, and it is in this context that she reads Dany Laferrière's *Pays sans chapeau* as representing a heterotopic space of freedom centred around Port-au-Prince. This hinterland occupies an interesting position, as it is defined not only spatially but also temporally: nights become the heterotopic hinterlands, where the previously subjugated Haitian population regains its agency and identity. Poręba then moves to a discussion of Lahens's *Douces déroutes*, which looks at Port-au-Prince and the rapid and chaotic urbanization responsible for the formation of hinterlands. Poręba emphasizes the discursive nature of hinterlands in both novels, which are not entirely dependent on topography, but on political, social, and ideological demarcations separating the hinterlands from the rest.

A similar postcolonial vein runs through Chapter 6, **Barbara Klonowska's** "Haven, Rebellion, Revelation: Australian Hinterlands as Heterotopias in Peter Carey's Novels", which demonstrates the ways in which various Australian hinterlands depicted in *Bliss* (1981), *True History of the Kelly Gang* (2000) and *A Long Way from Home* (2017) function as spaces that have the power to expose the repressed and traumatic Australian past of racial violence. Klonowska starts by pointing out that Carey often employs juxtaposition and contrasts to construct his fictional spaces, which stage the tension between heterotopias and the dominant social and political discourses. Such is the case with the Australian hinterlands, a heterotopic space which Carey uses to challenge the established social order. Heterotopias are presented as taking on a myriad of sometimes contradictory positions: spaces of repression as well as spaces of rebellion. The spatial relations in *True History of the Kelly Gang* show a contrast between the world of nineteenth-century Irish settlers and the outback, which becomes a haven for outlaws seeking refuge from the repressive society of law. In *Bliss* (1981), we find a similar contrast between an Australian heterotopian hinterland, in this case a utopian intentional community nestled in a rainforest, and a conventional middle-class suburb. *Long Way from Home* (2017), on the other hand, contrasts a geographically faithful depiction of the mainly white population of south Australia with the native Aborigine population of the north. In her reading of these novels, Klonowska traces the development of the concept of hinterlands from places of safety and openness to those of danger and incarceration, or, as she sees it, from a conceptualization of space as passive to one with agency.

In line with Klonowska and Poręba, **Marcin Tereszewski,** in Chapter 7, "The Ethical Call from the Hinterlands: Conceptualizing Waste in J. G Ballard's *High-Rise* and *Concrete Island*", concedes that hinterlands do not necessarily have to be located on the peripheries of cities, but can be formed within them as well. This is the case in the two novels under consideration, which depict heterotopic hinterlands in close proximity to the urban centre, and it is there that Ballard stages the subversive and disruptive effects of hinterlands. Part of the cityscape, and yet somewhere beyond it, both the titular high-rise and the concrete island are presented as sites of resistance against the prevailing values of the established culture. The protagonists of both novels find themselves at first stranded in and then voluntarily inhabiting these heterotopic spaces of disorder and societal chaos, each reflecting the ordered civilization outside its bounds. Tereszewski approaches this topic by way of waste studies (and, by extension, thing theory), which problematizes how discarded objects exhibit an ambiguous ontological status, especially in a capitalist environment. In much the same way that waste can be seen to reassert itself, hinterlands, which are also oftentimes rejected and invisible, have the power to reclaim their agency in Ballard's novels. Tereszewski interprets the ubiquitous presence of waste in both *High-Rise* and *The Concrete Island* as emphasizing the unique ontological status of the hinterlands being depicted.

Katarzyna Nowak-McNeice's Chapter 8, "Post-anthropocentric Hinterlands: Susan Straight's California", focuses on Californian heterotopias in two novels, *Take One Candle Light a Room* (2010) and *Between Heaven and Here* (2012), situating her discussion in the context of the Anthropocene and the destruction of the biosphere that characterizes it – the Sixth Great Extinction. Those ambiguously dispersed places represented in Straight's novels are a backdrop for post-anthropocentric subjects, who themselves testify to a dispersion of another kind, as they defy clear distinctions between human and non-human characters. The dissolution of rigid boundaries between humans and nonhumans is replaced by different connections and parallels, such as that between the land and the agents inhabiting it, or between the produce and the agent whose physical labour brings it into existence. This reconfiguration of agency is made possible by the heterotopic hinterlands where it is played out: in Straight's characterization, as Nowak-McNeice argues, the disruption of the distinctions between urban and rural zones, and a continuity between human and nonhuman agents, works against the cheapening of nature characteristic of the Capitalocene and suggests a model of community sustainability that transgresses the self-destructive scenarios rooted in anthropocentric, colonialist, racist, sexist, and speciesist practices.

All the chapters in this section approach hinterlands in terms of their heterotopic potential, regardless of whether the spaces in question exist (Haiti, Australia, or California) or are purely fictional. Hinterlands, often marginalized socio-economically, topographically, and culturally, are seen to stake a claim as heterotopic spaces, embodying Other, previously marginalized, voices, thereby also providing a source of innovation and regeneration.

Part III: Regenerative and nostalgic hinterlands

Part III interprets anew the main theme of the collection by turning its focus to the regenerative and nostalgic aspects of hinterlands, taking into consideration the movement implicit in nostalgia: back to the imagined centre of communal and individual identity, which – as is often the case with nostalgic longing – might never have existed. This imagined journey back is a journey to what is hoped to be the source of inspiration and regeneration. In the chapters in this section, the hinterlands become a lens through which grander social processes are highlighted, whether in con-tinental Asia or Europe, the Indian subcontinent, or the British Isles. All of these hinterlands become arenas for nostalgic representations of the hope for artistic, social, political, and individual rejuvenation and renewal.

In **Raffael Weger**'s Chapter 9, "(Re-)Constructing Identity along the Road through the Chinese Hinterland", this nostalgic turn is detected and analyzed in the Chinese context. Weger takes two examples of novelistic attempts at an interpretation of the idea of a hinterland: Gao Xingjian's *Soul Mountain* and Ma Jian's *Red Dust*. These two auto-fictional texts portray the experience of self-exile from the imperial centre to the vast hinterlands of the empire. In Weger's interpretation, Chinese hinterlands represent a contested space whose politicized and cultural status is revealed as inherently unstable and can be projected upon as a nostalgic space of authenticity, regeneration, beauty, simplicity, and ancestral roots – all idealized concepts that in the two auto-fictions support an underlying quest for the bedrock of Han culture. The larger questions of Han cultural roots prompt the two authors to simultaneously examine their individual identity, constructing it nostalgically, as Weger stresses, in the vast hinterlands from the point of view of a former urban dweller. Neither author ultimately manages to transcend his Han urban intellectual identity and both end up disillusioned with their quest for authenticity. Weger divides his close reading of the two texts into three parts, paying attention firstly to the representation of natural beauty (not common for authors of the era and resulting in a rather pessimistic picture of deforestation, climate change, and disastrous human intervention), secondly to interrelations between various agents (showing how an escape from politics turns out to be impossible, so that the politicization of private life with the constant threat of persecution is a reality the narrators have to contend with), and thirdly to local traditions and mythologies (in the context of so-called "root searching literature"). These different aspects of the journeys – through which a reinterpretation of tradition and concepts of natural beauty and human relations are represented – facilitate an understanding of the Chinese hinterlands as a literary construction of an ideal, rather than an actual, space.

In **S. M. Mithuna and Maya Vinai**'s Chapter 10, "Chenkalchoola: Reconfiguring the Social Imaginary of an Indian Hinterland", we change geographical location once again: their hinterland is located in the south of India, in Kerala. The authors of this chapter present a picture of the slums of Chenkalchoola – etymologically a red-brick baking site, and popularly named a colony – which is understood as both a specific locale and a community of its inhabitants who share the status of the dispossessed, the transient, and the excluded. The term *colony*, itself a loaded term that gains a special aspect in a country with a long history of colonial violence, designates Chenkalchoola as a site of otherness. In the region's social imaginary, as the authors stress, the place is a site associated with criminality and violence, and this perception influences the way its inhabitants are identified and treated. Mithuna and Vinai point out that paradoxically, belonging to a place like this hinterland banishes its inhabitants to the societal outskirts and might potentially result in discriminatory action, contrary to the usual process of not belonging resulting in marginalization and alienation. The case of Chenkalchoola is also interesting because it complicates the Western theoretical paradigms by the necessity of taking caste into consideration as a crucial aspect of India's societal makeup. The inhabitants of

Chenkalchoola are those excluded from the caste system – the official governmental classification known as the Reservation System – and thus slip through its rigid boundaries without social benefits and help programmes. Mithuna and Vinai focus on the only literary representation of this hinterland, which is an autobiographical text by Dhanuja Kumari S., *My Life in Chenkalchoola*, which was created with the help of one of Kerala's most important poets, Vijila Chirappad. A text documenting the story of struggle and resistance to systemic oppression directed against the dispossessed, it is also a testimony to the potential of this hinterland's population to rise up against what seems an unsurmountable combination of the societal prejudice and violence stacked against them. The chapter ends on a hopeful note, asserting the artistic and creative potential of the inhabitants of this hinterland. By contrast, the chapter that follows presents a more negative and a somewhat stifling capacity of the hinterland.

The last chapter in this section, **Paulina Pająk**'s Chapter 11, "Neither Peace nor Haven: Sussex as Virginia Woolf's Imagined Hinterland", takes us to the former imperial centre of Great Britain and presents its own local hinterlands located in Sussex. Starting with an overview of the processes of industrialization and urbanization and their impact on the natural and social landscape of Sussex in the years between the world wars, the chapter continues with a discussion of varied responses to these processes in order to bring into focus Virginia Woolf's reaction to the changes in the historical hinterlands, presented against the backdrop of these critical voices. Based on Woolf's miscellaneous fictional works and letter-essays, Pająk argues convincingly that the strategies Woolf uses – textual gestures that include irony and hybridity – situate these writings in a wider modernist tradition. The author traces Woolf's inhabitance in the region, such as at Asheham House in Beddingham, and Monk's House in Rodmell, and presents Woolf's views on the changing panorama in these and neighbouring places, documented in letters to friends and essays ostensibly planned for publication, and manifested in her attempts at saving the isolated and rugged character of the downs, which were quickly being transformed into an industrial hinterland. These multiple meanings of hinterlands add to the richness of the critical potential of the term, and Pająk's knowledgeable and perceptive argument is further amplified by the feminist reading of Woolf's landscape writings. Different forces at work – representing the postulated separation of city from non-city and the futility of such efforts, as well as of the middle class's mobility and attempts at curbing it – are made apparent in Pająk's analysis. Woolf is shown to have reflected deeply on these influences, as she observed the processes of industrialization happening in her closest vicinity and searched for evocative words to encapsulate her despair. Woolf's novel *The Years* and her final unfinished novel-play *Between the Acts* serve as a case in point and allow the author of the chapter to conclude that Woolf's miscellaneous, hybrid works disrupt the patriarchal, capitalist, and militaristic values cherished by many of Woolf's contemporaries.

Having thus taken us on a journey from Asia's hinterlands in China, through continental Europe's hinterlands in Slovenia, India's Kerala, and England's Sussex, the authors in this section illustrate in their analyses how ample and how critically poignant the term *hinterland* is. What connects the chapters in this section is their shared focus on the nostalgic aspect of the hinterlands, situated in various parts of the world. The geographical spread of the examples analyzed here suggests that perceiving hinterlands in a nostalgic manner is more of a rule than an exception. This, in turn, implies that the movement detectable in the very term *hinterlands* is not only a physical feature, but is an inherent property in the conceptual sense, as it designates a certain longing for the past constructed in communal and individual memory.

Part IV: Hinterlands revisited and reimagined

The section "Hinterlands Revisited and Reimagined" maps a spectrum of multimodal palimpsest cultural landscapes addressing locations in Central and Eastern Europe (Lower Silesia in Poland and Belarus further east) as well as in Canada (Kapuskasing) and the United States (Los Angeles). They are spaces either "swept into the maelstrom of urbanization" (Brenner and Katskis 24) or reduced to *territorium nullus* (Unangst 2022), and in that way, they are made available for acquisition, colonial expansion, and integration into newly formulated historical, imperial, and other political narratives (Kearney 1997; Demshuk 2012). These narratives as "necessary lies" (Eva Stachniak 2000), glossing over the inherent hybridity and complex past of hinterlands, produce landscapes of generalizations, like "the Midwest" or the "Recovered Territories", as well as enforce amnesia and a sense of oblivion. Imposing or demanding territorial identities of politically desirable citizens and creating illusions of fair policy (non-racial, democratic, solidarity oriented), these hinterland constructions envision their inhabitants as recipients of change who are deprived of agency – the Indigenous, the black, World War I interned as well as the post-World War II displaced. Whether referring to imaginary or real locations, these conceptual frameworks, originally in the service of deterritorialization and expansion, provoke revisions of their constructedness. Intersections of discourse, materiality, and human agency invite a re-reading with the dimension of memory, post-memory, loss, genocide, racial oppression, lost communal life, and suppressed cultural heritage to, ultimately, revise the possible uses of the term *hinterland* in contemporary contexts, notably that of "flyover country".

In their analysis of novels, non-fiction, films, and landscape materiality, the first three chapters of the section respond to hinterlands whose origin can be traced back to military conflicts resulting in massive de-territorialization followed by reterritorializations that transformed geographically defined locations, sometimes innocently called *heartlands* or *peripheries*, into places of production, forced labour, persecution, dispossession, and extermination. Whereas the European centre-hinterland polarity originates in the Second World War and its aftermath, the Canadian heartland remains a conflation of Ukrainian suffering and the painful history of Indigenous people. In all cases, both the memory of atrocities and that of ordinary communal life, the ways of "being in place", have remained suppressed for decades. The discussions the chapters pursue indicate that a recovery of these palimpsest layers, buried in the multimodal landscapes and remaining significantly absent from public memory, have been revisited and partly recovered in fiction, non-fiction, and films made after the fall of the Iron Curtain in Central and Eastern Europe. On the other hand, though the history of Austro-Hungarian immigrants from the provinces of Galicia and Bukovyna had already become the subject of research in the 1970s, its comprehensive recovery and its appearance in fiction took place in postmillennial publications addressing a wide spectrum of readers, including children and young adults.

Chapter 12 examines the process of re-discovering the Silesian landscape experienced by its post-war inhabitants, who had been forced to move westwards. Once a hinterland appropriated and redefined, it was a territory they found alien and treated for a long time as a temporary place of residence. Rather than becoming immersed in a close reading of a narrow selection of texts, **Ewa Kębłowska-Ławniczak** concentrates on the process of re-imagining and re-inhabiting this seemingly familiar landscape by recovering its multilayered complexity as reflected in a spectrum of phenomena including, initially, superficial musealisation and collectorship in the 1990s and, later on, a publication of testimonies (Karolina Kusznik 2019), memoirs, and autofiction (Marianne Wheelaghan 2021; Eva Stachniak 2000; Joanna Bator 2013), which enabled a gradual disentanglement of the local from the domination of grand narratives. The chapter shows how the cultural appropriation of the 1960s, with the classics ignoring the regional, gives way to a spate of publications including the early fiction of Olga Tokarczuk (*Drive Your Plow Over the Bones of the Dead*, 2009), Joanna Bator (*Sandy Mountain*, 2009; *Cloudalia*, 2010; *Dark, Almost Night*, 2014), and Marek Krajewski (the Eberhard Mock series starting in 2006) – writers who, in various ways, acknowledged the complexity of the region's multimodal landscape, sensing the affective presence (Rei Terada 2001, 6) of the so far invisible, and who made an effort to inhabit and "befriend" (Paweł Banaś 2009) what had gradually ceased to be a hinterland.

While Chapter 12 examines the way Lower Silesia was experienced by immigrants from the east, Chapter 13 concentrates on the return journeys of the World War II survivors and their descendants who after 1989 travel eastwards (southeastern Poland, Ukraine, and Belorus) to places of former habitation and destruction to reclaim a "lost place", to reread and re-examine the uncooperative hinterlands with the dimension of memory, postmemory, perpetrator memory and complicity. What they encounter is a visible, surface landscape without its landmarks, a place that has been cleansed and its local materiality imbued with memory lost so that its fragments have to be "unearthed", traced in the gestures of the body and explored tentatively through multidirectional links with other histories of violence. The hinterlands **Mona Becker** examines are dark, submerged "sites of the unknown" and they impenetrably echo the concept of a distant land "lying beyond what is visible or known" (Doolan 2019). Reading the novels of Rachel Seiffert (*The Dark Room*, 2001), Lisa Appignanesi (*The Memory Man*, 2004), and Jonathan Safran Foer (*Everything Is Illuminated*, 2003), the chapter shows hinterlands as spaces of confrontation, rediscovery, fictionalization, and reconciliation.

Canada's legacy of hinterlands as both wastelands and heartlands, a conceptual framework which treats the existing regions as primitive and waiting to be conquered/civilized, though bestowed with the singular beauty of wilderness, is the subject of Chapter 14. Physically and metaphorically, the distant heartland, examined by **Mateusz Świetlicki** in a collection of novels aimed at young readers, represents economic expansion where immigrants have to pay to be recognized as true Canadians (Clark and Skrypuch). The political violence and, ultimately, the loss of faith in Canada as a promised land (Lucik and Burton) symbolically wounded by its history of internment camps becomes, once again, silenced in the collective memory. A close reading of three novels that significantly address a broad spectrum of readers – Marsha Forchuk Skrypuch's *Dance of the Banished* (2015); Kassandra Luciuk and Nicole Marie Burton's *Enemy Alien: A True Story of Life Behind Barbed*

Wire (2020); and Pam Clark's *Kalyna* (2016) – the chapter follows the story of revisiting distant hinterlands, a theme explicitly thematized in *Kalyna*, bringing back an awareness of history buried in the heterotopic land that accommodates memories of internment side by side with images of grandiose natural beauty conflated with afterimages of the Ukrainian prairie.

The closing chapter questions and transcends the dominant reductive binaries of centre versus periphery (Williams 1973) in hinterland studies, but distinguishes between a "far" and a "near" hinterland, a concept proposed by Phil A. Neel (2018). **Sasha Pöhlmann** envisions hinterlands primarily as "swept into the maelstrom of urbanization" (Brenner and Katskis 24) to focus on what the author prefers to define as "internal hinterlands" – a conceptual frame more in line with the global perspectives developed by Brenner and Katsikis in "Operational Landscapes". Revising the traditional conceptual frame of hinterlands and proposing its expansion, the closing chapter sets out to elaborate on its meaning by connecting it to the related spatial discourse of "flyover country" – a partly urban, partly rural "in-between" ignored due to high altitude and non-stop communication – in order to address the hybridity of more recent global developments and "meta-regional imaginations". Discussing the adaptation of supposedly innocent geographical concepts, the chapter indicates their inherent predilection for imposing hierarchies and various forms of marginalization. In its examination of Paul Beatty's satire *The Sellout* on an allegedly post-racial USA, Pöhlmann argues bitterly that the novel's primary focus is on the return of the repressed in a country that imagines itself as post-racial. The discussion, drawing on a combination of geographical and cultural imagination and its mode of constructing cultural hierarchies, shows how this mode can be subverted to create an "internal hinterland" swallowed up by the urban space but not marginalized.

Works Cited

Amin, Ash, and Nigel Thrift. *Cities. Reimagining the Urban*. Polity Press, 2002.

Andrews, Hazel. "Mapping My Way: Map-Making and Analysis in Participant Observation." *Mapping Cultures: Place, Practice, Performance*. Ed. Les Roberts. Palgrave Macmillan, 2012, pp. 216–36.

Bachelard, Gaston. *The Production of Space*. Boston: Beacon Press, 1994.

Banaś, Paweł. *Oswajanie ziem odzyskanych. Dolny Śląsk na pocztówkach pierwszej powojennej dekady*. Korporacja Polonia, 2009.

Bator, Joanna. *Ciemno, prawie noc*. Foksal, 2013.

Brenner, Neil. *New Urban Spaces: Urban Theory and the Scale Question*. Oxford University Press, 2019.

Brenner, Neil, and Christian Schmid. "Planetary Urbanization." *Implosions/ Explosions: Towards a Study of Planetary Urbanization*. Ed. Neil Brenner. Jovis Verlag, 2014, pp. 160–63.

Brenner, Neil, and Daniel Ibañez. "The Agency of Design in an Age of Urbanization." *Critique of Urbanization: Selected Essays*. Bauverlag, 2017, pp. 224–36.

Brenner, Neil, and Martin Arboleda. "Coda: Critical Urban Theory, Reloaded?" *Critique of Urbanization: Selected Essays*. Ed. Neil Brenner. Bauverlag, 2017, pp. 268–89.

Brenner, Neil, and Nikos Katsikis. "Operational Landscapes: Hinterlands of the Capitalocene." *Architectural Design*, vol. 90, no. 1, January/February 2020, pp. 22–31. DOI: 10.1002/ad.2521.

Certeau, Michel de. *The Practice of Everyday Life*. University of California Press, [1984] 1997.

Cevasco, Maria Elisa. "Imagining a Space That Is Outside. An Interview with Fredric Jameson." *Minnesota Review*, vol. 78, no. 1, 2012, pp. 83–94.

Chisholm, George. *Handbook of Commercial Geography*, 4th revised ed. Longmans, [1889] 1903.

Cronon, William. *Nature's Metropolis: Chicago and the Great West*. W.W. Norton & Company, 1991.

Demshuk, Andrew. "Reinscribing *Schlesien* as Śląsk. Memory and Mythology in a Postwar German-Polish Borderland." *History and Memory*, vol. 24, no. 1, 2012, pp. 39–86. DOI: 10.2979/histmemo.24.1.39

Donald, James. "Imagining the Modern City: Light in Dark Spaces." *The Blackwell City Reader*. Eds. Gary Bridge, and Sophie Watson. Blackwell Publishing, 2010, pp. 323–30.

Doolan, Emma. "Hinterland Gothic: Subtropical Excess in the Literature of South East Queensland". *E-Tropical – Special Issue: Tropical Gothic*, vol. 18, no. 1, 2019, pp. 174–90.

Frost, Vicky. "*Hinterland*: Nordic Noir Done the Welsh Way – Box Set Review." *The Guardian*, 10 July 2014. Accessed 10 June 2019 https://www.theguardian.com/tv-and-radio/2014/jul/10/hinterland-box-set-review

Gandy, Matthew. *Concrete and Clay: Reworking Nature in New York City*. MIT Press, 2002.

Hansen, Kim Toft. "From Nordic Noir to Euro Noir: Nordic Noir Influencing European Serial SVoD Drama." *Nordic Noir, Adaptation, Appropriation*. Eds. Linda Badley, Andrew Nestingen, and Jaakko Seppälä. Palgrave Macmillan, 2020, pp. 275–94.

Harvey, David. *The Condition of Postmodernity: An Enquiry into the Origins of Cultural Change*. Blackwell, 1989.

Hedling, Olof. "After *The Bridge*? Adapting Nordic Noir Success into a Viable Audiovisual Industry in Southern Sweden." *Nordic Noir, Adaptation, Appropriation*. Eds. Linda Badley, Andrew Nestingen, and Jaakko Seppälä. Palgrave Macmillan, 2020, pp. 195–213.

Ingold, Tim. *The Perception of the Environment: Essays in Livelihood, Dwelling and Skill*. Routledge, 2000.

Jameson, Fredric. "Cognitive Mapping." *Marxism and the Interpretation of Culture*. Eds. Cary Nelson, and Lawrence Grossberg. University of Illinois Press, 1988, pp. 347–57.

Kearney, Richard. *Postnationalist Ireland: Politics, Culture, Philosophy*. Routledge, 1997.

Kusznik, Karolina. *Poniemieckie*. Wydawnictwo Czarne, 2019.

Lefebvre, Henri. *The Urban Revolution* Trans. Robert Bononno. University of Minnesota Press, 2003.

Lefebvre, Martin. "Between Setting and Landscape in the Cinema." *Landscape and Film*. Ed. Martin Lefebvre. Routledge, 2006, pp. 19–60.

Lynch, Kevin. *The Image of the City*. The MIT Press, 1960.

Merrifield, Andy. "Wither Urban Studies?" *Implosions/Explosions: Towards Study of Planetary Urbanization*. Ed. Neil Brenner. Jovis Verlag, 2014, pp. 386–93.

Mehzabeen, Evy. "Hinterlands." *The Wiley Blackwell Encyclopaedia of Urban and Regional Studies*. Ed. Anthony Orum. John Wiley, 2019, pp. 1–6.

Michel, Berit. *Mapping the City – Narrating 'Complexity': Urban Space in the Contemporary Anglophone Novel*. Wissenschaftlicher Verlag Trier, 2015.

Neel, Phil A. *Hinterland: America's New Landscape of Class and Conflict*. Reaktion Books, 2018.

Patel, Sujata. "The Making of Global City Regions: Mumbai: The Mega-City of a Poor Country." *The Blackwell City Reader*. Eds. Gary Bridge, and Sophie Watson. Blackwell, 2010, pp. 72–78.

Roberts, Les. "Landscapes in the Frame: Exploring the Hinterlands of the British Procedural Drama." *New Review of Film and Television Studies*, vol. 14, no. 3, 2016, pp. 364–85. DOI: 10.1080/17400309.2016.1189712 10.1080/17400309. 2016.1189712

Stachniak, Eva. *Necessary Lies*. Simon and Pierre, 2000.

Tally Jr., Robert T. "Introduction: The Reassertion of Space in Literary Studies." *The Routledge Handbook of Literature and Space*. Ed. Robert T. Tally Jr. Routledge, 2017, pp. 1–5.

Tally Jr., Robert T. *Spatiality*. Routledge, 2013.

Terada, Rei. *Feeling in Theory. Emotion after the "Death of the Subject."* Harvard UP, 2001.

Titelstad, Michael. "Writing the City after Apartheid." *The Cambridge History of South African Literature*. Eds. David Attwell, and Derek Attridge. CUP, 2011, pp. 676–94.

Unangst, Matthew. "Hinterland: The Political History of a Geographic Category from Scramble for Africa to Afro-Asian Solidarity." *Journal of Global History*, vol. 17, no. 3, 2022, pp. 496–514.

Vladislavić, Ivan. *Portrait with Keys: The City of Johannesburg Unlocked*. W.W. Norton & Co., [2006] 2009.

Wachsmuth, David. "City as Ideology." *Implosions/Explosions: Towards a Study of Planetary Urbanization*. Ed. Neil Brenner. Jovis Verlag, 2014, pp. 353–71.

Wheleelaghan, Marianne. *Niebiezka walizka. Pożegnanie z Breslau.* 2010. Trans. Marcin Melon. Canon Silesiae, 2021.

Wee, Lionel, and Robbie B.H. Goh. *Language, Space and Cultural Play.* Cambridge University Press, 2020.

Williams, Raymond. *The Country and the City.* Oxford University Press, 1973.

Wilson, Emma. *Cinema's Missing Children.* Wallflower Press, 2003.

Part I

Hinterlands as movement and transit

1 The transnational hinterlands of Los Angeles in Karen Tei Yamashita's *Tropic of Orange*

Dominika Ferens

Contrary to the urban studies tradition of focusing on the densely popu-lated and spatially bounded city, in the last decade Neil Brenner and Andy Merrifield, among others, have argued that there is nothing natural or inevitable about the growth of cities and that urban growth has depended on the systematic transformation of rural hinterlands "into zones of high-intensity, large-scale industrial infrastructure – *operational landscapes*" (Brenner, "The Hinterland Urbanised" 124, italics in the original). This observation may seem trite, yet it signals a shift of attention from the city to other areas of the planet, where "colossal, if unevenly developed industrial and environmental upheavals" have taken place as a result of the widespread belief that urban growth is inevitable and desirable (123). Although the upheavals are there in plain sight, until recently, urban studies scholars took little interest in them, and neither were they fully visible to academics in the social sciences and humanities. Brenner there-fore asks: "How can we visualize, and thereby politicize, the encom-passing but generally invisible webs of connection that link our urban way of life to the silent violence of accumulation by dispossession and en-vironmental destruction in the world's hinterlands and operational land-scapes?" (126).

Brenner attempted to make the webs of connection visible by means of NASA satellite maps of "operational landscapes", and by spearheading group projects like *Implosions/Explosions: Towards a Study of Planetary Urbanism* (2014). Three decades earlier, the Japanese American author Karen Tei Yamashita started writing fiction about "operationalized" landscapes and global "webs of connection". To her, such phenomena were perfectly visible because, though she was raised in Los Angeles, from 1974 to 1983 she had lived in Brazil, where she witnessed (to use Brenner's words) those "colossal … industrial and environmental upheavals" long before globalization got a bad name. Her first novel, *Through the Arc of the Rain Forest* (1990), depicted rural Brazil as a hinterland radically transformed

DOI: 10.4324/9781032617732-3

by the explosion of cities in Brazil and the United States. Yamashita fictionalized phenomena that rarely become the stuff of novels, namely, the effects of U.S. American economic expansion into a developing country: the extraction and export of Brazilian natural resources to the Global North, the denudation of the land, and the resultant climate change, all of which displace rural populations and turn city dwellers into compulsive consumers. Though far-sighted and daring in its geopolitical scope, Yamashita's ecocritical futuristic novel about Brazil was not widely read in the United States, perhaps because it was out of sync with reader expectations.[1] The timing may have been wrong, for similar novels published one or two decades later by William Gibson, Douglas Coupland, and David Eggers were enthusiastically received. Yamashita's ethnicity may have been a problem. *Through the Arc of the Rain Forest* had nothing to say about immigration to the United States, ethnic identity, and (resistance to) assimilation – issues that were important for Asian Americans in the 1990s. It may have also failed to meet mainstream readers' expectations that minority authors should write about their own ethnic enclaves; the fact that Yamashita had spent nine years in Brazil did not make her a credible authority on things Brazilian.

Her next novel, *Tropic of Orange* (1997), likewise challenged reader expectations, despite the fact that much of its action was set in Los Angeles, where Yamashita had grown up. In this novel, Yamashita imagined the aggravation of the problems signalled in *Through the Arc* in the wake of the 1992 North American Free Trade Agreement (NAFTA), which accelerated the flow of goods and money between the United States, Mexico, and Canada.[2] By reading *Tropic of Orange* alongside recent urban studies texts, I hope to draw attention to analogies in their authors' understandings of the relation between cities and their hinterlands, as well as their use of strikingly similar imagery to render that relation. If hinterlands are territories beyond that which is visible and known (Doolan "Hinterland Gothic"[3]; "Hinterland") – if they are usually out of sight and out of mind – literature like *The Tropic of Orange* has the power to bring them into view through a variety of tropes, parables, and symbolic tableaux. I am particularly interested in the aesthetic means Yamashita used to help readers conceptualize the impact of what Harvey Molotch called "the city as a growth machine" (Molotch 1976) on the hinterland and vice versa. I want to argue that Yamashita used magical realist deformations of space and time to help readers visualize disturbing phenomena that were mostly out of sight and out of mind in the early 1990s.

Other literary scholars, most notably Robin Blyn (2016) and Shouhei Tanaka (2020), have interpreted Yamashita's fiction as a critique of the political economy of globalization and neocolonial relations. Blyn pointed out that the novel "prefigures and significantly complicates the controversial vision of postmodern politics" proposed by Michael Hardt and Antonio Negri. In fact, *Tropic* of Orange "conveys its postmodern aesthetic as both an extension of neoliberalism and as an expression of the potential to change it" (192). Tanaka, in turn, discussed *Through the Arc* alongside *Tropic of Orange* as examples of what he calls "planetary petrofiction, novels that envision energy justice by locating oil's multi-scalar forms across geopolitical and geological histories" (191). Like Blyn, Tanaka acknowledged Yamashita's use of speculative fiction to make visible the approaching ecological catastrophe (191–92). But neither of these authors looks specifically at the politics and poetics of the hinterland in Yamashita's fiction, which are the focus of this chapter.

Tropic of Orange is a disaster novel set in the present or near future in Los Angeles and Mexico. Whereas in most stories of this kind disaster strikes at the beginning and coping with its aftermath fills the rest of plot, in *Tropic of Orange*, we encounter small symptoms of impending eco-nomic, humanitarian, and environmental catastrophes, which most of the characters manage to either cope with or ignore, until the final chapters. Structured like a Brazilian telenovela, the novel unfolds over seven days and features seven protagonists, each of whom occupies seven alternating chapters. Each of the seven strands of the story is narrated in a different style, ranging from street slang, through parable, to prophetic poetry and poetic prose. All the characters – two janitors, a journalist, a TV producer, a migrant, a self-appointed social worker, and a surgeon-turned-homeless man – are members of racial minorities. They lead parallel lives, some of which intersect. Three are named after Archangels (which seems appro-priate given the fact that the Spanish name of Los Angeles means "Our Lady, Queen of the Angels"). All seven are busy trying to protect some-body from harm and in the process, they fight losing battles against forces they barely understand. In the process, some form coalitions and try out new forms of transnational citizenship and commitment.

Usually read as an urban novel, *Tropic of Orange* has been called "the ultimate book about Los Angeles", one that fearlessly confronts the unimaginable complexity of this city (Foster i). I want to look beyond Yamashita's Los Angeles to its hinterlands, which have drawn less critical attention than the fictional city itself. In the colonial era, hin-terland signified the strip of land behind the colonial port. In order to function, cities have always relied on their hinterlands for food, water, energy and other natural resources, labour, recreation, and waste disposal. But the economies of contemporary megacities like Greater Los Angeles – which ranks as the largest industrial area in the United States – cannot be sustained by adjacent territories. Since Los Angeles is located on the westernmost edge of the United States, one would expect its hinterland to be a swath of land to the north and east of the city.

Yet, oddly enough, Yamashita's Los Angeles has practically no near (U.S. American) hinterlands, while it is fused with distant hinterlands that are not immediately recognizable as such because they are separated from the city by a border (Mexico) and an ocean (East Asia). On the one hand, Los Angeles has an insatiable appetite for hands, hearts, fuel, oranges, and drugs. On the other, its economic power allows it to corner the bicycle market in Singapore and absorb countless Vietnam War refugees who become part of its labour force. Economic growth in Los Angeles triggers crises in Mexico and across the Pacific, which then reverberate back in the city.

Mexico's status as a hinterland of Los Angeles is established at the outset of *Tropic of Orange*. In fact, Yamashita implies that Los Angeles should be read through its hinterland because she opens the narrative with a disorienting tableau of a barefoot woman sweeping the floor of a hacienda built on the Tropic of Cancer in rural Mexico. There is an aura of timelessness about this scene, for we are told that every morning Rafaela sweeps out of the house "a small pile of assorted insects and tiny animals – moths, spiders, lizards and beetles", which make "their way back into the house" during the night (3). But things are not what they seem: the sweeper turns out to be a Los Angeles janitors' union organizer, who has returned to her native Mexico temporarily, to oversee the construction of a Mexican American journalist's fanciful vacation home. If Rafaela stands for the prototypical migrant, passing unnoticed back and forth across the U.S.–Mexico border, then the American vacation home she sweeps can be read as a symbolic outpost of Los Angeles in the hinterland, and the "assorted insects and tiny animals" as migrants defying the sweeper and always returning.

Yamashita uses elements of magical realism to show the way Los Angeles forms a magnetic field or, to use Manuel Castells' vocabulary, a key node in the space of flows[4] in which people, natural resources, technology, manufactured goods, and money circulate in uneven patterns. Since many of these flows are invisible to the eye, Yamashita transforms them into the image of a landscape in motion. The Tropic of Cancer, imagined as a tangible line which cuts across Mexico, gets snagged on an orange that falls off a tree and is picked up by a migrant. From now on, the tropic is no longer a stable element of a grid but a taut line steadily moving northwards, compressing time and space, deforming the landscape, and making events that unfold in distant places collide. Meanwhile, Los Angeles is moving south. A homeless Japanese American character named Manzanar, standing on a freeway overpass, registers the spatial deformations as they begin to resound in the city. Since his calling is to direct the sounds of Los Angeles into a symphony, he thinks in terms of musical movements: "he knew that the entire event was being moved, stretched.

And he was quite sure that the direction was south. Yes, south, for the time being" (123). Yamashita's imagery of moving land masses bears a striking resemblance to that used by urban studies scholar Andy Merrifield when he explains that "the urbanization of the world is a kind of ex-teriorization of the inside as well as interiorization of the outside … The urban *unfolds* into the countryside just as the countryside *folds* back into the city" (542).

Not only is the landscape on the move but so are the people displaced from rural areas that are being "operationalized" by global cities. "We very well could be on the precipice of a historic displacement of people in the Americas toward the United States", a former U.S. national security adviser told the *New York Times* on October 1, 2021. Decades earlier, Yamashita visualized the impact of such a mass displacement as a tectonic shift that drags the Tropic of Cancer into California and folds the land-scape of Los Angeles, like drapery, by the sheer force of the migrants' determination to walk away from economic and ecological disaster in the South to the relative prosperity of the North:

> The entire City of Angels seemed to have opened its singular voice to herald a naked old man and little boy with an orange followed by a motley parade approaching from the south. Once again, the grid was changing … The valley was no longer only ten lanes across or one mile long; it was becoming the entire city and bigger than a tiny island or a puny country the size of San Bernardino. And the approaching parade was dragging in the entire midriff (and maybe even the swaying hips, burning thighs, and sultry genitals) of the hemisphere. (238–39)

The procession of migrants is playfully personified in this passage as an erotic body or, more precisely, its lower half, advancing with "swaying hips, burning thighs, and sultry genitals".[5] This collective body is unwanted by the "rational forces of the North", which shake their heads and rush to keep it from crossing the border: "The coordinated might of the Army, Navy, Air Force, Marines, the Coast and National Guards, federal, state, and local police forces of the most militaristic of nations looked down … and descended in a single storm" (239). Using a wide range of imagery, Yamashita shows that while the city and its hinterland are a continuum, the fact that they are separated by a national border reinforces an asymmetry between them. Rural Mexico is no longer rural: it is plugged into the internet and run by an international drug cartel whose headquarters are surrounded by corn fields. But the American megacity uses the border to dictate the terms on which the urban and the rural can meet. A similar point was made in 2013 by Brenner in the language of social science: the rural/urban divide no longer exists, for practically all "formerly marginalized or remote spaces are being enclosed, oper-ationalized, designed and planned to support the continued agglomeration of capital, labor and infrastructure within the world's large cities and megacity regions". This, in turn, leads to "polarization and sociopolitical struggle" ("Introduction" 26).

The asymmetry in the flows of people, goods, money, information, and ideas across the border, regulated by NAFTA, is already signalled in the novel's first dialogue, a long-distance telephone exchange between the sweeper Rafaela and her Mexican American employer Gabriel, concerning the price of toilet bowls. Gabriel wants Rafaela to install them in his vacation home. She points out that the same items are inexplicably much cheaper to buy in Los Angeles. "I went into town to price some toilet bowls and fixtures", she says. "You won't believe what they're asking. Maybe you ought to check out the prices over there. I'm going to make a list, and the next time you come down—". To which Gabriel responds incredulously, "You want me to bring toilet bowls down from L.A.?" (3). The reader is not told where the toilet bowls were manufactured, but their low price in Los Angeles suggests a U.S. corporation makes them in Mexico. By contrast, American Budweiser beer flows freely into Mexico, where it replaces local brands, even in village cantinas. When the migrant Arcangel stops at one on his way north, "all the hungry and miserable people in the cantina [are] eating hamburgers, Fritos, catsup, and drinking American beers" (131). Mexican smugglers exploit the porousness of the border: they use internet tracking technology, inject drugs into shipments of oranges, and conceal organs for transplants in milk-bottle coolers carried by nursing mothers onto planes bound for LAX. Human traffic is asymmetrical, too: Gabriel goes to Mexico for recreation and work without impediment, while crowds of labourers gather at the border, unable to cross into the United States.

Now that the urban has "unfolded" (Merrifield 542) into the Mexican countryside, the two become temporally and spatially fused. Tipped off by an informant, Gabriel tries to investigate the flow of contraband, dashing first to the Los Angeles airport to watch passengers getting off a plane, then to Mexico City, and finally to the cartel's headquarters, near his hacienda on the Tropic of Cancer. There, on a computer screen, he watches "a flashing indicator marked X" that

> moved around the map [of Los Angeles]. The indicator seemed to be located at the downtown freeway interchange. I calculated it would be right there in that homeless parking lot mess. I watched it move up what was now Limousine Way, blink toward the Music Center, and up Bunker Hill to Angel's Flight. What was it tracking? And how did this system get on Doña Maria's TV? Who else was watching this? (227)

The cartel's computer tracking system can be read in terms of the phenomenon Merrifield describes as "exteriorization of the inside as well as interiorization of the outside" (542). As Gabriel watches how the computer in Mexico steers the movement of contraband around Los Angeles, his confusion deepens with each second: "The commerce was on the ground; the threads pulling them around were in the air. Which conspiracy theory was this one? The cartel, if that was what it was, was a big invisible net. If I had a strategy, it would be to get in there and snarl the net without entangling myself" (245). Though Gabriel escapes from the cartel boss's house alive, he eventually gets entangled in the "expanding universe" of the world wide web, tracking the flows of money and goods: "I could follow a story or I could abandon it, but I could not stop" (249). At the end of the novel, the hard-boiled LA journalist is left flailing in the virtual world, unable to return to the warped but more concrete landscape of the city.

A powerful device Yamashita invented to give LA's southern hinterland a concrete form is the character Arcangel, a migrant who claims to be five hundred years old and to have "come from a long way away, from the very tip of the Tierra del Fuego, from Isla Negra, from the very top of Macchu Picchu, from the very bottom of the Foz do Iguaçu, but perhaps it was only a long way in his quixotic mind" (47). Arcangel claims to have been born before Columbus and to remember the entire colonial era. What makes him effective as the voice of the southern hinterland is the fact that every now and then he breaks into poetry reminiscent of that written by the legendary performance artist Guillermo Gómez-Peña (Gómez-Peña). Into a poetic form vaguely reminiscent of Walt Whitman's catalogues Yamashita compresses a postcolonial understanding of global economic flows that could not be conveyed in the conventional novel form. When Arcangel closes his eyes, he can see Central and South America as an "operational landscape" Brenner described as linked with the translational city's "silent violence of accumulation by dispossession and environmental destruction" (126):

Haitian farmers burning and slashing cane,
workers stirring molasses into white gold.
Guatemalans loading trucks with
crates of bananas and corn.
Indians, who mined tin in the Cerro Rico
and saltpeter from the Atacama desert,
chewing coca and drinking aguardiente to
dull the pain of their labor.
Venezuelan and Mexican drivers
filling their trucks with gasoline,

their cargos of crates
shipped by train,
by ship, and
by air and
sent away,
far away. (*Tropic of Orange* 145, italics in the original)

It is the clairvoyant Arcangel who spells out the function of the U.S.–Mexico border, as he stands on it "looking out across the northern horizon":

all 2,000 miles of the frontier
stretched across from Tijuana on the Pacific, ...
It waited with seismic sensors and thermal imaging,
with la pinche migra,
colonias of destitute skirmishing at its hard line,
with coyotes, pateros, cholos,
steel structures, barbed wire, infrared binoculars,
INS detention centers, border patrols, rape,
robbery, and death.

It waited with its great history of migrations back and forth – in recent history, the deportation of 400,000 Mexican

citizens in 1932,
coaxing back of 2.2 million
braceros in 1942
only to exile the same 2.2 million
wetbacks in 1953. (197–98, italics in the original)

Urbanism may be "planetary" but national borders preserve the asymmetry between the Global South and the Global North. This passage makes apparent the fact that the only thing keeping the megacity and its hinterland from physically "folding" into one another is the well-guarded yet porous border. Poetry allows Yamashita to shift the agency behind the litany of injustices from the U.S. authorities to the monstrous border itself, which makes the political critique more abstract but powerful nevertheless.

By repeatedly referring to the movement of oranges as commodities across multiple borders, and by making a specific orange carried by Arcangel from Mexico to the United States the novel's central metaphor, Yamashita firmly linked Southern California with Central and South America. Much is made of the fact that the orange comes from a tree brought to Mazatlán from Riverside, California, and that "it was a navel orange tree, maybe the descendant of the original trees first brought to California from Brazil in 1873 and planted by L.C. Tibbetts" (6). A fact Yamashita is undoubtedly aware of yet withholds from the reader is that oranges were first domesticated in China and came to the Americas with the Spanish Conquistadors. Just as the East Asian origins of the orange are elusive, so is the second distant hinterland of Yamashita's Los Angeles. Though today its economies rival that of the United States, in the nineteenth and early twentieth centuries, East Asia was an undeveloped hinterland that supplied the raw materials, labour, and agricultural know-how needed to sustain the growth of Los Angeles as a key economic and military outpost of the United States on the Pacific.

Yamashita subtly constructs East Asia as a space of U.S. American military, political and economic expansion, as well as a source of labour. She introduces several generations of Asian workers who helped to build Los Angeles and keep it running: Japanese, Vietnamese, and Chinese Singaporeans. The two Japanese American characters in the novel, Manzanar and Emi Murakami, are descendants of people who must have arrived in the United States before Congress passed the 1924 act banning immigration from Japan. Though neither of them reflects on the Murakami family history, their ancestors, like most Japanese on the West Coast, were probably farmers, market gardeners, or fishermen, who supplied the city with food. The older of the two has adopted the Spanish name Manzanar, invoking the World War II camp in the California desert, where he was incarcerated as a child. Trained as a physician, Manzanar belongs to a minority taught by the internment experience to assimilate to the white middle class through hard work and higher education. Yet we learn that before the start of the novel, Manzanar walked away from his successful surgical practice, unable to bear the strain of pretending to be well adjusted. He now sleeps in the shelter of a freeway and spends his days standing on an overpass in the centre of Los Angeles, conducting symphonies composed of the sounds of passing cars.

While Arcangel comes from and looks out on the city's southern hinterland, Manzanar's gaze sweeps the entire Pacific Basin:

> the great Pacific stretching along its great rim, brimming over long coastal shores from one hemisphere to the other ... From the North, that peaceful ocean swept from Vladivostok around the Japan Isles and the Korean Peninsula, to Shanghai, Taipei, Ho Chi Minh City, through a thousand islands of the Philippines, Malaysia, Indonesia, and Micronesia, sweeping about that giant named Australia and her sister, New Zealand. Manzanar looked out on this strange end and beginning: the very last point West, and after that it was all East. The inky waves

with their moonlit spume stuttering against the shore seemed to speak this very truth—garbage jettisoned back prohibiting further prog-ress. (170)

Unlike the Latino migrant Arcangel, Manzanar focuses on the present, studiously avoiding history, so his vision of the Pacific Basin is apolitical and ahistorical. He aestheticizes it in much the same way that he aesthe-ticizes the city. While his mind's eye penetrates the strata of pipelines, sewers, and electrical cables underneath the city, he seems unable or unwilling to see constant traffic between Asia and the United States via underwater optical fibres, satellites, and container ships. Nonetheless, Manzanar's figure, precariously poised on the freeway overpass, allows Yamashita to gesture towards the existence of the second distant hinter-land of Los Angeles.

It is through the story of another protagonist, Bobby Ngu, that Yamashita introduces a compressed history of U.S. American economic and military incursions into Asia. Bobby is a Singaporean who immigrated to the United States illegally as a child, when his father's business went bankrupt.

> Used to be, back in Singapore, Bobby had it easy. Dad had a factory. Putting out bicycles. Had a good life. Good money. Only had to go to school. One day, American bicycle company put up a factory. Workers all went over there. New machines. Paid fifty cents more. Pretty soon, American company's selling all over. Exporting. Bicycles go to Hong Kong. Go to Thailand. To India. To Japan. To Taiwan. Bobby's dad losing business. Can't compete. That's it. (18)

Since there are too many mouths to feed in the family, Bobby and his younger brother slip into a camp for Vietnamese refugees in Singapore, keep silent to disguise the fact that they don't speak Vietnamese, and are eventually transported to the United States. To the U.S. military, they are indistinguishable from Vietnam War refugees. Grateful to be an American and fully identified with the ethos of hard work and humility, Bobby is

> always working. Hustling. Moving … He can't stop. Daytime, works the mailroom at a big-time newspaper. Sorts mail nonstop. Tons of it. Never stops. Nighttime got his own business. Him and his wife. Cleaning buildings … Dump the stuff that's shredded. Wipe up the conference tables. Dust everything. Wipe down the computer monitors. Vacuum staples and hole punches and donuts out of carpets. Scrub the urinals. Mop down the floors. Bobby only stops for a smoke with the nighttime guard. (16)

Together with Rafaela, Arcangel, and boatloads of nameless Vietnamese, Bobby and his brother stand for the populations displaced by capital "operationalizing" the hinterland. And once they arrive, they make themselves serviceable.

The youngest arrival from the Asian hinterland is a Chinese girl, whose photo Mexican human traffickers present to Bobby as that of his cousin. Bobby drives from Los Angeles to Mexico, pays the cartel $5,000 for her release, and smuggles her into the United States in his car, though he suspects they are not related. Bobby's generosity is left unexplained, but the reader assumes that his sense of kinship with the Chinese girl stems from his experience of arriving destitute in Los Angeles as a child.

Since Los Angeles and its transnational hinterlands are all located around the Pacific Basin, the grand finale of *Tropic of Orange*, appropriately, takes place in an imaginary arena called the Pacific Rim Auditorium. There Arcangel, who renamed himself El Gran Mojado (The Great Wetback, standing for all undocumented migrants) and dressed up as a prizefighter, fights a surreal wrestling match with SUPERNAFTA (standing for the transnational economic system created by the 1992 trade agreement), who wears a titanium armour and spouts flames from his head like an oil rig.

> As NAFTA thrashed about the ring,
> Mojado's great wings flapped back and forth
> and back and forth,
> fanning a great storm,
> fanning the flames to cold smoke and
> stoking NAFTA to a live nuke.
> Everyone gasped as the great SUPERNAFTA imploded. (262, italics in
> the original)

Imploding in the arena, SUPERNAFTA takes down Arcangel/El Gran Mojado. The mock-heroic but deadly face-off between the antagonistic forces represented by Arcangel and SUPERNAFTA is Yamashita's most pointed commentary on the idea that progress is economic growth through globalization.

The fact that Yamashita ended the novel with the implosion of SUPERNAFTA against a backdrop of Los Angeles exploding brings to mind the imagery used by contemporary urban studies scholars who argue against the bounded notion of the city. As Neil Brenner points out, Henri Lefebvre used the phrase "implosion-explosion" in his ground-breaking essay "The Right to the City" (1968) to emphasize the drastic transformations of both urban and rural landscapes over the centuries. Paying homage to Lefebvre, Brenner borrowed this phrase for the title of the volume of collected essays *Implosions/Explosions: Towards a Study of Planetary Urbanism* (2014), illustrated with stark photographs not of cityscapes but of "operational landscapes": sprawling quarries with muddy access roads, a forest shorn by loggers, a salt lake partitioned into crystallizing ponds (Brenner, "Introduction" 18). Although as a fiction writer Yamashita provides neither data nor conceptual tools for academics, policy makers, and concerned citizens, and while she has somewhat different concerns than do the contributors to *Implosions/Explosions,* some of the questions they pose, summarized by Brenner, also seem to underlie *Tropic of Orange*:

- Can the spatial boundaries of cities be coherently delineated – whether in theory, analysis, or experience? Is a new formation of complete urbanization being consolidated in specific regions and territories?
- Is a planetary formation of complete urbanization being consolidated in the early twenty-first century? If so, what are its major experiential, social, spatial, and environmental expressions, and what are its socio-political implications?
- What are the limitations and blindspots of inherited and contemporary approaches to the urban question in relation to emergent worldwide urbanization patterns? What is the role of ideological (mis)representations of the city and the urban in historical and contemporary strategies to shape sociospatial and environmental transformations?
- If the traditional city is dissolving and urbanization is being generalized across the planet, can new forms of citizenship be constructed that empower people collectively to appropriate, transform, and reshape the common space of the world? (Brenner, "Introduction" 25)

While writing *Through the Arc of the Rain Forest* and *Tropic of Orange*, Yamashita must have pondered these very questions. In the former novel, she created a fictional case study of an "operationalized landscape", while in the latter she foregrounded the networks that tie such landscapes to transnational cities like Los Angeles. As a novelist rather than a geographer, she paid particular attention to the issue of empowering people in times of "planetary urbanism" and imagining new forms of kinship and citizenship. In her hands, the novel, which is traditionally organized around the intersecting life stories of two or three human characters, becomes a space for thinking about ways to cultivate mutual responsibility in times of compounded global crises, to "reshape the common space of the world" to make it habitable, even as it is being transformed by "planetary urbanism". Arcangel plays the role of folk hero and leader of a spontaneous demonstration, Buzzworm is a self-appointed social services counselor, Rafaela unionizes fellow-janitors,

Bobby goes on a mission to rescue an undocumented migrant, and Manzanar creates an aesthetic screen to protect himself from the assault of "planetary urbanism". Several of the protagonists die in the cataclysm when "the urban *unfolds* into the countryside" and "the countryside *folds* back into the city" (Merrifield 542, italics in the original). The novel ends when the line of the tropic is cut and Bobby can no longer hold on to its two ends. The moment he "lets the lines slither around his wrists, past his palms, though his fingers", he "flies forward", arms open in an "embrace", but the readers are not allowed to see what he is flying towards (263).

Notes

1 In an interview with Michael S. Murashige, Yamashita speculated about why she initially had such difficulties with finding a publisher and then a readership for *Through the Arc of the Rain Forest*: "It wasn't Asian American feminist literature; it wasn't magic realism; it wasn't science fiction" (323).
2 Though U.S. government sources deny this, NAFTA solidified an old asymmetry between Mexico and the United States, dating back to the colonial era, for it gave U.S. manufacturers access to cheap Mexican labour and the license to flood Mexico with American products, without granting people on both sides of the border symmetrical rights to travel and work.
3 To my best knowledge, the first and complex and sustained piece of literary criticism deploying the notion of the "hinterland" is Emma Doolan's dissertation *Hinterland Gothic: Reading writing Australia's east coast hinterlands as Gothic spaces* (2018), an excerpt of which has been published under the title "Hinterland Gothic: Subtropical Excess in the Literature of South East Queensland" (2019).
4 In 1996, just one year before the publication of *Tropic of Orange*, Manuel Castells wrote: "Our societies are constructed around flows: flows of capital, flows of information, flows of technology, flows of organizational interactions, flows of images, sounds and symbols. Flows are not just one element of social organization: they are the expression of the processes dominating our economic, political, and symbolic life .... Thus, I propose the idea that there is a new spatial form characteristic of social practices that dominate and shape the network society: the space of flows. The space of flows is the material organization of time-sharing social practices that work through flows. By flows I understand purposeful, repetitive, programmable sequences of exchange and interaction between physically disjointed positions held by social actors" (Castells, *The Information Age*, 412).
5 This image is clearly based on one of the novel's epigraphs, taken from Guillermo Gómez-Peña's poem titled "Freefalling Toward a Borderless Future": "standing on the map of my political desires/ I toast to a borderless future/ (I raise my glass of wine toward the moon)/ with ... / our Alaskan hair/ our Canadian head/ our u.s. torso/ our Mexican genitalia/ our Central American cojones/ our Caribbean sperm/ our South American legs/ our Patagonian feet/ our Antarctic nails". It may also have been inspired by Gómez-Peña's artistic performances.

Works Cited

Blyn, Robin. "Belonging to the Network: Neoliberalism and Postmodernism in Tropic of Orange." *MFS Modern Fiction Studies*, vol. 62, no. 2, 2016, pp. 191–216.

Brenner, Neil, ed. *Implosions/Explosions: Towards a Study of Planetary Urbanism*. Jovis Verlag GmbH, 2014.

Brenner, Neil, ed. "The Hinterland Urbanised?" *Architectural Design*, July 2016, pp. 118–27.

Castells, Manuel. *The Information Age: Economy, Society, and Culture*. Vol. I. *The Rise of the Network Society*. Blackwell, 1996.

Doolan, Emma. *Hinterland Gothic: Reading and Writing Australia's East Coast Hinterlands as Gothic Spaces*. Brisbane: Queensland University of Technology, 2018. PhD dissertation.

Doolan, Emma. "Hinterland Gothic: Subtropical Excess in the Literature of South East Queensland." *eTropic Special Issue: Tropical Gothic*, vol. 18, no. 1, 2019, pp. 174–91.

Foster, Sesshu. "Introduction." *Tropic of Orange*. by Karen Tei Yamashita. 1997. Coffee House Press, 2017.

Guillermo Gómez-Peña. guillermogomezpena.com Accessed 19 Sept. 2022.

"Hinterland." *Oxford English Dictionaries Online*, 2019. https://en.oxford dictionaries.com/definition/hinterland. Accessed 12 Sept. 2022.

Lefebvre, Henri. "The Right to the City." *Writings on Cities*. 1968. Edited and translated by Eleonore Kofman and Elizabeth Lebas. Blackwell, 1996, pp. 147–59.

Merrifield, Andy. "The Urban Question under Planetary Urbanization." *Implosions/Explosions: Towards a Study of Planetary Urbanism*. Ed. Neil Brenner. Jovis Verlag GmbH, 2014, pp. 164–80.

Moloch, Harvey. "The City as a Growth Machine." *American Journal of Sociology*, vol. 82, Sept. 1976, pp. 309–32.

Murashige, Michael S. "Karen Tei Yamashita." *Words Matter: Conversations with Asian American Writers*. Ed. King-Kok Cheung. Honolulu: University of Hawai'i Press, 2000, pp. 320–42.

Tanaka, Shouhei. "The Great Arrangement: Planetary Petrofiction and Novel Futures." *MFS Modern Fiction Studies*, vol. 66, no. 1, 2020, pp. 190–215.

Yamashita, Karen Tei. *Through the Arc of the Rain Forest*. Coffee House, 1990.

Yamashita, Karen Tei. *Tropic of Orange*. Minneapolis: Coffee House, 1997.

2 Mapping identity and memory in Phaswane Mpe's *Welcome to Our Hillbrow*

S. U. Kriegel

This chapter focuses on the relationship between hinterlands, memory, and mobility in *Welcome to Our Hillbrow* (2001) to analyse the complex formation of identity in South Africa at the turn of the millennium. The literary analysis will look at how the concept of hinterlands is used as a spatializing practice to negotiate questions of belonging on an individual as well as on a national level. The novel *Welcome to Our Hillbrow* serves as a starting point for such an inquiry, as it is widely recognized as part of the literary canon of a new South Africa after the end of apartheid. In this novel, Phaswane Mpe explores questions of (national) belonging through the main characters and their movement from the hinterlands to the South African metropolis of Johannesburg and later Oxford, England. The main characters insert the hinterlands into urban centres by inscribing their memories of the periphery through mobility into the cityscape. The hinterland becomes a spatializing practice that situates the individual characters in particular time and place, thus linking them to the genealogy of a new nation. By focusing on the function of hinterlands in the novel, the different ideas of collective identities in the discourse on the new South African nation become more visible. In addition, the nation's hinterlands are sites of cultural entanglement after apartheid (Nuttall 2009) that reach beyond the nation state and question the current postcolonial world order.

Hinterlands as spatializing practice

The term *hinterland* has recently received more attention (Topalovic et al. 2013), especially in the (post)colonial contexts (Korieh 2000; Curto 2003) of a few specific hinterlands. Regarding South Africa, with its continued public discourse on land reform and constrains on (social) mobility after apartheid, a focus on its (literary) hinterlands helps us to think through questions of belonging. It also helps us to understand how these must be negotiated against the lasting effects of inequality caused by colonization,

DOI: 10.4324/9781032617732-4

institutionalized racism, and the socioeconomic divide of capitalist rural-urban development.

Therefore, the chapter highlights the way a relational understanding of space and mobility can be combined with postcolonial studies and intersectional theory to achieve a more comprehensive understanding of South African literary texts that negotiate belonging. In addition, it emphasizes the value of the concept of hinterland for literary criticism and as a spatializing practice. Mobility theories add constructive insights to literary criticism, which so far rarely incorporates them (Aguiar et al. 4), even though mobility is a constitutive element of storytelling (Berensmeyer and Ehland 11). A short theoretical discussion is followed by a concise historical contextualization and a close reading analysis of *Welcome to Our Hillbrow* against the key concepts of hinterlands, mobility, and memory.

A concise conceptualization of hinterlands is hindered by the varying use of the term as literally referring to peripheralized places or metaphorically as unknown places out of sight. Both meanings, however, use the concept of the peripheral as a common denominator, which always includes notions of exclusion (Ameel et al. 9). Hinterlands were first defined from a geographic-economic perspective as those regions that served a (colonial) port and by extension resource extraction, which later made the doctrine of hinterlands an integral part of European colonizing policies (Uzoigwe 1976). The term is often associated with remoteness, a removal from cultural and economic centres, even from modernity, and in opposition to the urban. Nevertheless, the hinterland often lacks the wholesomeness of the countryside (Ndebele 1998). In addition, the hinterland's remoteness does not make it necessarily rural (Tsing 2015). In today's world, the hinterland can also be situated in suburbs and inner-city wastelands (Neel 2018). Even though global cities appear independent from their hinterlands, they are, in fact, still fed by them (Topalovic 2013) and are, therefore, functionally central. Hinterlands cannot be clearly demarcated from the centres of power that they border and definingly enclose (Ameel et al. 7). Since the application of the peripheral is fluid, it can be used to exclude voices and put people out of sight by situating them (metaphorically) in a hinterland and thereby removing them from the normative power of the centre. Perhaps the hinterland is best defined by the usage of the term as a means to situate a place and its people at a (normative) periphery while refraining from declaring them as outright "other". It seems easier to define hinterlands by what they are not than by what they are.

When hinterlands are understood as a means to demarcate difference, their borders become fluid and their fringes reach into the centres of power. The hinterland as space becomes a dynamic and relational concept with the possibility of being a simultaneous and interrelated process of materially embedded practices (Massey 2005). However, this under-standing of space assumes a co-constitutive relationship between space and mobility because one space needs to be defined in relation to another and mobility allows for the overcoming of differences between two spaces (material or immaterial) (Frello 2008). Therefore, to define a metaphorical or literal space of the hinterland depends on aspects of mobility and those always involve moments of control that (re)enforce power (Massey 149–50), especially in a (post)colonial context. In that sense, hinterlands become a kind of spatializing practice that is embedded in asymmetric power relations and contributes to the time and place specificity of belonging. When applied to South Africa, the concept of hinterlands was used to establish the urban as a central and most importantly white space. The black experience became situated in the remote periphery, negating black urbanization as beyond the norm, thus subordinating black lived experience to that of persons considered white. Yet, white urbanity depended on a workforce of coloured and black people and was thus tightly interwoven with the hinterlands that took such forms as townships and racially mixed neighbourhoods (Bremner 1998; Chipkin 1998; Crankshaw and Parnell 1998).

As a geographically central neighbourhood in Johannesburg, Hillbrow shows how the hinterland as a spatializing practice is an integral part in the discourse on belonging in South Africa. The district holds symbolic meaning, dominating Johannesburg's skyline with the Ponte Building and Hillbrow Tower, results of apartheid's efforts in white urbanization. Additionally, it is a known example of inner-city "urban decay" of for-merly "whites only" areas. From the 1980s on, the neighbourhood became increasingly racially mixed due to social and economic factors that made it attractive and possible for coloured and black workers to move closer to the city centre, their place of work. Today, Hillbrow is densely populated by people coming from the countryside or other African nations. Hillbrow carries symbolic relevance as a characteristic feature of Johannesburg, a locus of national culture in South Africa. Therefore, any story set in Hillbrow can be read as a commentary on discourses that go beyond the urban centre.

Set in the late 1990s, *Welcome to Our Hillbrow* incorporates autobio-graphical elements into an exploration of the way "home" communities can be constructed, maintained, and claimed. The novel is focalized through two characters: Refentše, a black man from the remote village Tiragalong in Limpopo Province, and Refilwe, a black woman and his ex-girlfriend from the same village. Both move independently to Johannesburg, Hillbrow, to pursue their higher education and careers, though Refilwe later moves on to Oxford, England. The narrative structure of the novel foregrounds the spatializing effects of hinterlands, memory, and mobility when it first follows Refentše's movements to and through the district in detail and, after his suicide, focuses on the memory that Refilwe constructs of him in both places by means of mobility. The narration traces how the hinterland becomes embedded in the city and relates its characters' struggle for belonging to the wider context of the nation and globalized world.

Mapping Hillbrow at the intersection of mobility, memory, and hinterland

In South Africa, the citizens' legal freedom of movement is one of the main achievements after apartheid. Mobility is not a good that is equally accessible to everybody. It reflects power differences (Beck 111) that privilege mobility over stasis and associate it with the more powerful. Hinterlands are often seen as remote, unimportant places of stasis, when in fact the centre depends on the resources that can be mobilized in the hinterlands. Both main characters embody these resources when they move from rural Tiragalong to Hillbrow. However, they take the memory of their hinterland origin with them to the city and go back and forth (physically and metaphorically) between the two spaces.

Tiragalong, as well as Hillbrow, are characterized using established literary tropes. The village is depicted as a backward, superstitious hinterland full of gossip and ignorant violence, as the quote about the murder of Refentše's mother shows:

> Tiragalong's story was constructed when your mother slipped and fell into your grave on that hot Saturday morning of your burial. As Tiragalong believed, only witches could fall into a corpse's grave on burial. Medicine men had confirmed that, in the good old days, such things only happened to witches after they had bewitched the deceased … . (Mpe 43)

After such a portrayal of the hinterland, one might expect a contrasting depiction of the city as progressive, tolerant, and civilized, but the opposite holds true. Hillbrow is characterized by the well-established modernist trope of vice in the city. It is a place of violence (7), disease, specifically AIDS (3), and betrayal, or as Refentše summarizes it, "this part of Quartz (street was) more harmless and pleasurable – to the extent that anything in Hillbrow could be either of these things" (8–9). Despite the use of these tropes that commonly help to establish the divide between centre and periphery, the novel makes it abundantly clear that both places are interconnected through people's mobility, when Refentše demands from his cousin, with whom he stays in Hillbrow after his arrival: "hadn't we better also admit that quite a large percentage of our home relatives who get killed in Hillbrow, are in fact killed by other relatives and friends – people who bring their home grudges with them to Jo'burg" (18). The characters carry their origins from the hinterland to the city and thus inscribe the hinterland into the cityscape that is to become their new home.

The hinterland becomes interwoven with the city through the main characters' movements that map Hillbrow and their active recollection of memories from their previous home. Cumpsty (2019) has commented on the act of pedestrian mapping and how it can be read as a way to resist marginalization and incorporate African epistemologies into the urban environment. This chapter then focuses explicitly on the role of hinterlands and memory in the process of inscribing the self into a new environment by means of mapping.

In the first chapter, which is conveniently called "Hillbrow: The Map", readers follow Refentše and his cousin on an introductory walk through the district. This process of orientation is articulated in the description of the walk and the conscious naming of each street that is passed.

There is Hillbrow for you!

If you are coming from the city centre, the best way to get to Cousin's place is by driving or walking through Twist Street, a one-way street that takes you to the north of the city. You cross Wolmarans and three rather obscure streets, Kapteijn, Ockers and Pieterse, before you drive or walk past Esselen, Kotze and Pretoria Streets. You will then cross Van der Merwe and Goldreich Streets. Your next port of call is Caroline Street. … On your right-hand side is a block of flats called Vickers Place … you will ignore the lift and walk up the stairs to the fifth floor where Cousin stays. (Mpe 6)

The described physical act of moving through Hillbrow relates the present cityscape to South Africa's racist regimes of the past by explicitly stating each street's name. There is power in naming things just as much as in not doing so and this power lies in the selectiveness of the process. The above-mentioned walk passes by Hillbrow police station, whose reputation was notorious under apartheid, yet the narrative voice does not acknowledge that (Knapp 89). This selectiveness can be read as refraining from direct engagement with the past to minimize the risk of essentialism or nostalgia. After all, the past racist regime's perpetrators, victims, and those in-between are still alive and need to live together in the present and future of a new nation.

For Refentše, the walk prompts memories of Tiragalong, which are used to situate these places next to each other. The hinterland becomes present in the same space-time that Refentše experiences and uses to orientate himself in Hillbrow (and South Africa's past). Recalling Tiragalong is a means to situate a claim to the city but at the same time it stresses the relationships that create Hillbrow and reach beyond its geographical borders into the hinterland, all the way to Tiragalong. Refentše acknowledges that when he demands from his cousin "hadn't we better also admit that quite a large percentage of our home relatives who get killed in Hillbrow, are in fact killed by other relatives and friends—people who bring their home grudges with them to Jo'burg" (Mpe 3). Belonging is presented as a complex process where memory and mobility converge in an individual's perception of home as the narrative voice later explains to Refentše:

> You discovered, on arriving in Hillbrow, that to be drawn away from Tiragalong also went hand-in-hand with a loss of interest in Hillbrow. Because Tiragalong was in Hillbrow. You always took Tiragalong with you in your consciousness whenever you came to Hillbrow or any other place. In the same way you carried Hillbrow with you always. (49)

Belonging in *Welcome to Our Hillbrow* is anchored in two geographically distinct places that are so heavily interrelated that one cannot exist without the other. Refentše's mapping and invocation of place-bound memories from Tiragalong create a hybrid space where the hinterland overlaps and merges with Hillbrow's streets and people. Thus, the hinterland is an integral means to construct the inner-city district of Hillbrow as "home". This hybrid space is also a borderland where the past and present meet, questioning imperial discourses of power and their lasting effects (Anzaldúa 1987; Mignolo and Tlostanova 2006).

For Refentše, the physical act of mapping binds his new surroundings to memory that allows him to relate to the new space. However, memory is also key, for Refentše, to claim Hillbrow as home.

> Refentše, child of Tiragalong (and, as you insisted in the days just before your death, also of Hillbrow), had never shared such (commonly held) sentiments. It was your opinion that the moral decay of Hillbrow, so often talked about, was in fact no worse than that of Tiragalong. (Mpe 17)

As his memory of the village fuses with the mapping of Hillbrow, the centre and hinterland become interrelated and interdependent in their existential meaning for Refentše, a "child" of both places. The memory of Tiragalong's "moral decay" exposes the immaterial similarities of the two geographically distinct places, highlighting the constructed nature of hinterlands and their peripheral character. In *Welcome to Our Hillbrow*, the ubiquitous violence, gossip, and ignorance question the artificial boundaries between the two spaces and their supposedly distinct place-boundedness. Refentše's movement integrates Hillbrow into a new narrative of origin for him. The concept of hinterland is used to create a notion of home as a highly interrelated place of simultaneous relations that situates its creator in place and time because, as Massey pointed out, "movement, and the making of relations, take/make time" (119) and are integral to claiming belonging. A relational and dynamic approach to hinterlands as spatializing practice focuses on relational arrangements of living beings and social goods that help us to define space and incorporate them in relationally ordered systems like a society (Löw 2006). These relations are impacted by processes of perception, memory, and imagination. Thus, memory becomes an integral part of social structures (Beck 110) and space making, especially regarding an individual's home making.

Creating nations, hinterlands, and memory

Regarding collective identities, *Welcome to Our Hillbrow* intimates that one's origin and memory are constructed, hence one's narrative of origin can be changed. This does not only hold true for Refentše, who becomes a child of Tiragalong and Hillbrow, but also for collectives and nations. The role of place for the development of new national identities in national literature has been recognized in East European countries after the end of the Soviet era (Macdonald 2013; Matajc 2014). A drastic change in the dominating system of rule entails that the past cannot be told in a linear narration. A sense of belonging through a shared origin becomes complicated. In South Africa, the end of apartheid disrupted established practices of collective identification. For a new shared identity to emerge, the disruptions need to be addressed and often place functions as a binding factor. A reclaiming and renegotiating of space is necessary to create the genealogy of a new nation to legitimize its existence after previous power structures have become obsolete. Practically speaking, places with symbolic relevance, like Johannesburg and Hillbrow, need to be shaped into a new home. The analytical focus on hinterlands uncovers those voices that were made peripheral by previous regimes and now move into the centre to claim their place in a new nation.

This process challenges established ideological and social barriers, since Hillbrow was demarcated as a white urban space. The conflict of separate collectives laying claim to the same district, and by extension to the nation, can be bridged by relying on different accounts of the past, where individual memory is perceived as complementary, an additional version of the official history (Wenzel 118). This process makes it necessary to approach space as interrelated and simultaneous to avoid a hierarchization of differing memories of a particular place thus making it more inclusive to differently privileged groups. Through the process of memory several perceptions of a place with symbolic importance can overlap in time and bind different people to a particular place in a sense of collective belonging. Fusing Tiragalong with Hillbrow allows Refentše to legitimately situate his origin in several geographically distinct places and supposedly distinct collectives.

The aesthetic strategy to use memory in combination with the spatializing practice of the hinterland constructs belonging for Refentše and explores the construction of collective identities as well as the question of who can live in the urban centres after apartheid. The answer might be found in the description of Refentše's jumping to his death from a balcony:

> the vibrating panorama of Hillbrow and all its multitudinous life stories, conducting themselves in the milk, honey and bile regions of your own expanding brain. Your head became incredibly painful. You heard the echoes of Welcome to our Hillbrow ... hitting relentlessly against your skull. Welcome to our Hillbrow ... Welcome to our Alexandra ... Welcome to our Tiragalong in Johannesburg .... (Mpe 79)

The overwhelming memories that accompany Refentše' death weave together his places of belonging. This is only possible by considering place as unbound, "as open and porous networks of social relations ... that imply 'identities' are constructed through the specificity of their interaction with other places rather than by counterposition to them" (Massey 121). The hinterland that supplies the goods and people for Johannesburg cannot be clearly separated from the metropolis. The boundaries are fluid and overlap because of the relationships and memories that mobile people form in their interaction with the spaces surrounding them. *Welcome to Our Hillbrow* has its main characters map the new urban surroundings through repeated walks, exposing the constructed nature of place and the artificiality of their racialized character. When mobility is linked to memory of the countryside home, it can potentially undermine hegemonic discourses of belonging (in political terms: citizenship) that are linked to racialized understandings of home. In South African history, the political discourse on hinterlands legitimized remote areas as "home" for a non-white population. The novel uses the memory of the hinterland, Refentše's rural origin, to join South Africa's past, present, and future in Hillbrow or, as the narrative voice puts it, "Your first entry into Hillbrow, Refentše, was the culmination of many converging routes ..." (Mpe 2). The novel integrates the notion of a peripheral hinterland into the new home in the city by turning it into a place of memory that is invoked by the cityscape and serves as reference point, especially for the relationships that are foundational to the main character's identity construction – or "feeling of being home". Hinterland as a spatializing practise in *Welcome to Our Hillbrow* works against a nostalgic and essentializing understanding of South Africa's past but also of space, when it comes to home, the city, and hinterlands, it legitimizes a presence in South Africa's past and future for black persons.

Carrying the colonial hinterland to the imperial centre

Welcome to Our Hillbrow belongs to a group of contemporary South African works of fiction that explore the intersection of racial, individual, and collective identity in their complex and often uneasy relationship to place. One of those complicating factors is South Africa's colonial past, which the novel addresses increasingly after Refentše's suicide, once the narrative focalization is shifted to Refilwe. In pursuit of a master's degree, Refilwe moves temporarily from Johannesburg to Oxford, Britain, before she returns to Hillbrow and eventually to Tiragalong to die of AIDS at home and be buried "in our land" (120). Her mobility from the global south to one of the most symbolic loci of Western knowledge and education can also be read through the hinterland as a spatializing practice. This expands the novel's commentary to a global postcolonial scale. The colonial policy of the hinterland placed African colonies at the periphery of the global north (Uzoigwe 1976). South Africa became the hinterland of the British imperial centre, a fact that had lasting socioeconomic effect. Refilwe's entry into Oxford reflects Refentše's arrival in Hillbrow.

> On her arrival in Oxford Brookes University, Refilwe was offered student accommodation at Morrel Hall in Marston, … . If you drove there from the corner of Gipsy Lane and Headington Road you would take the route to the city centre, drive past the main entrance to the Headington Hill Campus, and turn right into Marston Road. (Mpe 104)

Refilwe claims this place as hers when she arrives "at the corner of Gipsy Lane and Headington Road, where our University was" (100). In fact, just as with Refentše, her mobility through the city of Oxford, "the Seat of Learning" (99), brings the hinterland of the global south to the former imperial centre. Certain places that Refilwe encounters in Oxford remind her of "home", of Johannesburg and Tiragalong. Her movement through the different places that make the city evoke memories of a discursively peripheralized global south. Refilwe tells her acquaintances in

Oxford that "*Jude the Obscure* reminded her of *Sweeney's*, a pub in the Braamfontein Centre, just opposite the University of the Witwatersrand" (108). She becomes a "child of our Hillbrow and Tiragalong and Oxford", she is "a Hillbrowan. An Alexandran. A Johannesburger. An Oxfordian" (122).

If Refentše carries the hinterland into Johannesburg, as does Refilwe carry a global south into the "Seat of Learning", a centre of the global north. The novel, however, is even more ambitious and aims to involve the reader in this process of questioning established notions of periphery and centre or, more generally, closed and place-bound definitions of space. Over the course of the narrative, the use of the multivalent "you" changes its addressee multiple times, leaving the pronoun open for interpretation, as Carrol Clarkson observed in his discussion of identity formation in the novel (2005). "You" first addresses Refentše, and later shifts to Refilwe but it also functions to performatively address the readers. "Welcome to our … " can find its addressee within the text but it can also be directed outwards towards the readers. In this manner, the readers become involved in the narration's exploration of belonging and spatializing practices. They, too, can bring their hinterland to the reading of the novel and the questions of "home" that it raises.

In a paradoxical manner, the specific use of the address "you" can create distance and proximity because it puts places and people in close proximity regardless of their physical and geographic location. It confirms the simultaneity of space, when it places absent and present spaces next to each other, creating a certain ambiguity regarding the reality of space overall. Moreover, the use of the multivalent "you" underlines the ambivalence, instability, and interdependence of our understanding of different places and spatial categories, highlighting how one can use one spatial concept, like the hinterlands, in order to create another space, like home. The novel questions, in a globalized world, a peripheral perspective on the global south. There is no clear periphery when the character Refilwe moves from the Limpopo hinterlands to Johannesburg (as former British hinterland) then to Oxford (a British centre of knowledge and power), and claims it all as hers. In this regard, the novel challenges a core denominator of the common notion of hinterlands as being remote, excluded, and lacking agency.

Conclusion: Hinterlands as a means to question power

The concept of hinterland usually includes the notions of exclusion due to its peripheral character. *Welcome to Our Hillbrow* plays with that notion when it superficially establishes the rural Tiragalong as backwards, unprogressive, and distant and contrasts it with the one square mile district of Hillbrow in Johannesburg, as just as ignorant, uncivilized, and violent as the hinterland. Both places are intrinsically interrelated and become similar because of the relations of people and goods that move between the two places. Defining a hinterland is based on the privilege of power.

The concept of hinterland is used as a spatializing practice. In the novel, it is employed to construct the belonging of people that are not completely "other" but also do not yet fully belong to the centre of a new South Africa (Abdullah et al. 2021). The main characters' movement through Hillbrow relates their presence to the nation's racist past, while denoting its constructed character and insisting on presenting their selective narrative to the readers. Simultaneously, they inscribe their presence and their memory of the hinterland (by extension a part of their identity) into the cityscape to construct a home for themselves. The process further includes their voices in the genealogy of the nation that is represented by the symbolic cultural value of Hillbrow.

A relational, dynamic, and interrelated understanding of space stresses how the evocation of the hinterland in the centre leads to the overlapping, interrelation, and merging of different places and times the thus exposing the constructed and artificial nature of place. The novel pushes this exposure further when it brings the (post)colonial hinterland to a centre of power of the global north. The novel even goes so far as to include its readers in the process by addressing them directly through a multivalent "you", pointing to the need to question the racialized character of places and linear genealogies of nations and to bring one's own hinterlands to claim a seat at the table.

Works Cited

Abdullah, M.M., H.K.J. Singh, and O.M. Abdullah. "Decolonization, Neo-Apartheid and Xenophobic Violence in Phaswane Mpe's *Welcome to Our Hillbrow*." *Pretanika Journal of Social Sciences and Humanities*, vol. 29, no. 1, 2021, pp. 457–70. DOI: 10.47836/pjssh.29.1.25

Aguiar, Marian, C. Mathieson, and L. Pearce. "Introduction: Mobilities, Literature, Culture." *Mobilities, Literature, Culture*. Palgrave Macmillan, 2019, pp. 1–34. DOI: 10.1007/978-3-030-27072-8

Ameel, Lieven, J. Finch, and M. Salmela. "Introduction: Peripheral and Literary Urban Studies." *Literature and the Peripheral City*. Eds. Lieven Ameel et al. Palgrave Macmillan, 2015, pp. 1–17. DOI: 10.1057/9781137492883_1

Anzaldúa, G. *Borderland/La Frontera: The New Mestiza*. Aunt Lute, 1987.

Beck, Anna. "Subjective Spaces - Spatial Subjectivities: Movement and Mobility in Monica Ali's Brick Lane and Ian McEwan's Saturday." *Perspectives on Mobility*. Eds. Ingo Berensmeyer, and Christoph Ehland. Rodopi, 2013, pp. 107–24. DOI: 10.1163/9789401209649_008

Berensmeyer, Ingo, and Christoph Ehland. "Movement and Mobility: An Introduction." *Perspectives on Mobility*. Eds. Ingo Berensmeyer, and Christoph Ehland. Rodopi, 2013, pp. 11–27. DOI: 10.1163/9789401209649_003

Bremner, Lindsay. "Crime and the Emerging Landscape of Post-Apartheid Johannesburg." *Blank: Architecture, Apartheid and After*. Eds. Hilton Judin, and Ivan Vladislavić. NAi Publishers, 1998, pp. 49–63.

Chipkin, Clive. "The Great Apartheid Building Boom: The Transformation of Johannesburg in the 1960s." *Blank: Architecture, Apartheid and After*. Eds. Hilton Judin, and Ivan Vladislavić. NAi Publishers, 1998, pp. 250–67.

Clarkson, Carrol. "Locating Identity in Phaswane Mpe's *Welcome to Our Hillbrow*." *Third World Quarterly*, vol. 26, no. 3, 2005, pp. 451–59. DOI: 10.1080/01436590500033735

Crankshaw, Owen, and Susan Parnell. "Interpreting the 1994 African Township Landscape." *Blank: Architecture, Apartheid and After*. Eds. Hilton Judin, and Ivan Vladislavić. NAi Publishers, 1998, pp. 439–43.

Cumpsty, Rebekah. "Sacralizing the Streets: Pedestrian Mapping and Urban Imaginaries in Teju Cole's *Open City* and Phaswane Mpe's *Welcome to Our Hillbrow*." *The Journal of Commonwealth Literature*, vol. 54, no. 3, 2019, pp. 305–18. DOI: 10.1177/0021989417700232

Curto, José C. *Enslaving Spirits: The Portuguese-Brazilian Alcohol Trade at Luanda and ItsHinterland*, c. 1550-1830. Brill, 2003.

Frello, Birgitta. "Towards a Discursive Analytics of Movement: On the Making and Unmaking of Movement as an Object of Knowledge." *Mobilities*, vol. 3, no. 1, Mar. 2008, pp. 25–50. DOI: 10.1080/17450100701797299

Knapp, Adrian. *The Past Coming to Roost in the Present: Historicising History in Four Post-Apartheid South African Novels*. ibidem-Verlag, 2006.

Korieh, Chima J. "The Nineteenth Century Commercial Transition in West Africa: The Case of the Biafra Hinterland." *Canadian Journal of African Studies/La Revue canadienne des études africaines*, vol. 34, no. 3, 2000, pp. 588–615.

Löw, M. "The Social Construction of Space and Gender." *European Journal of Women's Studies*, vol. 13, no. 2, 2006, pp. 119–33.

Macdonald, Sharon. *Memorylands: Heritage and Identity in Europe Today*. Routledge, 2013.

Massey, Doreen. *Space, Place and Gender*. Polity Press, 1994.

Massey, Doreen B. *For Space*. Sage Publications Ltd., 2005.

Matajc, Vanesa. "'The Rhetorics of Space': Introduction.' *Neohelicon*, no. 41, 2014, pp. 3–12. DOI: 10.1007/s11059-013-0217-6.

Mignolo, W.D., and M.V. Tlostanova. "Theorizing from the Border." *European Journal of Social Theory*, vol. 9, no. 2, 2006, pp. 205–21. DOI: 10.1177/13 68431006063333

Mpe, P. *Welcome to Our Hillbrow*. Ohio University Press, 2011.

Ndebele, Njabulo S. "Game Lodges and Leisure Colonialists." *Blank: Architecture After Apartheid*. Eds. Hilton Judin, and Ivan Vladislavic. David Philips, 1998, pp. 119–23.

Neel, Phil A. *Hinterland: America's New Landscape of Class and Conflict*. London: Reaktion Books, 2018.

Nuttall, Sarah. *Entanglement: Literary and Cultural Reflections on Post-Apartheid Johannesburg.* Wits University Press, 2009.

Topalovic, Milica, et al. *Hinterland: Singapore, Johor, Riau.* Architecture of Territory/ETH, 2013.

Tsing, Anna Lowenhaupt. *Mushroom at the End of the World: On the Possibility of Life in Capitalist Ruins.* Princeton University Press, 2015.

Uzoigwe, G.N. "Spheres of Influence and the Doctrine of the Hinterland in the Partition of Africa." *Journal of African Studies*, vol. 3, no. 2, 1976, pp. 183–204.

Wenzel, Marita. "The Configuration of Boundaries and Peripheries in Johannesburg as Represented in Selected Works by Ivan Vladislavic and Zakes Mda." *Literature and the Peripheral City.* Eds. Lieven Ameel et al. Palgrave Macmillan, 2015, pp. 111–27.

3 Decrepitude, dispossession, poetry, and a no-place as a site of weak resistance

Twenty-first-century America as a hinterland in the films *Paterson* and *Nomadland*

Zofia Kolbuszewska

A joint discussion of the films *Paterson* (2016) directed by Jim Jarmusch, and *Nomadland* (2020), directed by Chloé Zhao, might at first sight appear rather misconceived and futile because the films differ in their territorial focus and cinematic genre. *Paterson* belongs to "slow cinema", and presents a repetitive mundane routine of a small-town bus driver, while *Nomadland,* whose protagonists travel all over the United States, is a docu-drama that belongs to the cinema of "structured reality". However, by juxtaposing the two films, this chapter seeks to bring out an often overlooked, yet, in the conception of Phil A. Neel, an inseparable and indispensable, if perhaps less consequential, element of hinterland topography – a desert, a no-place. When conceived of in both geographical and metaphorical terms, its significance as a site of the "weak resistance" against the "unity of separation" of hinterland inhabitants enforced by late capitalism is illuminated and reinforced.

Hinterland topography is shaped by the pressure of the post-industrial economy on the landscape and inhabitants of cities and countryside, both locally and globally. Neel's incisive analyses and scathing commentary, presented in the book *Hinterland: America's New Landscape of Class and Conflict*, offer a convenient vantage point from which to examine the representations of American hinterlands evoked in the films *Paterson* and *Nomadland* and interrogate the ways both films underscore salvaging communal values from the process of physical and social dereliction in contemporary America. Part-rural and part-heavily industrialized space (factory farms, massive logistics complexes, sites of power generation, and sites of resource extraction), the hinterland spreads as a "disavowed, distributed core distinct from the central city, its industries and services" (Neel 17), but "more integral to 'the

DOI: 10.4324/9781032617732-5

immediate process of production'" (17). The hinterland is thus defined by its distance from the "booming cores of the supposedly 'post-industrial economy'" (17). The "far" hinterland "is more traditionally 'rural'" (17) although nowadays it is "largely a space for disaster industries, government aid, and large-scale industrial extraction, pro-duction, and initial processing of primary products" (17–18). The far hinterland also includes "large urban zones of collapse" (18) such as the inner cities of the Rust Belt. On the other hand, the "near" hinter-land is largely suburban, yet should not necessarily be associated with white the affluent middle class that has recently been relocating to the gentrified city centres, while the suburban areas are populated at an accelerating pace by inhabitants who staff large logistics complexes that exist beyond the urban core, or who commute downtown to work in service industries (17–18). The bird's-eye view of the geography of the post-industrial economy in constant crisis reveals, as he observes, "small green zones nested in vast logistics-industrial spaces that extend laterally from these cores, dwindling finally to rural spaces crosscut by thin transit corridors" (97).

However, Neel distinguishes yet another territory in his hinterland topography – the desert, an area that is of no use to the post-industrial economy due to the earlier depletion of resources or legal inaccessibility. Created in the wake of industrial exploitation and characterized by the destruction of local economies and social networks of support, or off limits for corporations owing to their status as federal lands, desert areas become ideal loci of resistance to the dominating economy because "the real deserts are largely invisible from the metropolis—they are simply too far beyond its walls" (34).

Moreover, the desert offers its visitors a respite from participating in the production of "human waste", an opportunity that most of the exhausted and wretched hinterland inhabitants, considered by Zygmunt Bauman "wasted lives", are precluded from embracing:

> The production of 'human waste' … is an inevitable outcome of modernization, and an inseparable accompaniment of modernity. It is an inescapable side-effect of order-building (each order casts some parts of the extant population as 'out of place', 'unfit' or 'undesirable') and of economic progress (that cannot proceed without degrading and deva-luing the previously effective modes of 'making a living' and therefore cannot but deprive their practitioners of their livelihood). (5)

As inhabitants of the post-industrial world, the "wasted lives" may also be referred to as "the material community of capital" (Neel 20). The only connection they have with others in a world entirely at the service of capitalist production is their shared dependence on the exigencies of a ruthless economy premised on infinite growth, immediate gratification of the consumer, and ever accelerating speed (20). Only the cultivation of communal practices in defiance of the speed and wastefulness of liquid modernity is capable of disrupting and threatening to derail the swift and orderly streamlining of this "unity of separation" (20) that makes the capitalist production feasible. Communal efforts such as mutual emotional support, education, practicing non-commodified lifestyles, conservation, and recycling contribute to the seizing and repurposing of the impersonal infrastructure that economic mechanisms rely upon (47). The desert as an area abandoned, overlooked, forgotten, or inaccessible to before post-industrial economy constitutes a site of resistance which can be appropriated by various opponents of "the material community of capital" – for instance far-right militias whose response to the permanent economic crisis and the new geography of the hinterland to which it has given rise assumes various forms of partisanship (35). The partisan's pragmatic goal of building power in the midst of the crisis is different from that of the leftist "who instead focuses on building elaborate political programs and ornate utopias" (53).

Nomadland and *Paterson* demonstrate yet another model of resistance facilitated by a recourse to the desert's liminal status that helps incite acts of defiance against capitalist commodification, reification, and wasteful excess. Cherished return to a desert, no-place inherent in the topography enforced by the late capitalism, yet beyond the reach of its atomizing and alienating power, is a return to a site where relations between humans can evolve into a participation in creative activity, as well as mutual economic and emotional support. This, in turn, leads to the rise of an intentionally built communal culture; a culture that is not subordinated to the overwhelming rush of the time turned into a capitalist commodity. It is worth noting, however, that not only is the figure of the desert particularly fraught with utopian political significance, but it also evokes philosophical and poetical reflection on the transformative, regenerative, and creative potential of liminality and nothingness:

> The figure of the desert ... appears on the horizon of what Povinelli calls our 'Carbon Imaginary',[1] our habit of viewing everything in terms of birth, life, death and finitude. The Carbon Imaginary must contend with 'the problem of how something emerges from nothing and returns to nothingness; how the one (1) emerges from the zero (0) and descends back into it'. What Freud described in terms of the death instinct must be located on a geological and geopolitical and not just a psychosexual level. The zero retains a transformative potential ... . (Tynan 11)

As represented in both films, America emerges as a projection of the "Carbon Imaginary", a decrepit hinterland where post-industrial ruins, industrial facilities, and nature encroach on one another, forming a depressing yet uncanny hybrid landscape that serves as a backdrop, catalyzer, and agent in the lives of the characters who hold simple jobs in *Paterson* or most of the time are on the look-out for temporary, seasonal work in *Nomadland*. The viewer witnesses the very modest material conditions of their life set in a post-industrial landscape of a small town in *Paterson* and their impoverishment, dispossession, and the loss of their middle-class status in the wake of economic and social crises in *Nomadland*. The space contiguous to or situated beyond the hinterland, from a late capitalist point of view considered a wasteland, emerges in these films as a site of resistance to the social, cultural, and environmental havoc wreaked by the depletion of all kinds of resources in a country subordinated to the logistical, material, and philosophical exigencies of capitalist economy. Its policy of turning both humans and their environment into raw resources and commodities (Zuboff) has rent the delicate tissue of social solidarity and led to the decrepitude of the environment and dispossession of the labour force.

The artistic examination of life rife with social tensions and economic inequality as well as the interrogation of alterity and exclusion facilely lend themselves to reductive representations: they are frequently either divorced from the material reality of represented subjects due to aestheticizing romanticization or intellectual abstraction, or, conversely, err on the side of, so to speak, pornographic naturalism. The films *Paterson* and *Nomadland* deftly avoid these pitfalls, even as their aesthetic strategies inscribe themselves in the American poetic tradition that embraces both the Dickinsonian succinctness and precise philosophical scrutiny of the mundane, and the Whitmanian directness with its intensity of attention to the immediacy of everyday experience, rootedness in the reverence for the tangible texture of the world, and insight into the condition of common Americans. Jarmusch's film presents a microscale close-up of an American hinterland, whose staggering macroscale interrogated in *Nomadland* is shown as an ironic reversal of the liberating power of the American on-the-road myth. In twenty-first-century America, in the circumstances of rapidly growing economic hiatus between the rich and the poor – the already dispossessed, homeless, undocumented, and quickly dwindling middle class pushed beneath the poverty line – the revolt against the post-Wold War II American society's conformism and a quest for mythical regeneration give way to the entrapment of the seeming dynamism of the mobility of those in constant search for temporary jobs. Yet, under certain conditions, this hectic mobility can, paradoxically, turn out to be as liberating as a routinely repetitive bus route in the town of Paterson.

Paterson, loosely based on William Carlos Williams' epic poem *Paterson* (1946–1958, 1963), and some of his other poems, in particular "The Young Housewife" (1916), is Jim Jarmusch's tribute to American Modernist poetry and poetry in general. The city of Paterson featured in Jarmusch's movie, just as Williams' city of Paterson, New Jersey, can be construed as a holographic or fractal image of America. This is very much in keeping with the poet's conviction "that for art or poetry to be effective and universal it must adapt to local conditions" (Miller 183). Yet, rather than filtering reality through the consciousness of Dr Paterson, who in Williams' poem examines America's history and its "symptomatic" dreams, Jarmusch, even as he draws on a passage from *Paterson* in which Dr Paterson's thoughts are personified as bus passengers, prefers to entrust the doctor's consciousness into the custody of the bus driver who happens to be a poet, effectively making him the "lyrical I" of the film:

> Say it! No ideas but in things. Mr
> Paterson has gone away
> to rest and write. Inside the bus one sees
> his thoughts sitting and standing. His
> thoughts alight and scatter—
> (Williams 9)[2]

The doctor's thoughts, metaphorically presented in Williams' poem as riding on a city bus, metamorphose in Jarmusch's film into poetical reflections of the bus driver, inspired by watching passengers occupied with their daily routines and mundane problems.

The film presents at a slow pace a week in the life of that city bus driver, who is named Paterson and lives with his wife, Laura, in the town of Paterson, New Jersey. Each day's routine follows the same pattern: Paterson gets up early in the morning and goes to work, listens to the same mundane complaints of another bus driver, gets behind the wheel, and drives his bus along the same route. He enjoys listening to his passengers talk, revels in the cultural and racial diversity of the passenger crowd, attentively yet kindly observes their gestures and behaviour, and is always helpful and quietly reassuring when his assistance is needed. On his bus route and when walking to and from work he scrutinizes with renewed fascination the same minutest details of the decrepit urban landscape of downtown Paterson. During pauses, Paterson writes poetry in a notebook he always carries with him. After work, he takes Marvin, his wife's dog, for a walk and has a beer at Shades Bar, where he is greeted by regular patrons and the owner, Doc.

Laura, whose visual artistic sensibility finds expression in the exhilaration of decorating her environment and her baking, loves husband's poems. She keeps encouraging him to publish them or at least make copies, and finally, one day he reluctantly agrees. Unfortunately, Marvin gets to the notebook first, chews on it, and shreds its pages, destroying Paterson's poems. The following day, when the bus driver, dejected, contemplates the Great Falls of the Passaic River in Paterson – falls to which Williams devoted a whole section of his poem – he notices a Japanese man reading *Paterson*. Even though Paterson denies it, the Japanese person recognizes a poet in the modest man and offers him an empty notebook as a gift, pointing to the poetical appeal of blank pages, a creative potential inherent in emptiness; in nothing – in a metaphorical no-place.

Nomadland, in turn, belongs to the cinema of "structured reality" and "has been widely praised for its mix of poetry and realism" (Rose). It is a docu-drama adapted from a 2017 nonfiction book by the journalist Jessica Bruder, shot in actual landscapes and workplaces, whose cast is mostly made up of non-professional actors, or perhaps more precisely, non-actors playing themselves, except for Frances McDormand and David Strathairn. It follows developments in the life of Fern, a fictional character, who, after losing her job at the U.S. Gypsum plant in Empire, Nevada, which shut down in 2011, sells most of her belongings, which remind her of her recently passed husband, and purchases a van to live in. She crisscrosses the country in search for work. On the job in an Amazon fulfilment centre, she meets a woman who invites her to attend a fellow-nomads' desert convention in Arizona, organized by a Bob Wells – an actual person, the leader of the twenty-first-century American nomad community of elderly people living in campers, and its support network. There, Fern is introduced to an ecologically viable and economical way of living; participates in the recycling and exchange of kitchen utensils, tools, and other useful objects; and learns the survival skills and self-sufficiency a nomad needs to persist on the road in defiance of the late-capitalist corporate grip on America and the globalized world.

Fern makes friends with elderly people who have no medical insurance, thus their life expectancy is shortened, and people who earn too little money in their temporary jobs to pay both the rent and gas. Only a few of them have relatives to whom they can – reluctantly – turn for support. In order to be able to operate from their vans or campers, they are forced to travel all over the country in search of low-paying jobs in gigantic Amazon storage facilities, the tourist industry, fast-food restaurants, or food processing plants in remote locations. Forced to borrow money to fix her van, Fern visits her sister in California. After Fern falls out with the sister's bank manager husband about the responsibility of financial institutions for economic crises that lead to massive unemployment, poverty, home evictions, and homelessness, the sister confesses she envies Fern's courage and independence. Fern continues her foraging for a living and revisits the nomads' meeting place in Arizona, where she participates in the tribute to a dead friend. Even as this intensifies her mourning for her late husband, Bob Wells' words – that for the nomad community the promise of meeting again "down the road" defies the finality of goodbyes – offer her a consolation. *Nomadland* starts with a finality of the demise of a plant that embodies the seeming inevitability of economic stagnation with its apparently ineluctable unemployment, but the film's ending is open if not serene. Before hitting the road again, Fern returns to the nearly abandoned Empire, a town whose postal code has been cancelled, to dispose of the rest of her belongings kept in storage. In complete silence, she visits her office in the shut-down factory and the home she shared with her husband.

The community of nomads featured in *Nomadland* resist "the unity of separation" in their unique style. They are mostly elderly people who, unlike the young protagonists of Jack Kerouac's novel *On the Road*, have hit the road not by choice, but out of economic necessity. The contrast is best brought out in a passage in which the narrator makes an observation on what makes one of Kerouac's minor characters, Gene Dexter, take to the road: "crossing and recrossing the country every year, south in the winter and north in the summer, and only because he had no place he could stay in without getting tired of it and *because there was nowhere to go but everywhere*, keep rolling under the stars, generally the Western stars" (19, emphasis ZK).

The elderly van and camper owners, too, go everywhere because there is nowhere to go after they became homeless, divested of their life savings, and unable to find a permanent job. They, however, embody Bauman's "wasted lives", whereas the lives of Kerouac's protagonists were wasted in a different struggle, as a romantic gesture in a transgressive oedipal rebellion against the stifling and repressive culture and politics of the Cold War America. Even as they cover ever more territory and transgress the boundaries of normalized conformity, Kerouac's beatniks seek spiritual regeneration, if not actual political lucidity, or communal activism, because they "substitute[ed] mythology for political realities" (Pease 270); their countercultural gestures lacked historical consciousness (Pease 277).[3] It is hard to ignore the irony in the fact that Kerouac's characters were protesting against the political and cultural conformism of the America that was a beneficiary of the New Deal. Conversely, the protagonists of *Nomadland* have witnessed the dismantling of the New Deal, which removed all safeguards keeping them from sliding into poverty. That is why they need communal support, and they find it precisely in the desert, a no-place, a nowhere. Travestying the passage from *On the Road* invoked earlier, the dispossessed nomadic elderly, who travel everywhere across America in their vans and campers, indeed have a "nowhere" to go – they regularly return to a no-place in the Arizona desert to attend campers' rendezvous.

It is in that no-place of the desert that the nomads articulate their paradoxical, utopian yet concrete, communal reply to the condition of "the material community of capital". Unlike that of far-right militias, their response, although also articulated and shaped in the desert, consists neither in building power or pursuing violent partisanship, nor in proposing a utopian political program. Rather, very much in the spirit of William Carlos Williams' pre-New Deal individualist progressivism, they reinforce and intensify communal practices and return to "the 'smallness' of building with one's 'bare hands'" (Williams 2; Miller 171). It thus comes as no surprise to what extent Williams' poetic reflection on America – its culture, poetry, the American dream, and economy – evinced in the poem *Paterson*, pertains to the plight of the *Nomadland* community. Community-building education in survival, self-care, fixing and repairing, respectful handling of instruments, utensils, tools, and equipment, as well as recycling and ecological pro-activity evinced in the film fulfil the poet's injunction: "No ideas but in things" (Williams 9). Poetry in particular can be counted among those practices that not only do not rely on, but indeed defy, economic mechanisms underlying post-industrial capitalism and its strategies of enforcing "the unity of separation".

Among many intertextual references to modernist poets and writers, in Book V, part III of *Paterson* there appears an indirect allusion to W. H. Auden's "Musée des Beaux Arts", which emphasizes a complex relationship between artistic imagination and mundane existence, as well as lashing out at the careless insensitivity of the powerful and affluent to the plight of the ordinary man and the indifference to the rich texture of everyday life:

Peter Brueghel the artist saw it
from the two sides: the
imagination must be served—
and he served
dispassionately
It is no mortal sin to be poor—anything but this featureless
tribe that has money now—staring into the atom, completely blind—without grace or pity, as if they were so many
shellfish. The artist, Brueghel, saw them: the
suits of his peasants were of better stuff, hand woven, than we can boast
(Williams 228)[4]

The mention of Breughel's rendition in his paintings of the fabric worn by peasants not only brings out the poet's conviction that a hand-woven fabric exceeds in quality those industrially produced, but also emphasizes the materiality of the text, a word whose meaning derives from the Latin word "weaving" (etymonline). Thus, invoked materiality situates poetry in the world of things and makes it consequential in the reader's reality.

In this context, it is fitting to invoke another poem by Auden, "In Memory of W. B. Yeats" (1939), in which he reflects on poetry's strengths and weaknesses. Auden, however, writes despondently of poetry's insufficient agentic power, yet extolls its resilience: "For poetry makes nothing happen: it survives/In the valley of its making where executives/Would never want to tamper" (82). The poet pits poetry against the management of capitalist economy and observes that the world projected by poetry, "the valley of its making", is located beyond the capitalists' reach. Yet, the phrase "for poetry makes nothing happen" sounds like a pessimistic statement about the incommensurability of these two realities, the inconsequentiality of the poetic word in the world of things, economy, and politics. According to Auden, poetry, contrary to Williams' conviction, has no power to exert influence in the readers' material world and produce particular effects, even as it derives from the miserable circumstances of that world. Auden's stanza goes on to locate the sources of poetry in the local, the impoverished, and the desolate. These are to be found in "raw towns" like Williams' and Jarmusch's Paterson: "it flows south/From ranches of isolation and busy griefs,/Raw towns that we believe and die in" (Auden 82). Nonetheless, this anguished but compelling image might elicit unease and inspire – more in the spirit of Williams' vision of poetry – an alternative, positive reading of the phrase "poetry makes nothing happen". Perhaps it might be productive to change the accentuation from "poetry makes *nothing* happen" to "poetry makes nothing *happen*". In this way, the relocation of emphasis grants poetry the power of conjuring up "nothing" – a no-place; a site of possibility beyond the reach of the political and economic regimes; a metaphorical desert – a site of imagination and transformation as well as of regenerative potential. Such power of poetry is evoked in the film *Paterson* in the scene where the Japanese man points to the appeal of blank pages of an empty notebook he offers to the bus driver.

The power of poetry as a strategy of resisting the late-capitalist reduction of reality to economically assessed utility is also underscored in *Paterson* by the director's employment of devices and formal features that characterize the so-called "slow cinema". A subject of heated debates about whether it can be considered a politically vibrant and/or aesthetically engrossing, or just a self-conscious, complacent artistic phenomenon catering to cultural elitists (Çağlayan 3), yet dubbed as "perhaps the most exciting art cinema current in the twenty-first century" (3), slow cinema operates at the cusp of "global networks of production, exhibition and distribution and local articulations of native traditions" (4). It is characterized by numerous paradoxes: "inasmuch as the films are elusive, opaque and difficult to grasp, the discursive and theoretical framework in which they operate similarly eludes comprehension" (222). Aptly, the stylistic devices employed by Jarmusch underscore an aesthetic sensibility manifested in "the expansion, elongation and exaggeration of cinematic temporality and the valorisation of ambiguity" (224); a sensibility that finds expression in such conceptual tropes as nostalgia, boredom, and absurdism – generally viewed as touchstones of modernist art cinema (224). The director consciously adopts the modernist tropes of slow cinema in a film conceived of as a tribute to American Modernist poetry. Thus, *Paterson* is also from a formal point of view a transgressive excursion into the territory "where executives/ Would never want to tamper" (Auden 82). In celebrating the monotony of daily routines, the slow pace of camera movement and its panning shots defy individuals' alienation from networks of support and solidarity by visualizing unexpected, often poetically motivated connections. The camera insistently dwells on behaviour and relationships that appear absurd from the perspective of senseless rush of lives trapped in the treadmill of economic exigencies. The slow-cinema poetics of *Paterson* encourage re-imagining the ways of relating to the hinterland, as well as exploring utopian possibilities that emerge from occupying a no-place as a site of transformation inseparable from the topography of the hinterland.

Creativity and communal engagement, presented in Jarmusch's *Paterson* and Zhao's *Nomadland* as strategies of defying the capitalist economy's drive to turn out human waste, can also be considered an embodiment of Ruth Levitas' conception of "utopia as method" that may potentially lead to "the imaginary reconstitution of society". Utopia, a no-place, is viewed as an imaginary site inviting discussion and negotiation in order to "accommodate changes in the way in which aspirations for a better life may be expressed" (5). It is a situated method that "simultaneously critique[es] the present, explor[es] alternatives, imagin[es] ourselves otherwise and experiment[s] with prefigurative practice[s]" (219). Thus, a potentially reconstituted society is not a repressed precariat anymore but acquires cultural agency. This is precisely the vision of society that underpins the conception of "weak resistance" (Majewska), a term invoked by Ewa Majewska to describe the phenomenon of Polish women's 2016 "black protest" against the draft of a very restrictive abortion law (eventually instituted pursuant to the decision of the Polish Constitutional Tribunal in 2020). The conception of "weak resistance" draws on Vaclav Havel's ideas presented in his essay "The Power of the Powerless", and questions the necessity of adopting the strategy of heroic struggle in order to manifest resistance, political agency, and the solidarity of the excluded. While rejecting patriarchal male individualism, "weak resistance" draws on feminist materialism in that its focus is society understood as a network of interrelated elements characterized less by having no access to the means of production than by active participation in the field of cultural reproduction (Majewska). Majewska emphasizes the crucial importance of an artistic aspect of "weak resistance":

> Art occupies a crucial position in the reflection on weak resistance, first of all as the area of cultural production that, often in advance, provides diagnoses and gives expression to those problems of the contemporary world that have not yet acquired a recognizable political shape and a name communicable in the mass media, or that have not been postulated yet. (n.pag., translation ZK)

In *Nomadland,* the community of nomads puts up weak resistance in the nowhere of the desert, while the bus driver's weak resistance in *Paterson* is manifest in poetry as a way of life. It is showcased in the scene in the park in Paterson, New Jersey, by the Great Falls of Passaic River, that culminates in the Japanese fan of William Carlos Williams' poetry offering Paterson, the bus driver-poet, an empty notebook vibrant with poetic potentiality. Indeed, poetry does make nothing *happen*. The no-place of the *Nomadland* Arizona desert maps onto the empty notebook in *Paterson*; America characterized by hectic movement in *Nomadland* finds it slow-paced holographic, or fractal model in Paterson, New Jersey. Yet, the bus driver's attentiveness to the poetic potentialities of material aspects and personal relationships in his town reveals the twofold nature of Paterson, and therefore of America – a hinterland potentially coterminous with a no-place beyond the reach of executives, a centre of "weak resistance" to "the unity of separation" upheld by late capitalism. The films *Nomadland* and *Paterson* poetically interpret the topography of the American hinterland, and in an illuminating way demonstrate "weak resistance" put up by its inhabitants even as they themselves engage in an artistic practice that contributes to salvaging, recuperating, and virtually wrenching communal values from the process of physical and social dereliction in the wake of havoc wreaked by late-capitalist economy.

Notes

1 According to Povinelli, "The Desert is the space where life was, is not now, but could be if knowledges, techniques, and resources were properly managed" (16). She puts forward the concept of "Carbon Imaginary" as crucial for comprehending the figure of the desert. Povinelli claims that the "Carbon Imaginary" should be comprehended as "the restricted space between natural life and critical life" (26). In other words, it "reinforces a scarred meeting place where [biology and ontology] can exchange conceptual intensities, thrills, wonders, anxieties, perhaps terrors, of the other of Life, namely the Inert, Inanimate, Barren" (17).

2 Excerpt from *Paterson*, copyright ©1946, 1948, 1949, 1951, 1958 by William Carlos Williams. Copyright © 1963 by Florence Williams. Copyright © 1992 by William Eric Williams and Paul H. Williams. Reprinted by permission of New Directions Publishing Corp.
3 Although Pease develops his argument mainly in discussing Gore Vidal's American chronicles in the context of Vidal's critique of the American Exceptionalism and the lack of historical consciousness that had its bearing on 1960s antiwar culture and American countercultural movements' failures in general, his reflection can be extended to Kerouac's characters' oblivion (as well as to that manifested by his circle of friends) of historical circumstances that led to the rise of the American society's conformism after World War II.
4 Excerpt from *Paterson*, copyright ©1946, 1948, 1949, 1951, 1958 by William Carlos Williams. Copyright © 1963 by Florence Williams. Copyright © 1992 by William Eric Williams and Paul H. Williams. Reprinted by permission of New Directions Publishing Corp.

Works Cited

Auden, W.H. "In Memory of W. B. Yeats." *Selected Poems: New Edition*. Ed. Edward Mendelson. New York: Vintage Books, 1979, pp. 80–83.
Bauman, Zygmunt. *Wasted Lives: Modernity and Its Outcasts*. Cambridge: Polity Press, 2004.
Bruder, Jessica. *Nomadland: Surviving America in the Twenty-First Century*. W. W. Norton & Company, 2017.
Çağlayan, Emre. *Poetics of Slow Cinema: Nostalgia, Absurdism, Boredom*. Cham: Palgrave Macmillan, 2018.
Havel, Vaclav. "The Power of the Powerless." Vaclav Havel et al. *The Power of the Powerless: Citizens against the State in Central-Eastern Europe*. Ed. John Keane. New York: Routledge, 1985, pp. 25–92.
Kerouac, Jack. *On the Road*. 1957. New York: Viking, 2001.
Levitas, Ruth. *Utopia as Method: The Imaginary Reconstitution of Society*. Palgrave Macmillan, 2013.
Majewska, Ewa. "Słaby opór i siła bezsilnych. #Czarnyprotest kobiet w Polsce 2016." *Praktyka Teoretyczna*, 10 Nov 2016, https://www.praktykateoretyczna.pl/artykuly/ewa-majewska-saby-opor-i-sia-bezsilnych-czarnyprotest-kobiet-w-polsce-2016/. Accessed 25 Jan 2022.
Miller, Stephen Paul. "The Abstract Expressionist Housewife: Fracture, Transposition, Williams and the Three Phases of Modernism." *William Carlos Williams Review*, vol. 32, no.1, 2015, pp. 159–96. JSTOR, https://www.jstor.org/stable/10.5325/willcarlwillrevi.32.1-2.0159. Accessed 25 Jan 2002.
Neel, Phil A. *Hinterland: America's New Landscape of Class and Conflict*. London: Reaktion Books, 2018.
Nomadland. Directed by Chloé Zhao, Searchlight Pictures, 2020.
Online Etymological Dictionary, https://www.etymonline.com/online. Accessed 25 Aug 2022.
Paterson. Directed by Jim Jarmusch, Amazon Studios, 2016.
Pease, Donald E. "America and the Vidal Chronicles." *Gore Vidal: Writer against the Grain*. Ed. Jay Parini. New York: Columbia University Press, 1992, pp. 247–77.

Povinelli, Elizabeth A. *Geontologies: A Requiem to Late Liberalism*. Durham: Duke University Press, 2016.

Rose, Steve. "*Nomadland*: is 'structured reality' cinema an exciting new trend, or simply fake news?" *The Guardian* 28 Apr 2021, https://www.theguardian.com/film/2021/apr/28/nomadland-is-structured-reality-cinema-an-exciting-new-trend-or-simply-fake-news. Accessed 12 Jan 2022.

Tynan, Aidan. *The Desert in Modern Literature and Philosophy: Wasteland Aesthetics*. Edinburgh: Edinburgh University Press, 2020.

Williams, William Carlos. *Paterson*. New York: New Directions, 1963.

Zuboff, Shoshana. *The Age of Surveillance Capitalism: The Fight for a Human Future at the New Frontier of Power*. New York: Hachette Book Group, 2019.

Part II

Heterotopic hinterlands

4 Spaces of identity in Morocco
Maureen F. McHugh's *Nekropolis*

Marta Komsta

Introduction

Though predominantly associated with urban and rural studies, the term *hinterland* evokes multiple connotations in diverse research fields. In line with its German provenance ("hinter" meaning "behind"), the concept denotes a "tributary region, either rural or urban or both, that is closely linked economically with a nearby town or city" ("Hinterland"). In a similar vein, Evy Mehzabeen describes the hinterland as "an outlying area tied to a particular core through a network of economic relationships like trade, services, and functions" (Mehzabeen 816). Phil A. Neel, who differentiates between "far" (rural and post-industrial) and "near" (suburban) hinterlands, sees them as examples of "a disavowed, distributed core, distinct from the array of services and FIRE industries of the central city but more integral to the 'immediate process of production', in which labor meets capital and value is produced" (Neel 17). For that reason, the hinterland comes to represent spaces of socioeconomic exploitation as cornerstones of capitalist economy:

> Though sometimes geographically distant, most non-urban areas function as subsidiary zones for global capital and for the particular cities that happen to be closest to them – they are by no means outside the economy, and they therefore no longer constitute "peripheries" that are not yet fully subsumed into world capitalism. The global destruction of the peasantry has converted the periphery into a worldwide economic hinterland, defined by expulsion and exclusion. (Neel 17)

While these definitions accentuate the term's political as well as socioeconomic implications, my main interest lies with the semiotic ambiguity engendered by the hinterland's peripheral status. Though economically and administratively associated with the city core, the hinterland is, by definition, situated outside. Mehzabeen aptly notes that the hinterland

DOI: 10.4324/9781032617732-7

"needs to be understood not merely as a contiguous space serving a city but also as a space dependent upon the control of the city. Since the city is felt to be everywhere, *a hinterland becomes those spaces that the city is not*: having less control, power, concentration, and density of population" (820; emphasis added). Thus, the hinterland is "a peripheral space sub-servient to a dominating core" (Mehzabeen 816), which has far-reaching repercussions in the symbolic domain. Marked by semiotic instability and subversiveness, "a shifting terrain" (Doolan 2019, 177), the hinterland is a repository of Gothic sensibility, not unlike Yuri M. Lotman's anti-world of the periphery, "unstructured chthonic space, inhabited by monsters, infernal powers or people associated with them" (Lotman 140).[1] Situated beyond the urban centre, the hinterland is the liminal territory of those "elements [that] are always set *outside*" (Lotman 140), relegated, physi-cally and metaphorically, through the practices of systemic exclusion and repression to the peripheries of the given semiosphere.

From the historical perspective, the term points to a history of ex-ploitation and stigmatization; in Douglas Kerr's analysis of (post-)colonial representations in British literature, the term *hinterland*, rife with colonialist undertones, indicates "the 'back country' or interior, that uncertain territory that recedes away from the known and pos-sessed" (Kerr 11). As such, Kerr contends, it "extends 'our' sphere of property and knowledge and security, but extends beyond it, and is always to some extent disputed. We may assert our right over it, it may contain what we desire or fear, but it is an area of darkness – perhaps its heart, if it has a heart" (Kerr 11). The "darkness" of the hinterland points to its ontological and epistemological elusiveness, which, in turn, highlights the term's aptness in approximating those mental phenomena that reach beyond the limits of comprehension. Here I am following Victor Crapanzano's assertion, after Bonnefoy, that "the beyond is like shadows … : it cannot be contained. It slips away – to appear again just when we have thought, in relief or in despair, that we have finally done with it" (16). According to Crapanzano, the hinterland is the "imagined presence", transcending the boundaries of collective and personal imagination (17), which is established precariously upon the "absence of the accessible" (17). The hinterland belongs hence to the sequestered dimension of imagination that represents the innately indefinable "nonreal":

> What makes the inaccessibility of the hinterland terrifying is less its inaccessibility than its determining role in our perception of that which we take naively to be accessible: that which we actually perceive, experience, touch, and feel. Imagined – or, better still, imaginable – it remains elusive. … It is this elusiveness, this determining absence of the

accessible, which is terrifying; for that which we perceive is always determined ... by that absence, that imagined presence. (Crapanzano 17)

These overlapping contexts – geographical and psychological – form the crux of the essay's theoretical approach to the concept of the hinterland in Maureen F. McHugh's 2001 SF novel *Nekropolis*. The "exquisite if melancholy" narrative, set in twenty-second-century Fez, Morocco, accentuates the profoundly ambivalent attitude of a futuristic theocratic society towards rapid technological development, simultaneously denigrated and exploited by the said society in the name of preserving its homogeneity (McHugh 2001b).[2] According to Gerald Jonas, *Nekropolis* "posits two technological breakthroughs in order to explore the nature of freedom and the question of how we relate to those we deem somehow 'other'" (Jonas): the neurological procedure of "jessing", which enhances one's obedience towards their owner, and the creation of a type of androids, referred to as chimeras or, pejoratively, the harni. Hariba and Akhmim, the novel's protagonists, belong to the domestic staff of a wealthy Fezzian household, albeit on very different terms: Hariba, a young, "jessed" woman, is one of the house managers, whereas Akhmim, a male chimera, is a luxurious commodity and the overseer of the male section of the house. Narrated from multiple points of view, *Nekropolis* follows Hariba and Akhmim's clandestine relationship which forces the couple to abscond from their owner and eventually from the country in search of a better future as refugees in Spain, E.C.U. (the acronym presumably referring to the future European Union). The subsequent clash between the main characters and the conservative community is transposed onto the novel's spatial plane, represented first and foremost by the eponymous Nekropolis, the former burial district in Fez and home to Hariba and her impoverished family. Hariba's relationship with the Nekropolis, which comes to reflect the protagonist's transgressive identity, accounts not only for her low socioeconomic status but, significantly, her symbolic one, which becomes a determining factor in the protagonist's decision to undergo the procedure of jessing. The social stigmatization is further foregrounded in the case of Akhmim, whose posthuman corporality and, by extension, his Other-self contextualize him as the abject element, "an agent in the pay of the differential symbolic order" (Berressem 28), whom the society "must reject ... in order to be able to define and defend the boundaries of identity" (Kutzbach and Mueller 9).[3] With these formulations in mind, in this chapter I examine the identity of place/body as constitutive elements of the hinterland model in *Nekropolis* by positing a semiotic link between the territory of the Nekropolis and the protagonists' bodies as heterotopic "counter-sites" (Foucault 23), explored in line with what Kirby Farrell identifies as a relationship between identity and place, with the latter – the "landscape [that] is a form of psychic topography" (Farrell 118) – functioning as the reflection of the former. "In looking at landscape we are always investing it, however unwittingly, with our motives and values", Farrell contends. "This is why it makes sense to regard landscape not simply as an entity, but also as a tool or technique for managing the self" (Farrell 118).[4] In what follows, the body and/as place become/s a hinterland in McHugh's novel.[5]

The place: the Nekropolis

The fact that the main setting in *Nekropolis* is, quite literally, a necropolis points to the interpretative ambivalence of the novel's spatial model, engendered by the convergence of the cemetery's cultural status of "a burial ground and place for memorialisation" (Grabalov and Nordh) and its spiritual connotations, making it a particularly nuanced semiotic terrain situated physically in the realm of the here and now as well as in the ever-elusive metaphysical beyond.[6] The cemetery, a reservoir of memory that "may bridge the nebulous gap between subconscious and conscious motivation in the manipulation of form and space" (Francaviglia 509), is also a heterotopia, described by Michel Foucault as "a place unlike ordinary cultural spaces" due to its universal connection to all members and classes of a given society (Foucault 25). A heterochrony that marks "a sort of absolute break with … traditional time" (Foucault 26), the cemetery is a mirror of individual and collective memory; like heterotopia's subversive relationship with utopia, "the cemetery's memory is like the mirror and its reflection: real because of the physicality of the grave yet unreal and easy to distort" (Wright 55). In effect, the cemetery heterotopia reflects the society's collective memory in its utopian – non-real – form by means of which the communal selfhood is shaped. Collective identity, reified via the cemetery's symbolic as well as architectural organization, becomes an idealization of the society's past – a utopia cast in stone.[7]

In order to examine the complex interdependence of place and identity, McHugh's novel delineates the transformation of the Nekropolis' utopian latency into a heterotopic hinterland. Foucault's analysis of the historical changes in the cemetery's localization and its subsequent function – from "the sacred and immortal heart of the city" to "the other city" (Foucault 25) – ties in with the conversion of the former burial site into a district inhabited by "poor people who have left farms and small towns to come to the city" (McHugh 2001a, 6). The subsequent mechanism of "diversion", by means of which "an existing space may outlive its original purpose and the *raison d'etre* … [and] may thus in a sense become vacant, and susceptible of being diverted, reappropriated and put to a use quite different from its initial one" (Lefebvre 167), is associated here with extensive reappropriation of a seemingly uninhabitable territory into a domestic domain. As Hariba reminisces:

> I grew up inside the Nekropolis. We didn't have running water. It was delivered every day in a big lorritank and people would go out and buy it by the liter, and we lived in three adjoining mausoleums instead of a flat, but other than that, it was a pretty normal childhood. ... Next to my bed were the dates for the person buried behind the wall, 2073 to 2144. All of the family was dead years ago. No one ever came to this death house to lay paper flowers and birds. (McHugh 2001a, 8)

Reappropriation, the underlying principle of the spatial and symbolic organization of the novel's hinterland, is made evident in the description of Hariba's house, a former mausoleum, whose smells and objects, primarily associated with funeral arrangements, now signify domestic spatiality. Significantly, the secularization of sacred space, associated with the death houses, corresponds to the subversion of the utopian memory of the deceased by the memory of those still living, such as Hariba and her family:

> Our house always smelled of cinnamon and the perfume my mother used on her paper flowers and birds. In the middle death house there were funeral arrangements everywhere and when we ate we would clear a space on the floor and sit, surrounded. When I was a little girl, I learned the different uses of papers: how my mother used translucent tissue for carnations, stiff satiny brittle paper for roses, and strong paper with a grain like linen for arrogant falcons. (McHugh 2001a, 8–9)

The cemetery is hence remodelled into a hinterland inhabited by the city's outcasts, which also accounts for the extension of the cemetery's symbolic field onto the district's living populace. The name itself conveys a double meaning: though situated within the city's limits, the Nekropolis is defined as the periphery of the dead, whose dwellers are rendered symbolically non-existent to the rest of the society. While administratively a part of the city, the district is separated from the urban centre in several contexts – historical (a cemetery), symbolical (the realm of the dead) as well as socioeconomic (a slum area inhabited by the destitute) – becoming, in effect, a heterotopia where "all the other real sites that can be found within the culture, are simultaneously represented, contested, and inverted" (Foucault 24).[8] By the same token, since "sites of memory hold communal identities together – or divide them" (Crang and Travlou 161), the reappropriated Nekropolis, "a conservative place" (McHugh 2001a, 6), highlights the growing disparity between the traditionalist values of the novel's Moroccan society and the dynamic, changing selfhood of its younger members, for whom the former burial site represents a hinterland in both a literal and figurative sense as an impoverished district as well as regressive mentality associated with staunch laws and customs.

In what follows, due to the fact the Nekropolis has become urbanized through a population influx and socioeconomic osmosis with the adjacent neighbourhoods, its identity changes as well, as highlighted by Akhmim's expression of surprise during his first visit to the Nekropolis with Hariba: "'There are inns here?' Akhmim asks. 'Of course,' I say. 'People come from the country to visit their families. People live in the Nekropolis, we have stores and everything'" (McHugh 2001a, 56). Ahkmim's reaction and Hariba's explanation point to the tension that lies at the symbolic foundations of the Nekropolis' abject status as the home of the (living) dead, transplanted onto the fraught relationship between the collective symbolic domain and the actual lives of the district's inhabitants. This fracture is demonstrated in the character of Hariba's mother, "as old-fashioned as they come" (McHugh 2001a, 146), who represents the burden of memory and tradition imposed upon the female characters in McHugh's narrative. Tellingly, the mother's name does not appear in the novel, signalling the subjection of her individual identity to the communal selfhood. As illustrated in the single chapter narrated by this character (fittingly entitled "Duty"), her entire life has been modelled in acquiescence to the patriarchal demands of the traditionalist community: "When I was twelve, my mother died and our life was nothing but shame. We were children who no one watched. No one paid for our school. I know my father was with us when he came home from work, but in my memory it is only Zehra [her sister – note added] and me, trying to be women, trying to keep a home" (McHugh 2001a, 117). The extent of the elderly woman's obeisance to the stringent social norms is poignantly emphasized by her son, Fhassin, who accuses his mother of surrendering her identity to the confines of patriarchal morality: "your prison is the Nekropolis", he tells her (McHugh 2001a, 115). Fhassin's comment resonates acutely with the overarching mechanism of sociocultural subjugation that extends both over the Nekropolis and its inhabitants. Incarcerated for an adulterous affair with a married woman, Fhassin immediately recognizes the hinterland's peripheral status that renders it particularly susceptible to exclusion and repression, made even more evident in the tension between the traditionalistic paradigm and the lived reality of the people.

Thus, despite its conservative veneer, the heterotopia of the Nekropolis reveals its transgressive potential by becoming a shelter for Hariba and Akhmim; Hariba's seemingly sarcastic comment – "Funny that we are going into a cemetery to live" (McHugh 2001a, 56) – points to the implicitly abject nature of the Nekropolis which, from the perspective of the protagonists, is not unlike the "'unlivable' and 'uninhabitable' zones of social life" where Hariba and Akhmim, "those who do not enjoy the status of the subject" on account of their reappropriated carnality, seek refuge from the repressive jurisdiction of the religious state (Butler xiii). Within this "enacted utopia" of death houses (Foucault 24), the hinterland's essentially dissentious potentiality is actualized at the interstice between social identity and the intimate sense of selfhood as a counterspace of resistance. For Hariba's mother in particular, the return of her daughter, "sick and in disgrace" (McHugh 2001a, 103), highlights the fundamental incongruity between her strict religious upbringing and her experience of motherhood, the latter a hinterland stretching beyond the "imaginative horizons" of cultural precepts as the key factor in unshackling the individual from the communal self (Crapanzano 18): "When you are a mother ... you do things you don't know you can do", the elderly woman asserts. "When I had four children and no husband, I did things I never would have thought I could do. And now I will again" (McHugh 2001a, 109). The hinterland's subversive modality comes forth through various examples through which the former cemetery district subtly marks its counter-identity in relation to the dystopian state. Such acts and tokens range from the paper flowers that Hariba makes while in hiding or an orange given to Akhmim by another chimera that signals the willingness to help the efforts of Hariba's relatives and friends, who challenge the dominant system by aiding the outlawed protagonists at the risk of brutal persecution at the hands of the police. Taken together, while neither overt nor wide-reaching, these signals suggest the underlying presence of the hinterland's singular selfhood that transcends the culturally enforced regulations of the centre in the name of solidarity between the excluded and the oppressed.

The body: Hariba and Akhmim

Since McHugh's narrative highlights a symbolic correspondence between the Nekropolis and the two main characters, both the place and the body illustrate the inevitably flawed heterotopic reflections of the collective ideals. A hinterland made flesh, the body is then "a spatial site, and also a locus of values and norms" (Loos et al., 22) that "incorporates both materially real and unreal sites situated in one conflicted space" (Loos et al., 18). To reiterate Foucault's metaphor of the mirror, the body is subjected not only to the gaze of the individual looking at her reflection, but also to the values and judgements of her environment: "Foucault's mirror example retains its demonstrative power here; the self-perception of one's body is influenced by viewing oneself in a mirror, a non-real place.

This reassessment of self-perception, based on norms and values, is social in that it is dependent on social recognition" (Loos et al., 22). The scrutinized bodily heterotopia, "an embodied self" (Teather 8), is classified as belonging to or rejected from the symbolic domain:

> As a site of both one's own bodily lived experience and a site where social values and norms accumulate, the body is a junction where the Self and the Other become entangled. This has consequences for an individual's agency: although the corporeal body of the Self can be seen as autonomous, the societal norms and values of the Other, shaping its heterotopic elements, cannot. There is therefore not only an entanglement but also a tension between the individual and communal in the body. (Loos et al., 23)

The said tension is made apparent in the novel's opening passage, which demonstrates Hariba's resignation of bodily autonomy through the neurological procedure of jessing:

> How I came to be jessed. Well, like most people who are jessed, I was sold. I was twenty-one, and I was sold three times in one day, one right after another; first to a dealer who looked at my teeth and in my ears and had me scanned for augmentation; then to a second dealer where I sat in the back office drinking tea and talking with a gap-toothed boy who was supposed to be sold to a restaurant owner as a clerk; and finally that afternoon to the restaurant owner. (McHugh 2001a, 1)

As a procedure that engenders a lifetime of economic exclusion and exploitation of the jessed individual (since, as Hariba admits, she will have to "work fifty years" before being able to buy her freedom [McHugh 2001a, 2]), it becomes a crucial component of the social mechanism of disappropriation that divests the heterotopic body of individual agency. Lefebvre points out that, "[d]ominated by overpowering forces, including a variety of brutal techniques and an extreme emphasis on visualization, the body fragments, abdicates responsibility for itself – in a word, disappropriates itself" (Lefebvre 166). Hariba's former role in the collective identity (she mentions at one point that she "was a good student" with "good marks in math and literature" [McHugh 2001a, 3]) is disappropriated via her body, since jessed women are no longer considered eligible to marry and have children.

The inherently invasive nature of jessing and the ensuing stigmatization are concealed within a social discourse that highlights the procedure's purported usefulness. The language of the theocratic officialdom accentuates the benefits of jessing by evoking the implied emotional connection between the servant and her owner: "The Second Koran says that just as a jessed hawk is tamed, not tied, so shall the servant be bound by affection and duty, not chains" (McHugh 2001a, 5). The exploitative social structure in McHugh's novel blurs, albeit superficially, the socioeconomic and ethical inequality between the community and the disappropriated Other; accordingly, Mbarek, Hariba's owner, addresses the jessed woman as his daughter in order to disguise the transactional relationship between them. Similarly, disappropriated individuals come to internalize the social repercussions of jessing as implicitly valuable and, thus, desirable. When asked by Akhmim whether she recognizes "the difference between the compulsion and [her] own feelings", Hariba replies with the following: "Jessing changes the unruly brain, makes us feel the loyalty that we should. If I've chosen to have myself changed to feel loyalty, then it isn't really compulsion. And it makes service easier, if it's something my brain wants me to do. ... Jessing only heightens my natural tendencies, and makes a servant as trustworthy as kin" (McHugh 2001a, 7). In the case of the female protagonist, who admits to having had "a simple, rather conservative upbringing" (McHugh 2001a, 3), the unexpected relationship with Akhmim forces her to confront the influence of social conditioning that affects her decision to undergo jessing. By deciding to reverse the procedure, Hariba attempts to reclaim her subjectivity from the collective selfhood, described as "trying to be two people, one a good girl and the other a secret, hidden even from [her] own self" (McHugh 2001a, 52–53).

The most pronounced representation of the disappropriated body in McHugh's novel is Akhmim, the human/AI hybrid, whose physical appearance is aligned with his predominant function as "a pleasure chimera", designed and manufactured as a sexual artefact for their owners, being "the perfect lover" who "put[s] the needs of the human first and their needs second" (McHugh 2001a, 235). At the same time, he is described as "a technician's creation. An artificial combination of genes, grown somewhere" (McHugh 2001a, 11), "a biological construct" (McHugh 2001a, 4), "a very expensive, very pretty toy" (McHugh 2001a, 3), or, conversely, "an abomination" (McHugh 2001a, 153) or "blasphemy" (McHugh 2001a, 142). Akhmim is perceived by the religious community as an uncanny entity, "an embodied heterotopia" (Roux and Belk 7), whose singularity is anchored in the protagonist's selfhood, which violates the binary categories espoused by his environment.[9] Though designed as either male or female, the android's gender identity transcends duality: in contrast to what they see as intrinsically limited human animals ("Humans are rigid and *harni* bend. Humans have only one shape" [McHugh 2001a, 59]), the chimeras strive to re-attain the primordial unity they experience in their early childhood; as Akhmim recalls, "[w]e were all one, in the way of harni, almost indistinguishable, until we were five years old and we had to start sleeping in separate beds and going to different classes so we would differentiate. We cried. We were cast out of paradise and after that we were never whole again" (McHugh 2001a, 65). The chimera's unfeigned sense of oneness with his species ("I'm we", he affirms [McHugh 2001a, 84]) is a meaningful inversion of the fundamentally performative collectiveness of human society, satirized in *Nekropolis* via the concept of "bismek", elaborate AI role-play programmes popular amongst wealthy Moroccan families. Staged by Hariba's mistress as entertainment for her guests, bismek constitutes a heterotopia offering temporary respite from the strict moral rules:

> Interactive fantasies. The characters are generated from lists of traits, they're projections controlled by whoever is game-mistress of the *bismek* and fleshed out by the household AI. Everyone else comes over and becomes characters in the setting. There are poisonings and love affairs. The mistress's setting is in ancient times and seems to be quite popular. Some of her friends have two or three identities in the game. (McHugh 2001a, 14–15)

The trope of performance here indicates the general underlying principle of the Moroccan society in McHugh's novel. Akin to Hariba enacting the role of a dutiful daughter to her owner, the society itself operates as a performative model of communal Self, in which moral transgressions are relegated to staged identities that, as Hariba observes, "entertain themselves with suffering" without disrupting the established status quo (McHugh 2001a, 25). Likewise, the chimera's uncanny sense of self that marks him as "an abjected outside" (Butler xiii) forces the posthuman protagonist to submit to the collective selfhood by learning to perform traditional gender roles through which "the 'unconstructed' becomes bounded once again through a signifying practice" (Butler xx). As a result, young chimeras adapt to human society by emulating conventional roles and behaviours:

> Before we were separate, we didn't play like humans. After we were separated, we would mimic each other a lot. And sometimes we'd play pretend. We'd play that my sisters had been sold to a human, and because I was the boy, I had to be the rich man who bought them. I'd sit in the chair and order them to do things for me: "Brush my hair", or "Bring me my shoes". (McHugh 2001a, 65–66)

The novel further accentuates the androids' implicitly abject status in Moroccan society by positioning them as commodities categorized in accordance with their designated purpose; there are then "pleasure chimeras", such as Akhmim, as well as "nanny" and "labour" chimeras. The android is, to paraphrase Judith Butler, a body that does not matter; as such, it is relegated to the realm of the abject, which is exemplified by the excluded spaces of transgressive intimacy of the so-called "*harni* pile" (McHugh 2001a, 84). As Akhmim, who at one point in the novel becomes a prostitute, recalls meeting other sex chimeras in the brothel they are all employed at: "There is nothing to say, only skin. I sit down on the couch and we all touch and pet each other and I inhale young milky skin with its faintly cinnamon scent. I slide my shoes off and for the first time since I left the crèche to go to Mbarek-salah's, I'm we" (McHugh 2001a, 74–75). Their intimacy, perhaps because of its uncanny innocence, evokes repulsion as an abject act situated beyond the familiar symbolic realm: "you *harni* are disgusting", Akhmim is told by one his human co-workers, "I'd understand if you had sex … but this piling on top of each other is unnatural. Like rats in winter" (McHugh 2001a, 75).

Conclusion

What follows is the realization of the fundamental futility of re-appropriating the Other, who, though deceptively similar, remains in a realm beyond comprehension; after all, as Crapanzano asserts, "our constructions of the beyond are always slippery" (21). The protagonists' selfhood can be only approximated, but never fully comprehended as mutually incognizable hinterlands, situated outside the limits of one's imagination: "[Hariba's] otherness hits me most at moments like this when I'm understanding her well and I suddenly wonder how much of that understanding is just my assumptions of sameness, and then I wonder what she's really thinking and feeling", Akhmim explains. "Her face becomes familiar and strange. She's really a stranger in my life, this human, who has turned everything upside-down" (McHugh 2001a, 86). The narrative's last chapter, set in Málaga and entitled poignantly "In the Land of the Infidel", sees thus the end of Hariba and Akhmim's quest for freedom as well as marking the breakdown of their relationship, dismantled by the protagonists' matured awareness of each other's intrinsic incognizance, punctuated by the first and final act of sexual intimacy between them. Not long before Akhmim joins a small commune of fellow chimeras, Hariba is forced to acknowledge the fact that they remain ultimately unknowable to each other as hinterlands that can be explored only to a certain point:

> "Does it bother you when people call you a *harni*? Do you prefer chimera?"

[Akhmim] shrugs. "Not particularly. Whatever people call me, I'm still what I am".

"I don't see why it makes any difference".

"It's a human thing", he says. "Words shape your thoughts".

It's a human thing. I shudder and I don't know why. (McHugh 2001a, 217)

At the same time, Hariba's alienation in the Western Hemisphere is made apparent via her realization of the discrepancy between her previous sense of exclusion as a jessed woman within the Moroccan community and her new sense of Otherness as a refugee in Spain. Though she is cured of the neurological implications of jessing, her reclamation of individual agency is thwarted by the realization of the necessity of subjecting herself once again to the collective selfhood. Her new self relies on relegating her Moroccan past, whose evocation is "like a pain in [her] chest" (McHugh 2001a, 234), into the realm of the inaccessible, the hinterland of memory, which, much like the Nekropolis, is now the realm of the dead inhabited by the spectres of Hariba's family. This symbolic gap between the "concrete here-and-now" (Crapanzano 17) and the beyond is reiterated in the novel's final scene, which delineates a frontier between the protagonist's past and present identities that is as much psychological as physical. Instructed by one of her teachers to cut her long hair (condescendingly described as "naïve and immature" [McHugh 2001a, 255]), during the visit at the hairdresser's, the young woman looks into the mirror in which she sees a "new girl", who "looks like a Spanish girl who has Arab parents. She looks modern" (McHugh 2001a, 256). The moment is tinged with profound melancholy: Hariba's mirror reflection is a faux utopian representation of her symbolic and physical uprootedness in the western "land of the dead" (McHugh 2001a, 188). The coil of her hair, which Hariba collects from the hairdresser, is a memento of the protagonist's former, jessed self and a signifier of her alienation in the world that does not – and cannot – understand her plight: "I touch and I try to think of what to do with it. I could send it to Akhmim, but I don't know what it would mean to him. ... I could send it to my mother, but it would break her heart. ... I think it belongs to no one at all, this smooth coil of black hair, and I run my fingers over it. My tears are so hot, they're as hot as blood" (McHugh 2001a, 256–57). Akin to Hariba's lock of hair, the metaphor of the bodily hinterland in McHugh's novel eventually becomes a manifestation of the past as well as the horizon of the future that continuously informs the identity of people and places that have been left behind.

Notes

1 According to Emma Doolan, the hinterlands, "identified always only in relation to some other dominant centre, are peripheral zones – prime territory for the Gothic, whose narratives have in this sense always taken place in hinterlands, displacing menace over borders of time and space, elsewhere …" (Doolan 2019, 179).

2 It should be noted that the novel's setting is not related to actual Morocco, past or present. McHugh affirms that "[t]he Morocco of this book, while based on the country of the same name, is entirely a fictional creation" (McHugh 2001a, 257). However, though the fictional Nekropolis in Fez is modelled upon the actual one in Cairo, Egypt, its designated function is intended to be more universal than its geographical location; McHugh herself contends that she "found the old city where people live with death to be metaphorically rich, but [she] was careful never to work out the specifics" (McHugh 2001b).

3 I am using here the definition of collective identity as "the way that people define themselves in relation to others and the outside world, i.e. identities that are socially influenced" (Franco-Zamudio and Dorton 257). Hence, "collective identity encompasses both an individuals' self-definition and affiliation with specific groups or roles" (Franco-Zamudio and Dorton 256).

4 Similarly, Crang and Thrift posit the concept of "spatial selfhood" (Crang and Thrift 8) by means of which individuals establish their sense of self in relation to the spaces of the Other, real or symbolical, as "*a territory of self-identity* set against a radical and exoticised alterity" (Crang and Thrift 10; emphasis added).

5 I define space and place in accordance with the distinction proposed by Elizabethada E. Wright, after Michel de Certeau: "Place (*lieu*) excludes two things from being in one location simultaneously … Space (*espace*), on the other hand, is not a physical reality. It is created by operations and rules; it is a 'practiced place'. Like the mirror, place is the physicality; like the image, space is not" (Wright 54).

6 Grabalov and Nordh contend that "[c]emeteries' liminality lies not only in their spatial character but also in their ability to accommodate complex meanings, different from other urban spaces. Such liminality situates cemeteries between clear positions and static forms, both in public space discourse and in people's everyday lives" (Grabalov and Nordh).

7 In a rhetorical context, Wright asserts, cemeteries "seem silent, yet cemeteries are as silent as they are not. If one sees cemeteries as a rhetorical space, then there are thousands upon thousands of voices clamoring to be heard, a cacophony of remembrances are calling out" (Wright 60).

8 Likewise, Doolan notes that, "[l]ike the heterotopia, the hinterland, 'in order to be perceived' must first pass through another point 'over there'. The hinterland is 'the land behind; something, somewhere, else. Like the mirror space, the hinterland disrupts distinctions between inside and outside, over here and over there" (Doolan 2017, 10).

9 Roux and Belk describe embodied heterotopias as "the concrete enactment of utopias, not as distant from what they challenge, but in the very place that they originate" (Roux and Belk 7).

Works Cited

Berressem, Hanjo. "On the Matter of Abjection." *The Abject of Desire. The Aestheticization of the Unaesthetic in Contemporary Literature and Culture.* Eds. Konstanze Kutzbach, and Monika Mueller. Rodopi, 2007, pp. 19–48.

Butler, Judith. "Introduction." *Bodies That Matter. On the Discursive Limits of "Sex".* Routledge, 2011, pp. xi–xxx.

Crang, Mike, and Nigel Thrift. "Introduction." *Thinking Space.* Eds. Mike Crang, and Nigel Thrift. Routledge, 2003, pp. 1–30.

Crang, Mike, and Penny S. Travlou. "The City and Topologies of Memory." *Environment and Planning D: Society and Space*, vol. 19, no. 2, 2001, pp. 161–77.

Crapanzano, Victor. *Imaginative Horizons: An Essay in Literary-Philosophical Anthropology.* The University of Chicago Press, 2004.

Doolan, Emma. *Hinterland Gothic: Reading and Writing Australia's East Coast Hinterlands as Gothic Spaces.* Queensland University of Technology, 2017, PhD dissertation. https://eprints.qut.edu.au/115465/2/Doolan%20Hinterland%20Gothic%20exegesis.pdf. Accessed 5 Aug. 2022.

Doolan, Emma. "Hinterland Gothic: Subtropical Excess in the Literature of South East Queensland." *eTropic*, vol. 18, no. 1, 2019, pp. 174–91.

Farrell, Kirby. "Eschatological Landscape." *Land & Identity. Theory, Memory, and Practice.* Eds. Christine Berberich et al. Rodopi, 2012, pp. 117–39.

Foucault, Michel. "Of Other Spaces." *Diacritics*, vol. 16, no. 1, 1986, pp. 22–27.

Francaviglia, Richard V. "The Cemetery as an Evolving Cultural Landscape." *Annals of the Association of American Geographers*, vol. 61, no. 3, 1971, pp. 501–09.

Franco-Zamudio, Jamie, and Harold Dorton. "Collective Identity." *Encyclopedia of Critical Psychology.* Ed. Thomas Teo. Springer, 2014, pp. 256–59.

Grabalov, Pavel, and Helena Nordh. "The Future of Urban Cemeteries as Public Spaces: Insights from Oslo and Copenhagen." *Planning Theory and Practice*, vol. 23, no. 1, 2022, pp. 81–98, 10.1080/14649357.2021.1993973. Accessed 7 Sept. 2022.

"Hinterland." *Encyclopedia Britannica*, https://www.britannica.com/science/hinterland. Accessed 5 Aug. 2022.

Jonas, Gerald. "Science Fiction." *The New York Times*, 7 October 2001, https://www.nytimes.com/2001/10/07/books/science-fiction.html. Accessed 12 June 2022.

Kerr, Douglas. *Eastern Figures. Orient and Empire in British Writing.* Hong Kong University Press, 2008.

Kutzbach, Konstanze, and Monika Mueller. "Introduction." *The Abject of Desire. The Aestheticization of the Unaesthetic in Contemporary Literature and Culture.* Eds. Konstanze Kutzbach, and Monika Mueller. Rodopi, 2007, pp. 7–17.

Lefebvre, Henri. *The Production of Space.* Blackwell, 1991.

Loos, Martijn, Johanna Kaszti, and Rick van der Waarden. "The Body as Heterotopia." *Junctions*, vol. 5, no. 2, 2021, pp. 18–32.

Lotman, Yuri M. *Universe of the Mind. A Semiotic Theory of Culture*. I.B. Tauris & Co. Ltd, 1990.

McHugh, Maureen F. *Nekropolis*. HarperCollins, 2001a. Kindle edition.

McHugh, Maureen F. "PW Talks with Maureen F. McHugh." *Publisher's Weekly*, 30 July 2001b, https://www.publishersweekly.com/pw/by-topic/authors/interviews/article/38374-pw-talks-with-maureen-f-mchugh.html. Accessed 20 June 2022.

Mehzabeen, Evy. "Hinterlands." *The Wiley Blackwell Encyclopedia of Urban and Regional Studies*. Eds. Anthony M. Orum, et al., vol. II. Wiley Blackwell, 2019, pp. 816–21.

Neel, Phil A. *Hinterland: America's New Landscape of Class and Conflict*. Reaktion Books, 2018.

Roux, Dominique, and Russell Belk. "The Body as (Another) Place: Producing Embodied Heterotopias through Tattooing." *Journal of Consumer Research*, vol. 46, no. 3, 2019, pp. 483–507.

Teather, Elizabeth Kenworthy. "Introduction: Geographies of Personal Discovery." *Embodied Geographies. Spaces, Bodies and Rites of Passage*. Ed. Elizabeth Kenworthy Teather. Routledge, 1999, pp. 1–26.

Wright, Elizabethada A. "Rhetorical Spaces in Memorial Places: The Cemetery as a Rhetorical Memory Place/Space." *Rhetoric Society Quarterly*, vol. 35, no. 4, 2009, pp. 51–81.

5   Unravelling the Haitian hinterland as a twofold space

Dany Laferrière and Yanick Lahens

Izabela Poręba

The term *hinterland* is usually used to describe non-urbanized spaces, although a clear distinction between the two zones – urban and extra-urban – is not obvious, and certainly not strict. The boundaries between a *land* and what is *hinter*, behind or hidden, are becoming increasingly blurred and fluid (Neel). Hinterlands are also often seen as places that are essential to the prosperity and well-being of centres, but not fully visible and often located on the outskirts of cities. For example, factories, which are essential to maintaining certain standards of living in developed societies, almost always become invisible – they are often located in sub-urbs, or even further afield, in developing countries, where production is ongoing, often with little regard for environmental and labour standards (Matisoff).[1] Moreover, in this sense, colonies can also be read as imperial hinterlands – places where the production process was led by enslaved people, sustaining and ensuring the welfare of the "Centre" – but this process of alienation and exploitation was invisible to most Europeans in the eighteenth or nineteenth century. Yet the colonies obviously were not hinterlands from the perspective of their inhabitants, and factories were not hinterlands from the perspective of the workers. Such categorizations are always relative and dependent on the (discursive) existence of its opposite.

Therefore, the creation of the hinterland, although closely related to the demands of capitalism, is not just a contemporary practice, but is rather a constant need to reinvent the *spatial/spatialized Other*. Only by othering – that is, through dissimilarity, the processes of discursive and material concealment, privileging certain places and diminishing others – can space become a hinterland. This is both a material and discursive process, so to emphasize only one element of this becoming would lead to simplifications. No place is by definition a hinterland; it is impossible to distinguish certain topographical circumstances that, when fulfilled, will always entail the creation of a hinterland, e.g., not every space far from the coastline or the capital will serve as a hinterland (Pomeranz). The hinterlands are at

DOI: 10.4324/9781032617732-8

first manufactured, established, and relative, but then they are often transformed by the role they play in relation to the centre they support – so we can observe lands hollowed out in search of precious ores, people struggling with poverty or enslavement of various kinds. The land and its inhabitants are changing over time, as Achille Mbembe (169) describes: "This world also wears the cuts of the machine in its flesh and its veins. Crevasses, chasms, and tunnels. Crater lakes".

The hinterland is the spatial Other of the Centre (city, capital, etc.) created by both discursive and material practices. Accordingly, my understanding of the hinterland depends on three basic considerations: the hinterland is believed to be shaped in terms of time and perception, not just space; my approach depends on the Haitian context of literary and cultural analysis; and finally, I assume that a hinterland can be formed within the city, not necessarily on its periphery.

The first statement is based on the fact that hinterlands are usually depicted and analyzed as topographically delimited places, but I would argue that they are also highly dependent on temporal and imaginary conditions. This means not only that they are historical, and therefore politically and socially mediated, but also that they are *made*, through the means of language and politics. In this sense, I follow Michel Foucault's statement that "Space is fundamental in any form of communal life; space is fundamental in any exercise of power" (Foucault 152); space is where power relations or class differences are actually tangible and visible. Two spatial metaphors of class difference – the cauldron and vertical layering – that are used to describe Port-au-Prince in the novels of Dana Laferrière and Yanick Lahens will be discussed in this chapter. Both metaphors are means of exercising power in the Foucauldian sense. However, they are not limited to the spatial dimension, but are also historically and temporally grounded.

The focus of the chapter is the specific making-of hinterlands which can be witnessed in two postcolonial novels: Laferrière's *Pays sans chapeau* (2018; first published in 1996; translated into English a year later by David Homel as *Down Among the Dead Men*) and Lahens' *Douces déroutes* (2018). Both novels thematically take on the challenge of portraying contemporary Haiti, especially its capital. The narrator of Laferrière's novel is a writer who, after two decades of exile in Montreal, returns to his homeland, Haiti, with the specific goal of creating a literary representation of Haiti for readers around the world. One of the characters in Lahens' book, the French journalist Francis, arrives in Haiti with a similar intention – to capture the essence of the place in an article for the French press. However, the time gap of slightly more than 20 years between the publication of the two novels results in different portraits of Port-au-Prince. This difference, moreover, can be seen as a change that reflects different generational experiences of the Haitian writers – from Laferrière,[2] who gives voice to a generation of writers born under the dictatorial rule of Papa Doc, François Duvalier, and coming of age under his son, Jean-Claude Duvalier, often emigrating to the United States or Canada due to political persecution and censorship; to Lahens, who in her novel represents the younger generation, born during or after the end of Baby Doc's rule, with vague memories of the 1994 American military intervention, Operation Uphold Democracy. While both novels – at the level of fictional narrative and at the level of metanarrative – attempt to adequately portray Haitians and Haiti, they focus not only on the representations themselves, but also on the means of making such representations: "the book's [*Pays sons chapeau*] theme will be as much about *how* to represent Haitian reality as about the reality itself, and, as such, any truth that will be discovered will apply more to the modes of representation, and less to that which is represented" (Munro 187). By thematizing the representational purpose of narrative in the figure of a writer (Laferrière) or a journalist (Lahens) and abandoning the means of realist poetics, the authors draw our attention to the creation of representation.[3] This only further reinforces the need to take into account the geographical context of the hinterlands.

Finally, the last feature of the hinterland listed above is that it can intrude into places that are perceived as its reverse: cities and even the capital. Cities are not cohesive, nor are they fully visible and stable. That is why hinterlands tend to emerge within cities when they fragment or begin to grow rapidly – spatially or temporally. Moreover, inner-city hinterlands can be understood as heterotopian spaces, "places that do exist and that are formed in the very founding of society – which are something like counter-sites, a kind of effectively enacted utopia in which the real sites, all the other real sites that can be found within the culture, are simultaneously represented, contested, and inverted" (Foucault 24). I argue that these inner-city hinterlands are real places that are usually invisible or unknown, and only reveal themselves to the observer in certain moments of cognition. These acts of cognition occur in a different perspective than usual, for example, at a different time or by people who have not yet become accustomed to the space, such as immigrants. Such is the case in Port-au-Prince, as described by Laferrière, where there are two parallel spaces separated by the time boundaries of day and night. Moreover, the narrator, although born in Haiti, spends a lot of time abroad and is therefore no longer recognized by others as Haitian; nor does he identify as one. The intertwining of these two conditions – the day/night manifestation of the same space and the narrator's specific perspective of familiarity mixed with otherness – results in the recognition of a heterotopic, nocturnal Port-au-Prince in *Pays sans chapeau*. The same city that

Lahens describes reveals its downtown hinterland, sensitizing us to the fact that most people live in places that we avoid looking at.[4] It is by overcoming this invisibility that one can understand how the Haitian capital fabricates its hinterlands to hide what does not fit the official narrative – it is certainly no coincidence that *Douces déroutes* begins with a letter written by Judge Raymond Berthier shortly before he was assassinated because of evidence he uncovered that exposed lies and deceptions perpetrated by respected, nameless, possibly political figures. Exposing what has been deliberately hidden is a dangerous task. The beginning of the novel seems to inform readers, but this is exactly what the narrative accomplishes in its polyphony, allowing readers to peek not only at the surface of the Haitian capital, but also at its very bottom.

The making of a hinterland in the Haitian context

Pays sans chapeau concludes Laferrière's series of ten books about Vieux Os. The protagonist's name has been translated into English as Old Bones and is a pet name given to the writer by his grandmother. The book series tells the story of Vieux Os' emigration from Haiti just after the end of Papa Doc's dictatorship in 1971 and the rise to power of his son, Jean-Claude Duvalier, and ends with the hero's return to his homeland after twenty years of exile – in *Pays sans chapeau*. Upon his return to Haiti, Vieux Os wants to write a book about his homeland, a book that will "bring our [Haitian – X.X.] roots and our gods back to their rightful, honorable place" and therefore challenge the reputation of Haiti, which is "at its lowest point ever" (Laferrière 209). He can accomplish this task by describing and restoring the vodou gods through literature. The Haitian hinterland becomes the central core of this attempt to restore Haiti's reputation, as Vieux Os traces all dimensions of the nocturnal Port-au-Prince, especially zombis and glimpses of the afterlife. He is disturbed by the news his mother gives him shortly after his return – that an army of zombis is prowling the streets of Port-au-Prince at night, and that all the cemeteries are nearly emptied and therefore guarded by American soldiers. He consults the anthropologist J.-B. Romain (certainly Jean-Baptiste Romain, a physical anthropologist) to see if his mother's revelations are true. He also talks to the psychiatrist Legrand Bijou to further investigate the presence of zombis in Haiti and learns that the village of Bombardopolis in the northwest of the country is home to people who need to eat only once every three months. It would be interesting to know what cognitive conditions allowed Vieux Os to get close to the Haitian hinterland: where and when they made themselves known, and how they could be recognized. Their existence is real (although in the case of the novel, reality is of course mediated by fiction), but at the same time, the ability to perceive them is not obvious and requires the subject to know some special attributes (like being other in space) or to find themselves in the particular conditions in which this cognition takes place. It is here that the intersection of space and time will become crucial for grasping the process of hinterland formation:

> It's as if two countries were living side by side, without ever meeting. By day, a race of hard-luck people fight to survive. But at night, the same country is taken over by gods, devils, men changed into beasts. The real country: the struggle for survival. And the dream country: every fantasy of the most megalomaniac people on earth. (Laferrière 40)

Port-au-Prince is described by the narrator of *Pays sans chapeau* as a twofold place: during the day, a domain of reason, light, life, and the struggle for existence, and at night, a land of darkness, extra-rational cognition, dreams, and vodou.[5] The nocturnal Port-au-Prince is in fact a hinterland; moreover, it functions as a heterotopia. Its heterotopic capacity is evidenced by its relation to daytime Haiti. It is only through this Manichean difference that we can see that the Haitian hinterland performs this special, subversive function in relation to its mirror image – it transforms the rational into the irrational, revealing that what seemed real is in fact far from rational. One of these irrational rationalities is labour, which is exhausting and coercive, while barely giving people the means to survive, echoing the labour of slave ancestors. Another is the relativity of power inherent in the space, which we will now examine more closely.

The division of Port-au-Prince into "two countries… living side by side, without ever meeting" is also the result of a political settlement between the governments of Haiti and the United States. As the novel depicts, it all began with a threat issued by the Haitian president that once the Americans set foot in Haiti, a zombi army would be used to repel them (Laferrière 54; see Lauro 114, 135). When the Americans invaded the country, ostensibly in order to protect democracy and human rights (which certainly refers to the events of the 1994 U.S. peacekeeping operation; see Girard), the "young American leader" signed an agreement that "the American army would occupy the country during the day. The zombi army would have domain over the night" (Laferrière 54). It is not a spatial but a temporal divide that distributes power in Haiti. This new neo-colonial policy is even more camouflaged than previous ones because time, unlike space, is invisible and cannot be publicized by the international press. At first glance, this political decision to periodically turn nighttime Port-au-Prince into a hinterland, putting power in the hands of Haitians and their zombi army while everyone is dreaming instead of acting, may seem like a sign of Haitian subjugation. Especially when you think about it in a broader sense – nocturnal power is associated with superstition, darkness, and nature, all of which initially merged into Haiti's racist imaginary, which transformed vodou[6] into voodoo, zombis[7] into zombies. As Raphael Hoermann noted, "The figure of the zombie – in combination with allegations of cannibalism – has been prominently employed as such a Gothic trope of horror and terror to demonise Haiti and particularly its African Caribbean religion as a black savage practice" (Hoermann 2). The division of power seems to mask actual neocolonial subjugation.

However, it turns out that subjugation is not so obvious, as the hinterland becomes the site of a fearful and inaccessible space of freedom, which is therefore impossible to appropriate and explain. It is striking that almost every time the narrative mentions Americans, it happens in two possible circumstances, often simultaneous: to refer to the American occupation of Haiti or their irresistible need to explain the world, especially its nocturnal face. However, it is about more than taming otherness or the unbearable nature of irrationality, because it is about overcoming fears while proving that they were only phantasmagorical. How is it possible that villagers in Bombardopolis eat only once every three months, and what would it mean for the global capitalist system if people all over the world could not feel hunger? Why are cemeteries full of empty graves, and is there any truth to George Romero's *Night of the Living Dead* movies? Hence, it may be less surprising to hear Vieux Os' mother say: "It [this political arrangement – X.X.] served everyone well since the only thing that frightened the American soldiers… was having to go out into the Haitian night" (Laferrière 54). American soldiers hide in their barracks at night because everyone remembers the peculiar pop culture-driven images of zombies and voodoo upon arrival in Haiti, and are not eager to encounter them. It is by reconnecting with their cultural heritage and re-claiming the discourse of that culture appropriated by the Western popular culture imagination that Haitians can emancipate themselves from neocolonial rule.

The analysis of the narrative of Laferrière's novel revealed that the hinterland can be created like a heterotopia – in the clash between the real and the imaginary. Foucault's notion of heterotopia established it as a place that is on the one hand real and limited, but on the other one that represents, challenges, and inverts other existing realities. According to Foucault, the function of heterotopia is double: "either their role is to create a space of illusion that exposes every real space… as still more illusory… Or else, on the contrary, their role is to create a space that is other, another real space, as perfect, as meticulous, as well arranged as ours is messy, ill constructed, all jumbled" (Foucault 27). The hinterland's existence in Laferrière's novel can only be perceived under the right cognitive conditions (at night) and, like any created space, it involves a certain power and counter-power manifested in it. Furthermore, places of this kind are created only by difference: in contrast to day and reason, the space of night and magic could evolve. While usually the two aspects of the Janus face condition and sustain each other, the two faces of Port-au-Prince described in *Pays sans chapeau* have been radically separated, to the point where there seems to be no connection between them (hence, the narrator's observation that it occurred to him that the two countries of Haiti live side by side). Their reconciliation (which is Vieux Os' writing goal) might result in dealing with the identity crisis caused by the experience of neo-colonization.

Haitian identity and space are also the starting points for the narrative of *Douces déroutes*, as Lahens emphasized: "From there [Haitian capital – X.X.], I reflect on myself – I question history, myths, geography, the life force, the world as it is, with its inequalities, its misfortunes and its beauty, against all odds" (Lahens and Bardon). *Douces déroutes*, as the title suggests, "offers a bittersweet portrayal of current social and political conditions in Haiti" (Nzengou-Tayo 288). There is no main character in the story; instead, there is a group of friends, each with their own individual fears, troubles, and dreams they want to fulfil. What unites all the more or less separate threads of the narrative is, first, the fictional setting of Haiti, where everyone is trying to find a place to live, and second, the plot of the political murder of judge Raymond Berthier. The novel begins with a letter written by Raymond to his wife and ends with the four protagonists – Pierre, Ezékiel, Ronny, and Francis – accidentally discovering the identity of the judge's murderer when they witness an execution in Medequilla. But on a more fundamental level, this book is not a crime story – it is a novel about the island of Haiti and its people. Haiti is described from a historical perspective as the result of a tumultuous process of change in a "country consumed by fire" (Lahens 36). It is noteworthy that these descriptions of change, indebted in terms of time, duration, and rupture, in *Douces déroutes* are always shown through the transformation of space. Once again, time and space are inseparable, as in this passage:

> In the time of Pierre's childhood, this neighbourhood was still a rural village, silent and peaceful, where public entertainments were limited to patronal feasts, religious processions, altars of repose for the Feast of Corpus Christi. Then came the time of fences entwined with bougainvillea. Fences at first light as lace. Elegant flowered village was so beautiful that visitors compared it to certain suburbs of Tokyo, I'm telling you! And then came the heavy wrought iron windows, high stone walls and automatic entrance gates to houses. The time has come

for creeping, insidious fear. It was the precise time when the island began to crumble in their hands. Piece after piece. As an abandoned car on the side of the road. Each used as needed. As desired. Only a gutted carcass remains from the car. But it is still delusional, since the carcasses have a quite unexpected value on the international art market. We are an installation at the contemporary art biennale, where, you have to admit it, one can really see everything. Hear everything! We still inspire admiration. What a raw beauty! What a power! What a resilience! And whatever else you want! (Lahens 23–24)

The progressive processes of spatial fencing and separation are occurring in tandem with growing social anxiety and insecurity. Certainly, the metaphor of Haiti as a car used by successive rulers, modifying it to their own needs and stripping it down to the carcass, refers to the times of rapid political change in Haiti that have marked the country's political scene since the end of Jean-Claude Duvalier's rule in 1986. The more fragmented and isolationist Haitian society becomes, the more it resembles an abandoned carcass that may inspire pity and even admiration from the international press, like a museum exhibit, but in reality, it presents almost impossible living conditions for those at the bottom of the cauldron at any given time. The cauldron, which will be examined later in this chapter, is the most important metaphor for Haiti in Lahens' novel, symbolizing the class formation of this society.

The above-quoted passage also shows the rapid expansion of urban districts in Port-au-Prince. The result is the creation of hinterlands, places we do not look at or where it is better not to look, like those sideways or hidden alleys detailed and juxtaposed by Ézéchiel with inescapable poverty. One of the characteristics of urban sprawl is the disproportion between the number of people migrating to the city and the number of existing housing units, causing people to create such places for their own needs, often in an unplanned and chaotic manner. Thus, place of residence becomes an important determinant of class status, but, importantly, it only begins to matter in the context of the entire topographical configuration of Port-au-Prince. Again, as in Laferrière's novel, it is only by contrast that a place can become a hinterland. This shows the relative nature of the hinterland itself, which is established each time depending on the current politics (and interests of the government in question). Lahens, however, sees political practices of power not only in government policies of space management, but also in issues of access to space, and freedom and ease of movement within it. These issues are problematized through the figures of cars and their marketing campaigns in Haiti. One of these, a radio advertisement for the Audi Quattro, produced in 2015 with a primary focus on the

Haitian market, was heard by Cyprien. The ad, which is an homage to both Haiti and Audi, encourages people to "discover what makes Haiti the country of the Quattro":

> You are a magic island, The Pearl of the Antilles... You are a great wonder of verdant nature ... Irresistible! You always astonish and amaze ... Multicolored world, you are a brave, resilient people. You are a legendary, epic Nation. You are a Universe of creative geniuses, in painting, music, sculpture, craftsmanship ... You have a story made of human and natural poetry! You are the land of hospitality *par excellence* ... You are Haiti ... The country of the Quattro. (quoted after Walsh 194)

In Lahens' novel, the advertisement is transcribed only in fragments, but the effect is nonetheless powerful – one is struck by the absurdity of looking for a similarity between a new model of German car and Haiti, because the two words, placed side by side, "in the end, say nothing" (Lahens 15). It is the purpose of advertisements, Cyprien suggests, to transform the improbable into the quite plausible. The image of Haiti envisioned in this advertising performs a heterotopic function, but this time it is not an illusion revealing the illusory nature of the actual place (as was the case with Laferrière's portrait of Port-au-Prince at night), but rather another place, "as perfect, as meticulous, as well arranged as ours is messy, ill constructed, all jumbled" (Foucault 27). It functions as a *compensation* that, through the rhetoric of advertising, translates what is merely a utopian vision into a possible spatial Other of Haiti.

In both novels, the hinterland is located in the city of Port-au-Prince somewhat nearby, adjacent, revealing itself from time to time only to those who know how, when, and where to observe. In different ways, the narratives emphasize important factors that define hinterlands: they arise in specific spaces (they are not natural, but socially mediated and changeable) at specific times; their manifestation almost always involves some political power; it is their inaccessibility to everyone's consciousness that makes them particularly complex and intriguing; and finally, they are always becoming through difference. While many of the spatial hinterlands analyzed above fall into the category of Foucault's heterotopias – they are real (within fiction) spaces that simultaneously represent, contest, and subvert existing spaces – it is not clear what the purpose of such practices is. Foucault distinguished two possible functions of heterotopia – illusory and compensatory – but both can be observed in the novels. To understand how this is possible, the two spatial metaphors of Haitian society, the cauldron and vertical layering, must be examined in detail.

Spatial metaphors of Port-au-Prince

Society is often depicted through allegories of spatial relations and hierarchies between different social strata, as in the case of the social pyramid, where "Power is given to a few people at the top and each descending tier represents more people with a diminished level of power" (Sam), so the majority has the least power and turns into a discursive minority (Bendix 540), or the ladder: "stratification is shown solely by a set of eight equally sized and equally spaced rungs on a ladder, with the rungs varying only in the number of apples they possess" (Krieger 1099). Similar models of allegories depicting society can be found in the novels of Laferrière and Lahens. Importantly, like the aforementioned, they take the form of criticism of the current social system, especially inequalities in the distribution of power and wealth. It is worth noting that both of these allegories have an even more spatial dimension than the pyramid or ladder, as they directly coincide with the topography of Port-au-Prince. Thus, they become not only a visualization of abstract social relations, class conflicts, and alliances, but also a form of representation of these relations in space.

Port-au-Prince in *Douces déroutes* turns into a cauldron, in *Pays sans chapeau* – into a vertical layering, made possible by the specific terrain on which the capital is located, a form that has allowed social stratification to be reflected in a spatial form as well. The Haitian capital is made up of waterfront districts in the bay at the apex of the Gulf of Gonâve, and in the surrounding hills, where "Most of the Haitian elite (nearly all mulatto or nonblacks) live in the suburb of Pétionville in the 1,000–1,500 ft. (300–450 m) high hills southeast of Port-au-Prince" (Britannica). Thus, we can tentatively see that the natural conditions of the capital's location have been used to separate more or less segregated districts, with those in the hills being inhabited by the upper classes. This stratification is presented both by Laferrière and Lahens.

The detailed description of space can be found in *Pays sans chapeau* when the protagonist tries to briefly present what the capital city looks like:

LANDSCAPE... Alone in Port-au-Prince. I turned right for no reason and found myself at the top of Nelhio hill. The city at my feet. The rich live on the mountain slopes (the Black Mountains). The poor are jammed in together in the lower town, at the foot of a mountain of garbage. Those who are neither rich nor poor occupy the center of Port-au-Prince...

FIGURES
Fifty-six percent of the population occupies 11% of the land.

Thirty-three percent of the population occupies 33% of the land.
Eleven percent of the population occupies 56% of the land.
(Laferrière 34)

Based on this quote, horizontal lines can be drawn on a map of the Haitian capital to separate successive layers of vertically progressing prosperity. Moreover, one can even assume the size of the space available to each layer and its proportion in relation to population density. According to the narrative, this proportion is due to the unequal distribution of living space, as most of this space belongs to a statistical minority, the upper classes, and the bourgeoisie. The poor live "at the foot of a mountain of garbage", which is not a metaphor, but a recurring image in the novel's narrative – an image of all kinds of filth and sewage descending from the mountains into the slums. The presentist description of Port-au-Prince is also historicized, as evidenced by the following passage:

WAR

You can describe what's happened over the last twenty years in the area of housing in just one word: *war*. The population of Port-au-Prince has increased considerably with the constant influx of people of all social classes from the provincial towns. This movement has triggered a generalized panic in the city. The established Port-au-Prince bourgeoisie sought refuge in the mountains. The middle-class population quin-tupled while space remained constant. A frenetic game of musical chairs began. Anyone who lost his spot found himself, ipso facto, in the rats' nest of Martissant. (Laferrière 35)

Access to the home has been described as a "war", further empha-sizing the class struggle for space. This struggle, moreover, is triggered by urban sprawl, the uncontrolled influx of peasants into the city, which prompts the bourgeoisie to move away from the centre and fence off in estates that allow them to look at the city and its turmoil from a safe distance. Space remains "constant"; it cannot be stretched to accommodate the increasing number of residents, so all the social "rest" begins to crowd more and more under the hills, "in the rats' nest". This representation, like most allegorical images of social stratification, is a critique of the existing rules (or rather, lack thereof) of space management.

Similar criticism is even more acute in Lahens' novel. Once again, allegories of space take on significance as images of social class stratifi-cation. The key metaphor of the cauldron signifies Haitian society, in which the rich float in the foam and the poor and unfortunate sink to the bottom. As a rule, the poor and underclasses occupy the bottom of the cauldron, overwhelmed by the weight of the human mass filling the cauldron to the brim, but it only takes a moment of inattention or time spent on questioning the system itself for a person to join the lower classes: "Here, if you waste your time on sophisticated speculation about justice and injustice, moods and other nonsense, you find yourself at the bottom of the cauldron. One moment of tenderness and you are slipping due to lack of vigilance, and whoops, you fall" (Lahens 28). So it is possible to worsen one's social standing, but can the process be reversed? Two such cases are described in the novel: one is revolution; the other is private profit. Their logic, as depicted in *Douces déroutes*, is guided in two opposite directions. The first, revolution, stems from the realization of one's social position and the injustice of the current system. The second, private profit, is related to the complete disappearance of class consciousness.

The revolution is characterized in the novel as a periodically recurring process that loses its violent impulse and ends very quickly:

> Cyprien knows that the great virtue of the cauldron is that it keeps people warm. Sometimes a spark is enough for a virtue to turn into its opposite. Then the hatred takes over, and for a day or two the fiery gurgitation rises to the level of the foam. A day or two, that's it. Here hatred doesn't last long, it sinks to the very bottom. (Lahens 28)

One revolutionary spark could transform the ignorant masses into a group with a common purpose – to go beyond the cauldron, to reinvent all social policy, including its tangible, everyday dimension. However, this is not the case. This impulse is based on the affliction of hatred and, although very intense, is only temporary. This scenario of ephemeral revolution is, of course, reminiscent of the numerous political upheavals that have taken place in Haiti, and although some of them were openly launched in the interest of the people, especially those at the bottom of the cauldron, they ultimately failed to lead to real transformation (see Hallward; Quinn and Sutton).

Another example of upward shift is the individual success of Cyprien Novilus. He comes from a poor, rural family and sometimes recalls the five-kilometre walk to school he used to make every day in worn-out shoes – but as an intern at a law firm, he decides to dismiss that memory: "He doesn't plan on going back there. He offers these memories to ethnologists, fame-hungry poets and charitable organizations" (Lahens 29–30). When he becomes a successful lawyer, he argues that the cauldron is just a harmful *myth* invented by spiteful sociologists (Lahens 219).

As soon as one's own living conditions improve, those still faced by less fortunate others become less important.

Through the spatial allegories of Port-au-Prince as a cauldron and of vertical layering, Haitian writers tackle many problems of social organization and access to space. They show how different policies always work in the interest of a small group, and how difficult it is to achieve successful community action. Both allegories also operate at the level of disparities inherent in managing the specific topography of the capital. These allegories are thus part of a long tradition of depicting social relations in spatial form in order to critique them.

This chapter examined the specific embodiment of the hinterland in two Haitian novels to show that hinterlands are *made* rather than exist in themselves as certain spatially distinctive places located on the outskirts of urbanized centres. However, it is worth noting the dialectic inherent in this concept – that the hinterland simultaneously symbolizes something outside the centre, something hidden or invisible on a daily basis, but necessary to support and maintain that centre. This dialectic, while by definition partially reassuring of the contemporary power relationship, can also be used athwart – to subvert this power structure or at least make it visible again.

In both narratives, there are recurring questions about the purposefulness of stratifying spaces and fencing, about the (in)ability to move freely, and finally about what a city needs a hinterland for. In order to solve these problems, it is necessary to expand the properties that define hinterlands; hence, I argued that they are constructed not only in spatial, but also in temporal conditions and that they can also arise inside the city, since the basis for their distinction is the relationship between the centre and what is beyond. Such representational categories are *always produced by difference*: only in contrast to the daytime city can we fully describe the nocturnal city (with all the metaphorical meanings that these epithets imply for both narratives).

The hinterlands are not available to everyone. First, because not everyone *wants* to see them: in Laferrière's novel, for example, the rich residents of the mountainous districts are indifferent to where their waste goes; in Lahens' book, it is those who admire the beauty of poverty or those who have climbed the social ladder and stopped believing in the existence of a cauldron. Secondly, because not everyone *is capable* of seeing them, like the Americans who unsuccessfully try to rationally explain the lack of hunger of the villagers of Bombardopolis, because instead of understanding Haitian culture, they implement their own logic and modes of conduct. And thirdly, because not everyone *will be in the right place at the right time* to see them – in both novels the hinterlands are depicted only in specific places in Port-au-Prince at night.

Referring to Foucault's account of heterotopia, I showed that hinterlands perform a similar role – they simultaneously describe and subvert reality. Moreover, the hinterlands examined in the novels performed the illusory or compensatory functions as distinguished by Foucault. Either, like illusion, they exposed their own unreality to show how unreal the real is, or, in a compensatory function, they created unreal, perfect, and orderly spaces to show the imperfection and chaos of reality by contrast. Both of these mechanisms of relating to reality are in fact a form of criticism of what is represented. Laferrière and Lahens elaborate on this critique, explaining how irrationalism can also be part of the real, what it means to live in an inner-city hinterland, a place of non- or semi-existence (reminiscent of zombis), and why some symbols, always absorbing new meanings, no longer adequately represent Haiti.

Notes

1 Hiding the production process from view is, of course, not a modern phenomenon – in the nineteenth century in industrialized British cities, factories were hidden behind the facades of buildings erected on the main street.
2 This main plot of the novel is highly autobiographical because Laferrière, a young journalist for the radio station Haïti Inter and two newspapers *Le Nouvelliste* and *Le Petit Samedi Soir*, decides to go into exile to Montreal in 1976, following in his father's footsteps; see Izzo 126; Munro 179.
3 For further considerations on the complex relations between the real and the fictional, especially in the context of the autobiographical nature of the novel, see Mukenge and Kayembe.
4 Migrants in particular become a symbolically invisible group in this narrative; see Nzengou-Tayo.
5 This twofold structure was made even more visible by the construction of the book itself, organized in the form of the following alternating chapters entitled "Real Country" and "Dream Country".
6 In the chapter, I use the spelling "vodou" to describe a syncretic form of the Haitian religious belief system that has African roots and formed a basis for the commoning of the slave community in Haiti during the transatlantic slave trade. The term "voodoo", in turn, denotes a racist image perpetuated in Western popular culture, developed on the basis of the belief in superstition and black magic of Haitians or on the vision of cannibalism (Rushton and Moreman 2).
7 I accept the "zombi"/"zombie" spelling distinction proposed by Sarah Juliet Lauro and Karen Embry (87).

Works Cited

Bendix, Reinhard. *Kings or People: Power and the Mandate to Rule*. University of California Press, 1980.
Britannica. "Port-au-Prince." *Encyclopedia Britannica*, 22 January 2021, https://www.britannica.com/place/Port-au-Prince. Accessed 17 February 2021.

Foucault, Michel, and Paul Rabinow. "Space, Knowledge, and Power." Translated by Christian Hubert. *Foucault Reader*. Ed. Paul Rabinow. Pantheon Books, 1984, pp. 239–56.

Foucault, Michel. "Of Other Spaces." Translated by Jay Miskowiec. *Diacritics*, vol. 16, 1986, pp. 22–27.

Girard, Philippe R. "Peacekeeping, Politics, and the 1994 US Intervention in Haiti." *Journal of Conflict Studies*, vol. 24, no. 1, 2004, pp. 20–41.

Hallward, Peter. *Damming the Flood: Haiti and the Politics of Containment*. Verso, 2010.

Hoermann, Raphael. "Figures of Terror: The 'Zombie' and the Haitian Revolution." *Atlantic Studies*, vol. 14, no. 2, 2016, pp. 1–22.

Izzo, Justin. *Experiments with Empire: Anthropology and Fiction in the French Atlantic*. Duke University Press, 2019.

Krieger, N. "Ladders, Pyramids and Champagne: The Iconography of Health Inequities." *Journal of Epidemiology Community Health*, vol. 62, 2008, pp. 1098–104.

Laferrière, Dany. *Down among the Dead Men*. Translated by David Homel. Douglas & McIntyre, 1997.

Lahens, Yanick. *Douces déroutes: Roman*. Sabine Wespieser Éditeur, 2018.

Lahens, Yanick, and Agnès Bardon. "Haiti Questions Modernity Because We See Its Contradictions." *The Unesco Courier*, vol. 2, 2021, https://en.unesco.org/courier/2021-2/yanick-lahens-haiti-questions-modernity-because-we-see-its-contradictions. Accessed 17 June 2021.

Lauro, Sarah Juliet. *The Transatlantic Zombie: Slavery, Rebellion, and Living Death*. Rutgers University Press, 2015.

Lauro, Sarah Juliet, and Karen Embry. "A Zombie Manifesto: The Nonhuman Condition in the Era of Advanced Capitalism." *Boundary*, vol. 2, Spring, 2008, pp. 85–108.

Matisoff, Adina. "Manufacturing Malady: The Hidden Cost of a Product." *Asia Society*, August 2008, https://asiasociety.org/education/manufacturing-malady. Accessed 16 August 2022.

Mbembe, Achille. *Necropolitics*. Translated by Steven Corcoran. Duke University Press, 2019.

Mukenge, Arthur, and Emmanuel Kayembe. "Fiction et réalité dans *Pays sans chapeau* de Dany Laferrière: Entreautobiographie, autofictionet au-delà." *Literator*, vol. 37, no. 1, 2016, pp. 1–6. https://literator.org.za/index.php/literator/article/view/1290/2154

Munro, Martin. *Exile and Post-1946 Haitian Literature: Alexis, Depestre, Ollivier, Laferrière, Danticat*. Liverpool University Press, 2007.

Neel, Phil A. *Hinterland: America's New Landscape of Class and Conflict*. Reaktion Books, 2018.

Nzengou-Tayo, Marie-José. "*Douces déroutes* by Yanick Lahens." *Journal of Haitian Studies*, vol. 25, no. 2, 2019, pp. 288–290.

Pomeranz, Kenneth. *The Making of a Hinterland State, Society, and Economy in Inland North China, 1853–1937*. University of California Press, 1993.

Quinn, Kate, and Paul K. Sutton, editors. *Politics and Power in Haiti*. Palgrave Macmillan, 2013.

Rushton, Cory James, and Christopher M. Moreman. "Introduction: Race, Colonialism, and the Evolution of the »Zombie«." *Race, Oppression and the Zombie: Essays on Cross-Cultural Appropriations of the Caribbean Tradition*. Eds. Christopher M. Moreman, and Cory James Rushton. McFarland & Company, 2011, pp. 1–12.

Walsh, John Patrick. "Haïti, le pays du Quattro? L'imaginaire de l'environnement urbain de *Douces déroutes*, ou Yanick Lahens et le spectacle de l'inégalité." *Les Cahiers d'Outre-Mer*, vol. 279, 2019, pp. 193–213.

6 Haven, rebellion, revelation

Australian hinterlands as heterotopias in Peter Carey's novels

Barbara Klonowska

Peter Carey's fiction is best known for his experimental historical novels (including probably the most successful *Oscar and Lucinda* or *Jack Maggs*); slightly less popular internationally are perhaps his more contemporary texts set in and presenting the past and present of his once home country. Interestingly, these books often display a sharp picture of Australia and the community torn by internal conflicts and repression, both political and cultural, between the metropolitan, (sub)urban south and the rest of the country, and the various forms of resistance and reaction that these tensions produce. Ranging from post-hippie communes that challenge the middle-class ideal of suburban bliss, through the bush and the outback that represents the heartland of the continent, to the remote deserts that reveal its ugly politics, Carey's novels tend to construct Australia as a site of repression and/or rebellion. Generically, many of his novels may be classified as picaresques: through the complex adventure-driven plots involving travels, chance meetings, and surprising turnings of events, they represent not just the lives and times of their fictional protagonists but also glimpses of Australia and its problems and politics. Northrop Frye defines picaresque as a literary form whose aim is to reveal "the actual structure of society" (Frye 310): its social relations, problems, or conflicts. Picaresque, then, acts as a sort of a textual mirror set against a given society, reflecting but also interrogating its values, lifestyles, and politics. Frequently in Carey's fiction, they are the dominating themes of his novels.

Another characteristic feature of Carey's writing is the form of the novels that are often based on juxtapositions and contrasts. This strategy is manifested first of all in the construction of narration and point of view, which often involve two alternative narrators and perspectives juxtaposed in separate sections (e.g., in *Oscar and Lucinda* or *Parrot and Olivier in America*). Yet, the principle of contrast may be perhaps extended to include the construction of fictional space, equally often presented in antithetical terms. In several of Carey's novels, fictional

DOI: 10.4324/9781032617732-9

spaces are based on contrast and construct opposing alternative spaces that reflect or contradict dominating values, be they political or social. This tendency is also revealed in the contrast between the metropolis and the hinterlands, characteristic of some of his novels and reflecting the contrast between different sets of values, lifestyles, and ideas. Thus, the representation of hinterlands is revealing as, on the one hand, it points to the "actual structure of society", and on the other, it actively challenges it and criticizes or suggests some alternatives.

The very concept of hinterlands is intuitively understandable yet, as Robert Lee notes, it has no simple or straightforward definition (Lee 4). The narrow one describes it as a service area of a port (Lee 4) and the territory that supplies the goods; in urban studies, it describes "variegated non-city spaces ... which include diverse types of settlements" (Brenner and Katsikis 24). Yet the concept functions far beyond these narrow technical meanings and is used as a frequent metaphor that resorts to geography to make a cultural point. In its broader sense, hinterlands are conceptualized as spaces opposed to or located beyond the metropolitan centres (cf. William Cronon's *Nature's Metropolis*), as rural or remote areas, or simply peripheries and margins. Read ideologically, they may be perceived as spaces of struggle for recognition and hegemony, as areas of colonial or capitalist extraction, or as sites of marginalization and exclusion. Hinterlands, thus, may be conceptualized horizontally as places located beyond the geographical centre, or vertically as spaces in which dynamic processes take place. In this second conceptualization, they may be interpreted – together with the centres – as fluid and co-dependent categories, both present simultaneously and forming a functional unit.

In the Australian context, the notion of hinterlands acquires yet other specifically local meanings, the first of which is connected with tourism. Parts of Australia, especially those on the east coast such as Queensland's Sunshine Coast and Gold Coast hinterlands, or the Byron Bay hinterland of northern New South Wales are often described as hinterlands and advertised as spaces of leisure and pleasure, sites of holiday-making and contact with nature, providing an escape from the bustle of urban life (cf. Sarah Bristow). Against this seemingly unproblematic conceptualization one may, however, also posit another meaning of Australian hinterlands: that of spaces of colonial struggle, sites of the extermination of First Nations, and confinement of racialized others. Thus, hinterlands may be also read as sites of memory and violence, a dark reverse of sunlit centres that, when examined, bring to light matters suppressed or unwanted.

All of these meanings of the term *hinterlands* – the one that conceptualizes them as a land beyond, remote and wild, an escape and retreat, and the dark quasi-Gothic place of repressed trauma – seem pertinent to Carey's fiction that constructs such sites as a part of the juxtaposition contrasting them with more urban or "civilized" spaces. Carey's novels describe both spaces characteristic and typical of Australian past and present and those which, located in the hinterlands, the outback, or the bush, actively contradict and interrogate them. Hinterlands become a textual double, a dark crooked mirror set against the dominating discourses of power or society, which pose questions about the validity of their values. They constitute the sites of the other – other values and other ways of living and being. The notion of a counter-space or another space that both reflects and challenges the existing *status quo* draws on Michel Foucault's concept of heterotopia, which similarly describes the process of constructing alternatives to the existing power structures, not in the distant future or alternative reality but in the existing world. Foucault points out that while utopia is literally a no-place, that is a place that physically does not exist, a site without a place (Foucault 24); in contrast, heterotopia is a place that does exist in reality and "in which the real sites... are simultaneously represented, contested, and inverted" (Foucault 24). Hence, the name "hetero-topia": another place, a different place, a counter-site reflecting upon the common real places. As Foucault points out, "its role [is] to create a space that is other, another real space, as perfect, as meticulous, as well arranged as ours is messy, ill constructed, and jumbled" (Foucault 27). Heterotopias, constructed within the existing world, hint at the possibilities of other orders, logics, and arrangements located not in the future, the past, an alternative reality, or geographically distant locale but in the here and now. Their function is to raise an awareness of the possibility of other ways of being and living, perhaps better suited to human needs. Heterotopias, then, become counter-sites of resistance and sites of hope, offering alternatives, if not practical then only mental, to the existing solutions. They may also, however, act simply as mirrors, reflecting and forcing to reflect upon the present *status quo*.

This chapter will analyse the construction and function of thus conceived spaces of hinterlands represented in three of Peter Carey's novels: *True History of the Kelly Gang* (2000), *Bliss* (1981), and *Long Way from Home* (2017). Referring to the function of heterotopias as that providing the impulse to interrogate or pose alternatives, it will examine how hinterlands are used as a contrast and alternative to the existing historically spaces described in the novels and the social and political discourses that the fictional counter-spaces aim to challenge. Ranging from shelter, to haven and to revelation, Carey's hinterlands provide several kinds of mirrors set against Australian society and politics.

Hinterlands as shelter – *True History of the Kelly Gang* (2000)

True History of the Kelly Gang, probably the best known and most celebrated of the three novels discussed in this chapter, recounts the life and times of the eponymous hero – the legendary Australian bushranger and rebel. Situated in southern Australia in the years 1870–1880, the novel's background, against which the subsequent exploits and rebellions of the main protagonist are played out, is the process of shaping Australia as a nation state rather than an ex-penal colony. The novel sets the action in small towns and villages, describing how descendants of Irish convicts try to find themselves a place among the rich nobility of English origin and how their efforts, more or less legal, come to nothing and reduce them to the increasing poverty and crime. The novel represents Australia of the 1870s as a place still dominated by colonial rules and by the everyday discrimination and petty persecution of Irish ex-convicts. The fate of the main protagonist, Ned Kelly, told in his own voice, recounts his life from his childhood till his capture and hanging, and it becomes a metonymy of many other Irish people like him who were systematically discriminated against, pushed into numerous conflicts with the police, and made victims of systemic persecution. In the novel, Kelly becomes a sort of a Jean Valjean figure, as if taken from *Les Misérable*: a small crime committed out of poverty sets the protagonist on a trajectory, leading him towards the life of a lawless man, a rebel, thief, and murderer. Yet, despite his crimes, the novel presents Kelly as a man of dignity who desperately craves justice denied him and who rebels in the name of justice – even against the law. In Australia, as Dorothy Simmons suggests, his story has become a myth and Kelly himself may be read as "a man-myth whose role evolves with [the] evolving consciousness" (Simmons 419).

Spatial relations in Carey's novel contrast the world of the white settlers of English and Irish origin – small towns and farms – with the outback and the bush towards which the protagonists retreat to find shelter and hide from the police. The bush becomes for the protagonists the place of escape and rebellion, the camp of Harry Power, to whom young Kelly is first an apprentice in the thieving business, and then of the Gang who hide there from the forces of law. Hidden in dense bush, hardly visible, the huts of bushrangers are places of safety and temporary relief. More importantly, however, they are also spaces of freedom from the oppressive society and its law, according to which a poor man – especially of Irish origin – will always lose. Thus, in the novel, hinterlands become a heterotopia of safety, justice, and freedom: a place alternative to the existing colonial system, which oppresses and criminalizes the poor and those with the ex-convict past.

Interestingly, in the monologue of the main protagonist, there are only few very short descriptions of the outback itself. Little space is devoted to the presentation of landscapes, plants, and animals (the latter feature only as a source of food). Although the novel mentions numerous place names – apart from the towns, also names of woods or mountain ranges – their textual presence is signalled only and treated as a background and scenery behind the protagonist's life, rather than a subject in itself. Little space is devoted to the hardships and even danger of living in the bush, living off the land, sharing it with numerous species of snakes and other animals, or with other bushrangers. This briefness may be partly explained by the structure of narration: most of the novel consists of a quasi-stream-of-consciousness monologue of the eponymous hero who retells his life in a manuscript addressed to his baby daughter; as the narrator focuses mostly on actions and conversations, little of the landscape gets recorded. The outback for Kelly is the place of hiding and it is presented only as such, with little space devoted to its description or contemplation. The space is treated instrumentally, as a place serving certain functions for the pro-tagonist and embodying particular ideas for the novel; it hardly merits itself. The unsentimental treatment of space may recall the observations of Paul Shepard about the equally un-nostalgic native people's attitude to the natural environment. As he notes, "the nomad does not dote on scenery, paint landscapes or compile a natural history … his life is so profoundly in transaction with nature that there is no place for abstraction or aes-thetics … Nature and his relationship to it are a deadly-serious matter" (Shepard *Man in the Landscape* qtd. in Krakauer 183). Perhaps for the protagonist of the novel, the bush is equally "natural" – it is an environment he has to hide and survive in rather than an object of con-templation. His attitude to it is pragmatic rather than sentimental.

It seems, then, that hinterlands in this text are conceived as an idea rather than an existing place that may be represented in fiction. *True History of the Kelly Gang* constructs the outback as a counter-space of resistance towards the colonial centre, showing the former as an oasis of safety and freedom and the latter as a site of prejudice and oppression. This ideological opposition expressed at the level of spatial relations points to the injustices and harm inflicted by the colonial politics which treats unequally Australian subjects, first pushing some of them into crime and then punishing them with all due severity. Constructing the outback hinterland as a heterotopia of safety, justice, and freedom (contrary to the mainstream representation which shows it rather as a place of risk and danger), the novel treats it as a textual mirror that reflects the pitfalls of the colonial politics. Hinterland, then, construed as a site of contestation and rebellion, serves as a counter-space of interrogation and pro-blematization of the values professed by the colonial discourse, revealing the latter as a machine of systemic oppression crushing non-fitting individuals and leaving them no chance to lead a dignified life.

Hinterlands as h(e)aven – *Bliss* (1981)

A somewhat similar representation of the hinterlands, though more complex and ideologically charged, may be found in Carey's first novel *Bliss*. Its action is set in an unnamed city located in southeastern Australia, probably in the 1970s, but the spatio-temporal setting remains deliberately undetermined, thus bringing the novel close to a contemporary fairy tale with its generalizing rather than strictly local and limited meaning. Still, the simultaneous number of references to the then-Australian reality with its architecture, lifestyles, jobs, and problems firmly anchors the text in the convention of comic realism. The novel, just as *True History of the Kelly Gang*, contrasts two spaces and two ways of living and being with their specific values: the pleasure and leisure of a comfortable suburban life with the alternative heterotopia of the hinterlands and its simple, healthy, and organic lifestyle. The contrast, then, between the mainland and the hinterland – in the case of this novel, one of the Australian rainforest areas – is ideologically charged and reflects the fundamental for the novel contrast between two ideas of life.

The unnamed city is represented as a site of consumerism, money, and success obsession. The protagonists, middle-class, middle-aged advertising agents, are portrayed as career-obsessed and hardly reflective people whose ambition is comfortable life, money, and social ambition. The external sign of their success is a house in the suburbs, dining in city restaurants, and wearing expensive clothes; it is also a dream of making a career in New York. Driven by ambition and success, which seems to provide them with a state of bliss, they overlook its side effects: drug addiction, alcoholism, health problems, mental disorders, and ruined family relationships. They are also unaware, until the moment of a closer contact, that this comfort is based on and secured by a strong and unpleasant mechanism of oppression, represented by the police and psychiatric institutions; both of them feature in the novel as sadistic forces, hardly helpful and disciplining and punishing. The idea of a comfortable suburban life, then, is analyzed and discredited in this novel: although professed and dreamed of by many, it is exposed as a false bliss – limiting rather than liberating, especially for the less privileged members of the society. For women, isolating them from their workplace and delegating to the role of a housewife and a mother, the ideal of suburban life deprives them of a chance to pursue their own ambitions, careers, and independent life. For youngsters, a suburban house becomes a prison from which they want to break free as soon as possible. For successful businessmen, it is a boring, limiting place. As Don Fletcher observes, "suburbia was perhaps always a flawed notion of utopia … [and] in Australian literature suburbia has quite consistently been seen as Hell or as a metonym for death, negatively compared to either the testing and character-building bush or the aesthetically inspiring or at least vibrant working class inner city" (Fletcher 40). The suburban ideal of life in the novel turns out literally deadly – in the fantastic plot twist, this life ends in a cancer epidemic that threatens to kill the inhabitants of the suburban paradise. All of the protagonists try to escape from it, either through work, alcohol, drugs, or erotic affairs; most of them fail and literally die; only for the main protagonist the escape, via a series of comic and dramatic picaresque adventures, turns out possible.

The other space constructed in the novel and juxtaposed with the city life is the place in the hinterland, in the unnamed and intractable rainforest located ca. 500 miles away from it. This is the site of the Bog Onion Road commune, set deep in the outback, far from any signs of civilization, independent from and indignant of city life. The settlement consists of a group of huts, fields among the forest, and beehives; its inhabitants live off the land and are self-sufficient in terms of food and services; they avoid any contact with the state, its offices, and regulations, although sometimes they trade with nearby communes and towns selling their products. Their isolation from the city life is intended and cultivated: they deem the city unhealthy and lethal; instead, they profess a healthy lifestyle consisting of organic, self-grown food, physical work, freedom of habits, simple life, and communal involvement. With time, they increase their isolation, growing more and more trees to cut themselves off completely and become unreachable by any road and intractable from the air. They also develop their own rituals and myths, which help them reassert themselves as a community. As the narrator observes, "they were the refugees of a broken culture who had only the flotsam of belief and ceremony to cling to … they were hungry for ceremony and story" (Carey 1996, 291). The commune, both in its everyday habits and the myths they construct, tries to create a completely opposite ideal of life where there is no police and law as there is no crime and violence; they also reject all the values of late capitalism: money, careers, materialism, rat race, excessive possession, together with the poisonous side effects of the "civilized" life, such as illness and oppression. Thus, the rainforest commune is constructed as a viable alternative to the lethal city life: it is safe and saving, if only because untouched by the cancer epidemic sweeping through the city.

Interestingly, although described in more detail, the space of the commune is equally undetermined. The descriptions are limited to those of trees mostly, and – apparently – incorrectly chosen, as according to the critics, the non-existent species of trees are inserted into the seemingly accurate descriptions of nature (cf. Siwoń 127). It is quite incomplete, too, as strangely enough, this is the place completely deprived of animals, both friendly and hostile: there are no snakes here, no wombats or kangaroos, with only scarce occasional birds. Likewise, little is known about the exact location of the commune, except that it is situated in an unnamed and never located rainforest. This indeterminacy and imprecision suggest that, just as in the case of the unnamed city, the commune is not so much a mimetically described, really existing space (though communes like that existed in Australia and Carey himself lived shortly in one of them), but rather an idea and a model of life contrasted with that represented by the city.

Describing the hinterland and a commune located there, *Bliss* constructs a counter-space to the suburban flawed ideal, an alternative of authentic bliss suggesting a different possibility of living and being. Rainforest hinterlands presented in this novel may be interpreted as a heterotopia challenging capitalist and consumerist values and lifestyles, which in turn are shown as limiting and lethal. Far from mimetically describing existing places, city-lands and hinterlands constructed in this novel represent contrastive ideas of life, with the preference given to the latter.

Hinterlands as a dark mirror – *Long Way from Home* (2017)

Still another representation of the hinterland and its ideological function one may find in the latest novel by Carey, *A Long Way from Home*. Set in 1953, first in southern Australia (Victoria), then following the route of the really existing Reddex Trial (a car endurance rail), the plot of the novel makes a *tour de Australia*, tracing the actions of the protagonists as they travel from the south up north, then west, and south again, parallel to the coasts of Australia, yet deep in the hinterlands and wild parts of the continent. Just as previous novels by Carey, this text also contrasts two kinds of spaces juxtaposed antithetically: the "white" Australia of the south and southeast with the "black" Australia of the north. The key events in the novel take place deep in the interior of the northwestern Kimberley region still inhabited by native Aboriginal tribes. This novel provides the most complex and nuanced example of the hinterlands among the three analyzed texts; in contrast to the previous two, it uses mimetic descriptions of places, specific place names that can be located on a map, and accurate distances, thus offering a textual representation of actually existing spaces. Similar to the previous novels, however, it also treats these two spaces ideologically, as textual mirrors reflecting not only the external aspects of spaces but also their deeper ideological implications.

The "white" Australia of the south and southeast is represented in the novel by such cities as Bacchus Marsh, Melbourne, or Adelaide and is construed as a land of comfort and safety. Nice, orderly designed cities, spacious houses, mild climate, lush vegetation, greenery, lawns, avenues, monuments – all of them create a friendly urban space welcoming to people and fostering their safe and easy existence. The protagonists and their dwellings are perhaps not rich but comfortable enough – they are equipped with all modern conveniences, services, and technology, be it transportation, medical care, or educational possibilities. The Australians who live there have a chance to lead comfortable, risk-free lives, to enjoy safety and pleasures, and to develop their interests and passions. The protagonists are exclusively white; as one of them remarks, being 26, he has never seen a native person in his life; the first Aboriginals he meets are the ones who help during the race (Carey 2017, Part II, chpt. 6, loc. 2171). The "white" Australia, then, is racially uniform, safe, and comfortable, and in the novel represents the modern idea of life.

The novel contrasts this somewhat idyllic space with the Kimberley region, or the "black" Australia: the hinterlands, which constitute the reverse of the white southeast. In the novel, it is represented as a land of poverty, frugality, and oppression, coupled with harsh climate, heat, and aridity, which make this space hard and difficult to inhabit. Its inhabitants – the Aboriginal tribes – are treated by the white farm owners as creatures between animals and slaves. In the 1950s, First Nations are still not recognized as Australian citizens and are merely allowed to settle on a given site in return for unpaid work for the "owner", who owns both the land and them. In scenes reminiscent of Conradian *Heart of Darkness,* the novel represents the systemic oppression and discrimination of the native inhabitants who have no property rights; are subject to the limitations as to the freedom of movement; have to work in return for scarce food; have no proper education, save for the most basic course of English; and are strictly forbidden to drink alcohol. They have no proper houses, either, living in provisional shelters with no conveniences or services. Most painfully, however, in numerous episodes, they are shown as subject to all kinds of abuse and violence, physical, sexual, or legal. The Kimberley region and the Quambly Farm become the Australian heart of darkness, as similar oppression, exploitation, and horror seem to be taking place there. As Stephanie Convery observes, in this novel, Carey tackles "the living legacies of colonialism in Australia, including genocide, slavery, rape and the Stolen Generation" (Convery).

In this text, then, in contrast to the previous two, the hinterland is not the place of natural idyll or a safe shelter – to the contrary, it is the dark double of the centre. The heterotopia of the hinterlands presented here is conceived not as a desired alternative to the existing *status quo* that completes the latter with better values and features. Rather, it is a dark mirror dragging into the light the notions and actions unreflected, undesired, and officially repressed: both systemic and casual racism, discrimination, and violence. The hinterlands in *A Long Way from Home* reveal and criticize the still colonial policy of the state of Australia towards its native inhabitants; it is a nightmare land where both the present and the past show the horrors of the colonial politics. In contrast to the previous two novels, it is the land of memory, too. While both *True History of the Kelly Gang* and *Bliss* treat the hinterlands as a sort of a *tabula rasa*, a clean slate waiting to be taken and used by various colonizers, with no resistance to them, no life of its own, and no previous history, in *A Long Way from Home* the land has its independent, much older, and more complicated existence. In the plot, its past literally comes out of the ground, exposing human bones and archaeological remnants of previous inhabitants and the atrocities committed there; cave painting and sacred places show the complex life of the people whose existence has been palimpsestically covered by a new layer of "white" settlement. Erased from the centres, the past reappears in the Gothic-like fashion in hinterlands revealing long-buried atrocities. This complex presentation problematizes comfort and ease and interrogates the unexamined smooth vision of the past cherished by the "white" Australia presented in the story. The heterotopia of the hinterlands constructed in this novel, then, comes closer to the Gothic repository of the repressed notions and the practice of exposing and exploring them in fiction rather than to the uncomplicated idyllic model of the desired way of life.

Hinterlands as an alternative and criticism

This necessarily cursory examination of the construction of space and the representation of hinterlands in three of Peter Carey's novels demonstrates, first of all, their highly constructed rather than mimetic character. *True History of the Kelly Gang* and *Bliss* show little interest in the mimetic representation of the hinterlands; rather, they are focused on the latter's role of vehicles for the ideas they embody in the texts. Ideologically conceived hinterlands point to the values and features lacking in the dominating discourses: the lack of justice, equality, and solidarity (as in the *Kelly Gang*); the lack of authenticity; and the harmful consequences of consumerist lifestyle (as in *Bliss*), or the lack of humanity and equality (as in *A Long Way from Home*). Their function, then, seems to be that of textual mirrors set up against prevailing trends and values of represented times: historical in *True History of the Kelly Gang*, not quite past (*A Long Way from Home*) or present (*Bliss*). These mirrors reflect, interrogate, and criticize the centres, or centre-lands, either posing alternatives to be at least considered (as in *Bliss*), or pointing to the lacks, wrongs, and evils of the existing *status quo* (*True History* and *A Long Way from Home*). Hinterlands act as Foucauldian heterotopias: spaces of otherness, either of other possibilities, or other interpretations of the past.

Analyzing three instances of constructing hinterlands as heterotopias, one may also observe their evolution and growing complexity. While their representation is relatively brief and sketchy in the first two novels, in the latest one they gain a much more extensive textual importance. Likewise, their portrayal seems to evolve: from the rather abstract treatment based on the idea to a more expanded, even mimetic presentation; from one, ideological function only to many diverse functions. This change affects, too, their conceptualization: hinterlands change from the places of safety and escapism to the risky and dangerous spaces of the latest novel; from the open, innocuous spaces posing no danger and offering shelter to the space that traps the protagonist, imprisons him, and prevents him from leaving. This shift, then, may be described as a move from the passivity of space which is taken by man and used for his/her own benefits to the space which has its own agency and the power to irrevocably change the life of its inhabitants. The growing complexity and agency demonstrate the emancipation of hinterlands from the barely described abstract sites into the territories equally central, active, and influential as the "main" lands. This shift may suggest that the notion of "hinterlands" is not necessarily always a stabilizing category – to the contrary, it may destabilize the seemingly rigid division between the centre and the periphery pointing out that their conceptualization depends very much on the perspective and politics of those who describe them.

The evolution of spatial relations observable in the three analyzed novels, in turn, might also signal a change of poetics in Carey's fiction. In the most recent text, described by reviewers in contrast to the previous two as his "late style masterpiece" (Preston), Carey seems to turn away from postmodernist representation consisting of the creation of abstract spaces to a more detailed, almost mimetic description of extra-textual places, acknowledging the autonomy and subjectivity of both hinterlands and the people inhabiting them. In so doing, the latest novel may be seen as a move from an instrumental treatment of space (centre-lands and hinterlands alike) to the more profound respect towards the particular spaces, their cultures, peoples, and pasts. Australian hinterlands tend to grow into increasingly more complex and more autonomous territories than the abstract and ideological heterotopias of Carey's earlier fiction. This move might be perceived as a radical change yet simultaneously one may perhaps argue that it is also to some extent a characteristic feature of Carey's poetics, which tends to hover between postmodernism and more traditional concepts of storytelling. In his analyses of Carey's writing, Christer Larsson observes that although "Carey's novels are usually treated as works of postmodern fiction ... this [opinion] is obviously appropriate, but it can also be limiting", adding that apart from using postmodernist techniques "he is also skilled in more traditional methods of story-telling, and this blend of innovation and tradition makes his novels extremely complex and intriguing" (Larsson 176). Thus, the different conceptualizations of space, those close to postmodernist poetics in earlier novels, and those approaching more traditional realistic fiction in the later one should not perhaps come as a surprise but rather be treated as a conscious choice of a different, more ethically oriented attitude dictating a different selection of writing techniques. The poetics and politics of representation of hinterlands may be then interpreted as one of the instances of Carey's characteristic combination of various modes of writing and the proof of the artistic and ethical complexity of his novels.

Works Cited

Brenner, Neil, and Nikos Katsikis. "Operational Landscapes: Hinterlands of Capitalocene." *Architectural Design*, vol. 90, no. 1, 2020, pp. 22–31.

Bristow, Sarah. "The Most Memorable Things to Do in the Gold Coast Hinterland. Queensland Guide." 2020 www.queensland.com/au/en/places-to-see/destinations/gold-coast/how-to-do-the-gold-coast-hinterland. Accessed 2 March 2022.

Carey, Peter. *A Long Way from Home*. Penguin Random House Australia, 2017. E-book.

Carey, Peter. *Bliss*. 1981. Vintage, 1996.

Carey, Peter. *True History of the Kelly Gang*. 2000. Vintage, 2002.

Convery, Stephanie. "'You Wake Up in the Morning and You Are the Beneficiary of a Genocide.' Interview with Peter Carey." *The Guardian*, 2017 18 November. www.theguardian.com/books/2017/nov/18/peter-carey-you-wake-up-in-the-morning-and-you-are-the-beneficiary-of-a-genocide. Accessed 15 May 2020.

Cronon, William. *Nature's Metropolis: Chicago and the Great West*. Norton, 1992.

Fletcher, Don. "Utopia in Peter Carey's *Bliss*." *Social Alternatives*, vol. 26, no. 1, 2007, pp. 39–42.

Foucault, Michel. "Of Other Spaces." Translated by Jay Miskowiec. *Diacritics*, vol. 16, no. 1, 1986, pp. 22–27.

Frye, Northrop. 1957. *Anatomy of Criticism*. Princeton UP, 2000.

Krakauer, Jon. *Into the Wild*. Pan Books, 1996.

Larsson, Christer. "'Years Later': Temporality and Closure in Peter Carey's Novels." *Australian Literary Studies*, vol. 19, no. 2, 1999, pp. 176–85.

Lee, Robert, and Paul McNamara, eds. *Port Cities and Their Hinterlands: Migration, Trade and Cultural Exchange from the Early Seventeenth Century to 1939*. Routledge, 2022.

Preston, Alex. "*A Long Way from Home* Review." *The Guardian*, 2018 15 January. www.theguardian.com/books/2018/jan/15/a-long-way-from-home-peter-carey-review. Accessed 27 November 2021.

Simmons, Dorothy. "Our Ned: The Makeup of Myth." *Antipodes*, vol. 28, no. 2, 2014, pp. 416–25.

Siwoń, Krzysztof. "W Australii, czyli w piekle. *Święty spokój* Petera Careya i Raya Lawrence'a." *Od Banjo Patersona do Meliny Marchetty. Adaptacje literatury australijskiej*. Eds. Alicja Helman, and Martyna Olszowska. Fundacja Terytoria Książki, 2016, pp. 125–37.

7 The ethical call from the hinterlands

Conceptualizing waste in J. G. Ballard's *High-Rise* and *Concrete Island*

Marcin Tereszewski

Defining hinterlands presents a set of problems that can be partially mitigated by steering the conversation away from questions about "what are hinterlands?" towards questions of "what do hinterlands do?". It would seem that the intrinsic ambiguity of the concept is precisely the source of its power to reframe not only how we think about urban processes but how we relate to what has been discarded; that is, to waste, to garbage, as well as to hinterlands, which take the form of wastelands. The intersection of the nascent field of waste theory and the concept of hinterlands opens a fruitful avenue to consider the possible ethical implications contained in such ambiguous spaces. By focusing on the discarded spaces found in J. G. Ballard's *High-Rise* (1975) and *Concrete Island* (1974), this chapter argues that waste can be read as more than a static prop, but as an "actant", a kind of vibrant presence that asserts itself in relation to the protagonists. Developing the significance of waste in relation to the hinterland status of Ballardian dystopian spaces allows us to draw a parallel between the two: just as there is nothing like a clear demarcation separating civilization from its antipodes, waste from modernity, there also exists a clear ethical dimension in how both waste and hinterlands act upon the subject.

One approach to defining hinterlands is firmly rooted in geographical and cultural placement around notions of centre and periphery. Phil Neel takes this route by locating them away from the "booming cores of the supposedly 'post-industrial' economy" (17). These hinterlands, as he states, are "often a heavily industrial space – a space for factory farms, for massive logistics complexes, for power generation, and for the extraction of resources from forests, deserts, and seas" (17). In other words, these are spaces far removed from cultural, residential and commercial centres. Another important distinction made by Neel is between "far" hinterlands and "near" hinterlands. Far hinterlands include traditionally rural areas and "large urban zones of collapse", such as abandoned industrial cities.

DOI: 10.4324/9781032617732-10

"Near" hinterlands are, as the name suggests, closer to the urban core and include suburbs, "towering apartment centres that ring the city" (18). Neil Brenner and Christian Schmid, in turn, offer a slightly different approach. They call attention to the twenty-first century as an age when the urbanizing process has become all-encompassing, "a process that has seriously called into question the inherited cartographies that have long underpinned urban theory and research" (161). As a result of this process, various transformations have taken place, among which we find "the disintegration of the 'hinterland'" (161). Though the concept is never fully fleshed out, we see that it is no longer conceptualized in strictly geographical terms. It is now situated within a framework of planetary urbanization, which posits that spaces traditionally designated as non-urban territories – that is, beyond the inter-city or suburban peripheries – have become integral to the functioning of a global urban mosaic. What is more, as Christian Schmid argues, the process of urbanization has also undergone changes: no longer is it concentric, i.e., developing from a clear urban centre, but "undirected", as a result of which "overarching, polycentric urban regions are taking shape. Extremely heterogenous in structure, they include old city centres as well as once-peripheral areas" (67). This understanding of hinterlands signals a clear departure from what is considered in critical urban theory as an untenable tradition of viewing cities as self-contained entities, "internally integrated but externally differentiated from surrounding hinterlands" (Wachsmuth 362). With the challenge to the metro-centrism of urban studies, the focus has shifted to questions of how such places function outside the traditional categories defining urban.

Ballard's hinterlands occupy a position at the interception of these two approaches. On the one hand, we could classify them as "near" hinterlands, seeing that they are never far removed from the urban centre; sometimes – as we will see in *Concrete Island* – they are situated in the forgotten areas of urban space or, as in *High-Rise*, they are interwoven into the fabric of the urban. As such, the urban/hinterland (or centre/margin) distinction in Ballard's fiction also appears to be fluid. On the other hand, what is also of interest in our reading of Ballard is the destabilizing effect of the depicted hinterlands exemplified by waste, refuse, and whatever has been rejected from cultural and capital circulation. Waste in its uselessness exists outside the capitalist category of use-value, sharing a similar ambiguous ontological status as hinterlands, whose use-value is also called into question.

The significance of waste in culture, anthropology, and in literature has relatively recently become the subject of inquiry. According to Susan Signe Morrison, waste studies addresses the question of "the central role humans play in generating, ignoring, coping with, and analyzing waste in its various manifestations" (7). There is a visible anti-anthropocentric and anti-capitalist vein running through much of the core literature regarding discard studies, giving rise to two main dominant points of consideration: that waste is both a by-product of overproduction, which is inherent in capitalism, and that waste is also conceptualized in capitalist terms, i.e., as stripped of the use-value that had once defined it. Thus, without being anything in particular, waste becomes everything in general – destabilized and dismantled matter.

Waste studies provides a helpful context in which to think about hinterlands as places that, having been refused and discarded themselves, share a similarly ambiguous ontological status. In this respect, the question of defining waste is pivotal, however impossible to answer equivocally. For John Scanlan, "Garbage indicates the removal of qualities (characteristics, or distinguishing features) and signals the return of everything to some universal condition" (14). Garbage, much like the hinterlands, exists in the unseen and forgotten zones, pushed from view, undistinguishable in its form. When something becomes refuse, it is stripped of its use-value and by extension of its meaning. The hinterlands can thus be regarded as a repository of everything that has been rejected by the political body, such as excrements and waste – the former common to animals, the latter specific only to humans. These unique articulations of hinterlands have made themselves manifest not just at any time in human history but during the Capitalocene, the time of capitalist domination, when our relationship with objects, and by extension to places, has been defined according to their use-value. This is a development of Myra J. Hird's claim, also quoted in Morrison's study, that "Waste has become the signifier of the Anthropocene, inaugurating the only epoch that centralizes humans" (123). Not only is waste a by-product of capitalist ideology, but the way in which it is conceptualized is inseparable from the underlying capitalist and anthropocentric goals of expansion, mastery, and perfectibility.

In its aim to redefine waste in anthropological and philosophical terms, waste studies draws on and overlaps with new materialism. The broader theoretical context of waste studies includes such fields as object-oriented ontology (OOO), stuff theory, posthumanism, actor-network theory, and thing theory, to name just a few. What all these theoretical approaches share is a re-evaluation of our relationship with the world of inanimate objects. Thing theory is particularly relevant to our discussion on waste, as it proposes treating matter not as if it were the subject of human activity, but as having "agentic capacities" in its own right. Jane Bennett asks: "How, for example, would patterns of consumption change if we face not litter, rubbish, trash, or 'the recycling,' but an accumulating pile of lively and potentially dangerous matter?" (vii). Matter thus regarded is not passive and inert, but vital or "vibrant" to use Bennett's term. This perspective opens an ethical dimension by challenging the anthropocentric relation with our environment. The governing idea is that we come to know an object in a new way when it is no longer of use to us. Bill Brown, one of the main theorists of thing theory, argues that a shift of an object's relationship with us shifts – such as from usefulness to obsolescence – permits the confrontation with what he – following Heidegger in "The Thing" – calls "the thingness" of the object, the underlying material presence that remains beyond our control (it is unnameable, interminable, of no use-value). This confrontation ultimately suspends our default (anthropocentric) relation to the world predicated on mastery and control, revealing in effect the innate "thingness" of objects. Bill Brown emphasizes the importance of this relationship in defining objects in terms of their agency or lack thereof:

> We begin to confront the thingness of objects when they stop working for us: when the drill breaks, when the car stalls, when the windows get filthy, when their flow within the circuits of production and distribution, consumption and exhibition, has been arrested, however momentarily. The story of objects asserting themselves as things, then, is the story of a changed relation to the human subject and thus the story of how the thing really names less an object than a particular subject-object relation. (Brown 2001, 4)

A provocative illustration of this point is offered by Gay Hawkins in *Ethics of Waste*, where he recalls a scene from *American Beauty*, in which we see a recording of a plastic bag wafted by the wind. What would in most circumstances be an irrelevant piece of trash here takes on a poetic dimension, the plastic bag lyrically floating as if dancing on air (Hawkins 2006, 21). This potentially ambiguous dimension of waste did not go unnoticed by the Surrealists (e.g., Marcel Duchamp, Antonin Artaud) and later by postmodernist artists (e.g., Damien Hirst), who were quick to incorporate waste into their installations and artwork as a means of questioning the criteria by which we designate something as waste.

The role played by waste in surrealist art bears a resemblance to its function in Ballard's worlds, which are littered with things and places that have outgrown their usefulness. The list of Ballardian settings has become all too familiar to the point of becoming a cliché: the drained swimming pools, the abandoned shopping centres and hotels, empty nightclubs, deserted airfields, and motorways. It could be argued that these bleak wastelands and leftover spaces are precisely what render a setting Ballardian. While evoking dystopian, post-apocalyptic themes, they, perhaps more interestingly, invite an examination of our relationship with our surroundings, particularly with the objects and places in our environment. Ballard's fiction does not directly grapple with the ecological and social consequences of urbanization and capitalism in a manner appropriate to a science fiction novelist. As a New Wave science fiction writer, he focuses on the psychological aspects of urbanization by drawing on a rich surrealist and modernist tradition, which allows him to present the psychopathological consequences of postmodern and global urbanization.

Though the dystopian settings encountered in Ballard's fiction can be viewed in geographical terms (deserts, industrial wastelands, ruins, etc.), their status as hinterlands is amplified by the ubiquitous presence of waste, whose ontological status – as discussed above – can be seen as correlating to that of the hinterlands. In much the same way as objects become waste once they lose their use-value, these Ballardian hinterlands also reveal their "thingness" as a result of having become obsolete.

Even a cursory survey of the extremely broad range of settings in Ballard's work reveals that his stories are rarely ever set in an urban or nonurban environment in the strictest sense. In Iain Sinclair's study of Ballard's *Crash*, Ballard is quoted saying the following:

> I regard the city as a semi-extinct form. London is basically a nineteenth-century city. And the habits of mind appropriate to the nineteenth century, which survive into the novels set in the London of the twentieth century, aren't really appropriate to understanding what is really going on in life today. I think the suburbs are more interesting than people will let on. In the suburbs you find uncentered lives .... So that people have more freedom to explore their own obsessions. (Ballard qtd. in Sinclair 1999, 84)

Ballard associated the urban with order and centrality; therefore, departure from that urban centrality opens the possibility of randomness and freedom. With the exception of a few short stories (e.g., "Billannium"), the setting for the vast majority of his work is rarely ever a city, but rather the outskirts, the fringes, the suburban enclaves, travel resorts, motorways, high rises, junkyards, that is, interstitial zones which undercut the urban/nonurban dichotomy, places that Marc Augé refers to as non-spaces. This is precisely the case with the so-called urban disaster trilogy, which portrays only the fringes of urban space: the M4 motorway in the case of *Crash*, a modern high-rise outside London in the case of *High-Rise*, and a forgotten patch of land between motorway embankments in *Concrete Island*. All of these spaces share a common theme. Having lost their moorings, they are examples of non-places created by supermodernity. Augé defines these non-places as transitory zones, where humans pass anonymously with no experience of dwelling and rootedness. These places are characterized by concrete and artificial surfaces; they are the supermodern manifestation of hinterlands.

The hinterland in Ballard's *Concrete Island* is the Crusoe-like abandoned island, situated in "the waste ground between three converging motorway routes" (Ballard 2011, 11). It is there that the protagonist, Robert Maitland, a middle-aged architect, finds himself stranded after crashing his car through the barriers of the M4 motorway. A representative of the well-to-do middle class, an architect at a prospering firm, Maitland wakes up in his crashed Jaguar in a totally new environment, himself now useless and abandoned, much like the island itself. Maitland's first instincts are to somehow find an escape from this wasteland and return to the civilization above, but his injuries and steep embankments prevent any progress on that front. As the days pass, he begins to explore his surroundings, meets its inhabitants – a tramp by the name of Proctor and Jane Semour, a homeless woman, who takes him in, nurses his wounds but also impedes his escape. Eventually, Maitland begins to settle into his new environment, forgetting about his wife and professional responsibilities. Though Maitland's eventually aborted attempts to escape the island move the plot along, it is the island itself that becomes a character in its own right.

Two aspects of this island reinforce its hinterland status. Firstly, although located "at the centre of this alienating city", it remains virtually invisible to the cars passing above. Invisibility seems to be an inherent trait of hinterlands in general. Regarded as places outside the established value system, they attract no attention. Secondly, the ubiquitous presence of refuse, which – much like the hinterland island itself – has no inherent use-value and no explicit function, serves to further reinforce the hinterland as belonging to an order beyond capitalist values. The descriptions of the island often emphasize the abundance of waste:

No grass grew under the overpass. The damp earth with waste oil leaking from the piles of refuse and broken metal drums on the fare side of the fence. The hundred-yard-long wire wall held back mounds of truck tyres and empty cans, broken office furniture, sacks of hardened cement. Builder's forms, bales of rusty wire and scrapped engine parts were heaped so high that Maitland doubted whether he would be able to penetrate this jungle of refuse even if he could cut through the fence. (Ballard 2011, 39)

The island can be seen as the dumping ground for all the waste generated by consumerism and urbanized civilization. It is the necessary, albeit invisible, consequence of capitalist production, encouraging some critics, for instance, Sebastian Groes, to apply Ren Koolhaas's idea of Junkspace to this particular environment (Groes 129). In his 2002 article "Junkspace", Koolhaas describes this uniquely modern space in the following way:

> If space-junk is the human debris that litters the universe, junk-space is the residue mankind leaves on the planet. The built... product of modernization is not modern architecture but Junkspace. Junkspace is what remains after modernization has run its course, or, more precisely, what coagulates while modernization is in process, its fallout. Modernization has a rational program: to share the blessings of science, universally. Junkspace is its apotheosis, or meltdown... Although individual parts are the outcome of brilliant inventions, lucidly planned by human intelligence, boosted by infinite computation, their sums spell the end of Enlightenment, its resurrection as farce, a low-grade purgatory. (175)

Scanlan (20) draws attention to the Dantean reference reinforcing the idea that Junkspace, seeing it as an in-between space (between Paradise and the Inferno), prone to the ontological ambiguities liminality entails. What is important in this comparison is the reason for their existence; these junkspaces are the by-products of capitalist production, they are the necessary "fallout".

As Maitland begins to settle on the island, it becomes clear that it exerts an almost mesmerizing effect on him and, as a consequence, his objective shifts from escape to domination. He begins to discern similarities between himself and the island to the point of actually identifying with it.

> Identifying the island with himself, he gazed at the cars in the breaker's yard, at the wire-mesh fence, and the concrete caisson behind him. These places of pain and ordeal were now confused with pieces of his body. He gestured towards them, trying to make a circuit of the island so that he could leave these sections of himself where they belonged. He would leave his right leg at the point of his crash, his bruised hands impaled upon the steel fence. He would place his chest where he had sat against the concrete wall. At each point a small ritual would signify the transfer of obligation from himself to the island. (Ballard 2011, 70)

His elegant clothes and flashy car, remnants of the conspicuous con-sumption he had once engaged in, serve no purpose on the island and have the same value as the detritus littered all around him. A transformational moment takes place here, one that is ethical (and ecological) in nature, as the protagonist is invited by these circumstances to divest himself of a subjectivity rooted in a capitalist-based subject/object duality and to see himself as fundamentally on equal footing with his surroundings. What this hinterland wasteland made possible was a kind a re-evaluation of the protagonist's relation with the surrounding world, one which, if analyzed psycho-analytically, led to what Andrzej Gasiorek describes as a "recovery of the self" (114). On numerous occasions, Ballard emphasizes the active role Maitland's surrounding have, especially the natural environment with wet leaves that "wound across his skin, as if reluctant to release him" (Ballard 2011, 68). Further, "Maitland followed the swirling motions, reading in these patterns the reassuring voice of this immense green creature eager to protect and guide him" (Ballard 2011, 68). The grass is made animate with almost an animalistic quality: "The grass lashed at his feet, as if angry that Maitland still wished to leave its green embrace. Laughing at the grass, Maitland patted it reassuringly with his free hand as he hobbled along, stroking the seething stems that caressed his waist" (Ballard 2011, 68).

On one of his exploratory journeys of the island, Maitland comes across a unique articulation of waste, namely, ruins. Scattered among all the other objects of waste were ruins of a former WWII air-raid shelter, a derelict pay-box of a former cinema. "Parts of the island dated from well before World War II. The eastern end, below the overpass, was its oldest section, with the churchyard and the ground-courses of Edwardian ter-raced houses" (Ballard 2011, 69). On the one hand, these remnants of the past appear to be indistinguishable from the rest of the waste on island; however, their very presence is also a testament to the past retaining its hold, even though civilization has outgrown them. Waste as ruins presents a wholly unique set of dilemmas. Cecilia Enjuto Rangel explains that "ruins seem to permeate the modern landscape as a lingering trace of what cannot be recycled" (23). They are what resist full integration into con-temporary ideology and thus are not only a reminder of a past, but on a more ontological level, they defy assimilation. The main characteristic of ruins is that they are neither here nor there, neither in the past nor in the present – suspended somewhere between two worlds. This characteristic serves Ballard well, as, by association with these ruins, he is able to stage the dual nature of the protagonist. Displaced from his route activities and socially constructed identity as an architect, husband, and father, Maitland's relation with his new hinterland environment forces upon him a re-evaluation of his identity.

Whereas in *Concrete Island*, the protagonist is violently flung into an urban wasteland, the protagonists in *High-Rise* find themselves in a place which by design is meant to be the polar opposite of a wasteland – a modern high-rise, the epitome of civilization, comfort, and order, a kind of building the Swiss architect Le Corbusier, whose aesthetics were to have a great influence on the tower blocks built in London during the 1970s upon which the eponymous high-rise is modelled, famously called "a machine for living in". An embodiment of civilization and order, this machine for living gradually begins to malfunction, beginning with the garbage chutes, power outages, and ending with the total disrepair of the whole building. These seemingly insignificant malfunctions instigate a process of social disintegration among the tenants, who eventually succumb to their most tribal and atavistic impulses. In this space of hygiene and modern living, waste, almost like the repressed other pushing its way through to the conscious self, plays a crucial role in the gradual disintegration of the high-rise's meticulously constructed environment as well as the social structure of those inhabiting it.

Amidst this social breakdown, it is waste that reinforces this decline into chaos and "renders palpable the devolution into civil unrest" (Dini 125). Waste and all the issues surrounding it incited the first disagreements among the tenants of the high-rise: faulty and blocked garbage chutes, animal waste in the hallways, and complaints from the building manager about the type of garbage that was being disposed. As an example, he recounts, "the fifty-year-old owner of the hairdressing salon *was* endlessly redecorating her apartment on the 33rd floor, and *did* stuff old rugs and even intact pieces of small furniture into the chute" (Ballard 2012, 50). The building manager, who is initially overwhelmed with maintenance work, also notices the increased amount of strange garbage originating from all the apartments: "Some of the people generate the most unusual garbage – certainly the kind of thing we didn't expect to find here" (50). The steady accumulation of garbage, either due to the building's faulty garbage disposal system or the carelessness of the tenants, increases the hostility among the tenants – from petty squabbles this hostility eventually escalates to murder and rape.

The role and presence of waste also changes with the devolving conditions in the high-rise. In the further stages of social collapse, the tenants are depicted as coexisting with waste:

> Along corridors strewn with uncollected garbage, past blocked disposal chutes and vandalised elevators, moved men in well-tailored dinner jackets. Elegant women lifted long skirts to step over the debris of broken bottles. ... The scents of expensive aftershave lotions mingled with the aroma of kitchen wastes ... marking the extent to which these civilised and self-possessed professional men and women were moving away from any notion of rational behaviour. (Ballard 2012, 113)

No longer is waste an instigator of feuds and violence, as it simply becomes part of the accepted environment and is in a way reintegrated into the social fabric. In effect, the established norms by which we classify objects as useful and not useful are suspended, and thus the category of waste no longer holds any meaning.

As life in the high-rise devolves into a series of tribal battles for territory, punctuated with violence, rape, and cannibalism, objects which once had meaning and purpose take on a whole different reality. At one point, after prolonged exposure to this new environment, Dr. Robert Laing struggles to remember the original function of his "derelict washing-machine and refrigerator, now only used as garbage bins" (Ballard 2012, 176) as "everything [is] either derelict or, more ambiguously, recombined in unexpected but more meaningful ways" (Ballard 2012, 176). Objects that once held purpose and significance have now "taken on a new significance, a role that he ha[s] yet to understand" (Ballard 2012, 176) in much the same way Maitland's possession took on new significance in *Concrete Island*. As objects are stripped of their use-value, their "thingness" begins to emerge, challenging the preconceptions with which we define our place in relation to them. In his 1950 lecture "Das Ding" ("The Thing"), Heidegger states that "the thingly character of the thing does not consist in its being a represented object, nor can it be defined in any way in terms of the objectness, the over-againstness, of the object" (165). Things become objects because of their use-value in society; that is, the purpose that they are given, but that use-value has nothing to do with its inherent thingness, which is why it is necessary to make a clear distinction between an object and a thing.

Interestingly, the tenants are free to leave the anarchy of their high-rise at any time – either to go to work or to assume their regular everyday chores – but they are always drawn back to the building. Their lives are divided into two completely different experiences of reality: the disrupted reality within the high-rise and the ordered reality outside it.

> [T]his brief period away from the apartment building was almost dreamlike in its unreality. … Even the debris scattered at the foot of the building, the empty bottles and garbage-stained cars with their broken windscreens, in a strange way merely reinforced his conviction that the only real events in his life were those taking place within the high-rise. (Ballard 2012, 74)

Of these two experiences of reality, that of the high-rise assumes the category of "real" and everything else is regarded as "unreal", a conviction that is curiously reinforced by waste. The effect of dirt and waste is further explained by the following description of Laing's overall decline:

He picked at the thick rims of dirt under his nails. This decline, both of himself and his surroundings, was almost to be welcomed. In a way he was forcing himself down these steepening gradients, like someone descending into a forbidden valley. The dirt on his hands, his stale clothes and declining hygiene, his fading interest in food, and drink, all helped to expose a more *real* vision of himself. (Ballard 2012, 122, emphasis mine)

Defined as objects existing outside the capitalist category of use-value, waste, and dirt are presented as being capable of momentarily suspending the distinction between reality and unreality. Waste exerts its agency by calling attention to its existence as things in the Heideggerian sense, thereby exposing the constructedness of the surrounding world and implicitly reaffirming the idea of authenticity as a rejection of capitalist fiction, in this case, represented by the ordered reality outside the walls of the high-rise.

This leads us to the location of the high-rise. Following Neil Brenner's observation about the "disintegration of the 'hinterland'" mentioned earlier in this chapter, it is worth noting that the high-rise occupies a once hinterland area which has since been co-opted by residential development. Along with other high-rises nearby, "they were set in a mile-square of abandoned dockland and warehousing along the north bank of the river" (Ballard 2012, 15). The eponymous high-rise is not situated in the centre of the city, but on its outskirts, in otherwise abandoned and purposeless wastelands. This is in line with Brenner and Schmid's thesis that "around the world, the erstwhile 'hinterlands' of major cities, metropolitan regions and urban-industrial corridors are being reconfigured as they are func-tionalized ... to facilitate the continued expansion of industrial industri-alization and its associated planetary urban networks" (162). There is an underlying suggestion in this localization. It is only when the constructed reality created by the architectural assumptions of the high-rise begins to disintegrate that the protagonist, otherwise cool and isolated, begins to realize the "unreality" of life outside the destruction and affirms his connection with his environment – but on more equal terms. The high-rise could be seen as an encroachment on the hinterlands, an encroachment that is spectacularly rejected.

In conclusion, a recurrent theme in Ballard's work is the hypnotic effect certain places (in this case hinterlands) have on the protagonists, who choose to forfeit their established lives in favour of remaining in such places. We see this in the case of the tenants in *High-Rise* and we see this again with Maitland in *Concrete Island*. Both of these novels enact a departure from the rules and structures regulated by capitalist principles towards what is presented as a more authentic experience of reality made palpable by the confrontation with the thingness latently residing in surrounding objects. This is an ethical confrontation, as it opens the possibility of existing outside an anthropocentric relation to the objective world. In much of Ballard's work, one can find protagonists undergoing a process of reintegration into the biosphere, into an environment stripped of any vestiges of civilization, where the societal rules no longer hold sway. In order to stage this reintegration, Ballard had to avail himself of a particular relationship between the protagonist and his surroundings for his heterotopic hinterlands to come into being. Neither the term *heterotopic* nor *hinterland* points to a precise description of this place, which is why Ballard identifies it with discarded objects and useless places. The presence of waste in its myriad variations allows Ballard's protagonists to live outside the established social and capitalist order while attaining a certain kind of freedom which comes from a revised relationship to the surrounding world of objects. Waste as a defining feature of these hinterlands heralds a rupture in the established capitalist-centred narrative, allowing for an opening of an ethical relation with the environment based on mutuality, instead of mastery, with the human no longer occupying the centre but instead constituting an integral part of its biosphere. Acknowledging waste can, therefore, go some way towards denaturalizing the capitalist claim to universality. In other words, the ethicality of waste literature, in asking us to acknowledge what has been denied, redefines our relation to things and places that have been refused by established cultural norms. Waste stands in for the other that remains unmasterable and thus beyond the reach of signification based on use-value.

Works Cited

Augé, Marc. *Non-Places: Introduction to an Anthropology of Supermodernity.* Translated by Jon Howe. London: Verso, 1995.

Ballard, J. G. *Concrete Island.* London: Fourth Estate, 2011.

Ballard, J. G. *High-Rise.* New York: Liveright Pub, 2012

Bennett, Jane. *Vibrant Matter: Toward a Political Ecology of Things.* Durham, NC: Duke University Press, 2010.

Brenner, Neil and Christian Schmid. "Planetary Urbanization." In *Implosions/ Explosions: Towards a Study of Planetary Urbanization.* Ed. Neil Brenner. jovis Verlag, GmbH, 2014, pp. 160–163.

Brown, Bill. "Thing Theory". *Critical Inquiry*, vol. 28, no. 1, 2001, pp. 1–22.

Dini, Rachele. *Consumerism, Waste, and Re-Use in Twentieth-Century Fiction: Legacies of the Avant-Garde.* London: Palgrave Macmillan, 2016.

Enjuto Rangel, Cecilia. *Cities in Ruins: The Politics of Modern Poetics.* West Lafayette: Purdue University Press, 2010.

Gasiorek, Andrzej. *J.G. Ballard. Contemporary British Novelists*. Manchester: Manchester University Press, 2004.

Groes, Sebastian. "The Texture of Modernity in J.G. Ballard's *Crash*, *Concrete Island* and *High Rise*". *J. G. Ballard: Visions and Revisions*. Eds. Jeanette Baxter and Rowland Wymer. London: Palgrave Macmillan, 2011, pp. 123–141.

Hawkins, Gay. *The Ethics of Waste: How We Relate to Rubbish*. Maryland: Rowman & Littlefield Publishers. 2006.

Heidegger, Martin. "The Thing." *Poetry, Language, Thought*. Translated by Albert Hofstadter. Harper Perennial Modern Classics, 2001, pp. 161–184.

Koolhaas, Rem. "Junkspace." *Obsolescence*, vol. 100, 2002, pp. 175–190.

Morrison, Susan Signe. *The Literature of Waste: Material Ecopoetics and Ethical Matter*. London: Palgrave Macmillan. 2015.

Myra, J. Hird. "Waste Flows." http://discardstudies.com/discard-studies-compendium/. Accessed: 20 Sept. 2022.

Neel, Phil. *Hinterland: America's New Landscape of Class and Conflict*. London: Reaktion Books, 2018.

Scanlan, John. *On Garbage*. London: Reaktion Books, 2005.

Schmid, Christian. "Patterns of Pathways of Global Urbanization: Towards Comparative Analysis." *Implosions/Explosions: Towards a Study of Planetary Urbanization*. Ed. Neil Brenner. jovis Verlag, GmbH, 2014, pp. 203–217.

Sinclair, Iain. *Crash: David Cronenberg's Post-mortem on J.G. Ballard 'Trajectory of Fate'* London: British Film Institute, 1999.

Wachsmuth, David. "City as Ideology." *Implosions/Explosions: Towards a Study of Planetary Urbanization*. Ed.Neil Brenner. jovis Verlag, GmbH, 2014, pp. 352–371.

8 Post-anthropocentric hinterlands
Susan Straight's California

Katarzyna Nowak-McNeice

The times in which we are living are variously called the Anthropocene, the Capitalocene, the Plantationocene, the Chthulucene, and the very multiplicity of the terms suggests a certain anxiousness and slipperiness related to the era. The most widely embraced moniker, the Anthropocene, implies the primacy of the human and his hubris as the decisive factors in the catastrophe; the Capitalocene and the Plantationocene both point to the belief in an unencumbered growth and unstoppable expansion, resulting in the accumulation of capital in the hands of a very few and an ever-growing gap between them and the rest of the world, whereas the Chthulucene directs our attention to the multiplicity of forces shaping our planet, neither prioritizing nor excluding humans. While these different names give slightly different weight to the underlying conditions, they all point to one common factor, which is humanity's destructive potential that is threatening to annihilate the living planet. All terms also suggest that going beyond anthropocentrism is a necessary first step, however difficult (or close to impossible) it might be. Commenting on these problems, Rosi Braidotti in *The Posthuman* reminds us that "Finding an adequate language for post-anthropocentrism means that the resources of the imagination, as well as the tools of critical intelligence, need to be enlisted for this task" (82). Mindful of this crucial insight regarding the need to invent new vocabulary to envision post-anthropocentric agency, in the present text I propose that preliminary steps towards such agency are portrayed in Susan Straight's work. In this chapter, I focus on ambiguously dispersed spaces where such agency is performed, represented in Susan Straight's trilogy that encompasses *Between Heaven and Here* (2012), *Take One Candle Light a Room* (2010), and *A Million Nightingales* (2006). These spaces are neither rural nor urban; neither at the centres of capitalist production, nor removed from them. Dispersion not only characterizes space but crucially facilitates the dissolution of clearly definable distinctions between human and nonhuman characters, becoming the arena for post-anthropocentric characterizations.

DOI: 10.4324/9781032617732-11

Straight's novels undertake the issue of responsibility for the land, questioning the nature of possession, and in doing so, they portray animal figures that take on the meaning not just of marginal figures or metaphors, but rather, become a reminder of the entanglement and continuity between human and nonhuman animals, which, in turn, portrays an entanglement between spaces that can be categorized as hinterlands, following Phil A. Neel's definition. Neel stresses that a hinterland

> is not an exclusively "rural" space, and it is by no means truly secondary to global production. Instead, it often acts as a disavowed, distributed core, distinct from the array of services and FIRE [i.e. finance, insurance, and real estate] industries of the central city but more integral to the "immediate process of production", in which labor meets capital and value is produced. (18)

In Neel's assessment, hinterlands are ambiguous spaces: not entirely central and not quite marginal either. The similarly characterized Californian hinterlands of Straight's fiction are presented against the backdrop of the Capitalocene, and their representation suggests a recognition of the need to go beyond the human, which Straight's prose proposes, becoming an argument in the current discussion of the problems with the definition of the era we are witnessing.

The destruction of habitats and the loss of biomass on the overheating planet, termed the *Sixth Great Extinction* or the *Holocene Extinction* that we are witnessing at the moment, all contribute to the changing understanding of the territories of human expansion, comprising cities and their hinterlands, understood as complex, entangled, inseparable entities, along the lines of Jennifer Robinson's postulate, which is that "it is the wider city-region, rather than just the 'city', that offers the territorial context for much contemporary economic activity", effectively disrupting "any easy delimitation of the spatial extent of cities" (120). Susan Straight's prose depicts these intertwined spaces and intricate connections between them and the communities living there; it becomes a testimony to the impossibility of distinguishing between entities traditionally differentiated as "people" and "places"; as well as "people" and "animals", and a subversive suggestion of a need to reconfigure these categories in the Capitalocene.

A California writer superbly attuned to the local landscapes and fine-grain representations of local fauna and flora, Straight focuses on characters who do not always choose California as their home, but are flung there as a result of geopolitical processes captured by the term *Plantationocene*. In this essay, I focus on two parts of Straight's Rio Seco trilogy,

Take One Candle Light a Room (2010) and *Between Heaven and Here* (2012), whose central characters are descendants of slaves, violently incorporated into the economic structures of the American South, who migrate to California in order to escape the oppressive system of the plantation economy. While the first part of the trilogy, *A Million Nightingales* (2006), is set in Louisiana (and hence remains beyond the scope of this essay), the other two are set in California, a locale important to the writer and central to her fiction. In these two works, Straight paints a portrait of a fictitious community (based on Riverside, where she lives) whose multi-vocal story of survival uses the elements of animality and physicality to challenge the anthropocentric distinction between the human and the nonhuman, and their interactions within their environments, challenging the understanding of urban areas as separate from hinterlands, and the processes shaping them as different either in scale or in character.

Take One Candle Light a Room, the second part of the Rio Seco trilogy is set in California, and it traces the lives of the descendants of the characters portrayed in *A Million Nightingales*. The protagonist, a Black woman who calls herself FX, Fantine Antoine, whose light skin grants her an unreadability she uses to her advantage, lives in Los Angeles and works as a successful travel writer. The choice of the protagonist allows Straight to make references to far-flung corners of the world, suggesting an understanding of the city aligned with Robinson's, which undermines the establishment of any clear-cut borders of cities. Robinson argues that "even cities whose boundaries were defined by physical walls were maintained through flows and connections with hinterlands, with other cities, with distant parts of the world" (120). Robinson offers an interpretation of the city according to which its borders are fluid – and, historically, have always been – in addition, suggesting that they extend to far regions of the globe.

Such a fluid view of the city is close to the one presented in *Take One Candle*. It becomes apparent when, in a globalizing gesture, Fantine makes connections which traverse continents and stretch across time: "The tall grass from India that had travelled here on a ship and then been turned into white crystals. ... Sparkling. A cube, in a glass saucer, on a marble table in Paris" (221). A specific product: sugar made from cane, affords her an opportunity to think about the connections across the globe. Sugar travels, like people do, and it carries within it the burden of history. Even though the labour that enables the white crystals to appear on a café table in France is not referenced directly, it is suggested through a series of imperatives: "Cut it down, burn off the leaves, grind out the juice, boil it for hours, to get a white crystal" (221). The connection between the product and the agent whose physical labour brings it into existence is thus made explicit; similar to the connection between the city where the product ends up and the stretches of the globe where it is manufactured – the hinterlands to the centres of world commerce and culture, such as Paris, Los Angeles, or London.

The connection between the product and the producer is an organic link, to be understood as an effect of emotional investment in the product that becomes unified with the producer in the process of creation. When a teenage protagonist complains about working in the family field, saying grumpily, "This isn't a plantation," her father responds characteristically, "'Oui,' he said, his face never changing. 'I grow you'" (135). She is re-minded of this pronouncement, "I grow you" (172), when faced with choices pivoting on loyalty to her community; choices which involve defining her family in a way that would encompass not just blood rela-tives, but those whose investment in a place is carried through stories passed on between generations. The protagonist comes to understand loyalty to the place to be the only differentiating factor that matters: "There were only two kinds of people. Those who stayed home, and those who left" (278). Fantine, a traveler and a travel writer, is made aware of the fact that her professional success does not count for much, and that it is loyalty that is regarded the highest by those disenfranchised and desti-tute agents whose own attachment to the place is discredited by the global economic forces. "It had taken me years to learn that my absence was almost as unforgivable as drug addiction or imprisonment" (126), she admits, as she realizes that a fierce loyalty to the community and the land are the central values that have guaranteed the physical as well as cultural survival of her ancestors. The protagonist's realization might be also understood as a suggestion of the parallels between the land and the people inhabiting it that extend beyond the customary familiarity. Rather, Straight's prose suggests that people inhabiting the vague regions of his-tory – those never in a position to become important players of historical processes; those disregarded by the forces of the global economy, yet those whose labour and whose very existence is crucial to the Capitalocene defined by Jason Moore as a "multispecies assemblage, a world-ecology of capital, power, and nature" (10) – all inhabit spaces designated as hinterlands. Their ambiguous status parallels one another.

Following Neel's distinction between "far" and "near" hinterlands, one can distinguish such ambiguous spaces in Straight's prose. Specifying the distinction he is making, Neel argues,

The far hinterland is more traditionally "rural," though now the "rural" is largely a space for … large-scale industrial extraction, production, and initial processing of primary products…. Though largely rural, the far hinterland also includes large urban zones of collapse…. The "near" hinterland, by contrast, encompasses the foothills descending from the summit of the megacity. It is largely "suburban" in character, though this is something of a misnomer given the term's connotation of middle-class white prosperity. Much of the urban population in the U.S. (and in the world generally) lives in this near hinterland. (17–18)

Such hinterlands, far and near, where the distinctions between rural and urban spaces are effaced and their functions fluctuate, stripping them of lasting characteristics, are represented in Straight's novels as well. For example, the stretches of road leading downtown go towards places "where the county hospital's old brick buildings stood like a factory that fabricated people no one wanted" (125), suggesting not only industrial processes, but also their inherent dehumanization. Urban "zones of collapse", as Neel terms them, also appear in Straight's prose:

Construction workers were gutting an old bank and a SRO hotel. Signs for luxury lofts were lit with spotlights on the roofs. Thousands of homeless people had packed their tents and bags and boxes and coats and melted into invisibility when the sun rose high enough—now they came out with the approaching end of the workday like emissaries sent among the rest of us. (31)

The new luxury buildings replace old, dilapidated ones; but the space meant for the powerful and affluent is inhabited surreptitiously by the disempowered and destitute, making the space ambiguous and impossible to pin down. Similarly, the temporal planes merge and mingle, for even though the signs of past poverty are supposedly erased by present affluence, they are brought back into view in the form of the people pushed to the margins of the capitalist society who refuse to remain hidden.

Ultimately, for the protagonist of *Take One Candle*, past and present also mingle to reveal the future: the journey back to the ancestral grounds, to Louisiana, is a journey to confront one's past, understood in both an individual and a communal sense, and to recognize where one's future might lie. The novel suggests that what gives one a sense of peace is the path of loyalty to situated, localized wisdom, which relies on a recognition of the common fragility of all animals, human and nonhuman alike, living in ambiguous spaces that protect them and guarantee their survival, even though their very existence is not always legitimized. The ancestral stories are implemented with modern knowledge of the global economy that covers all corners of the world, yet remains connected to the producers in an organic way. Globally conceived, the communities we build are different, but equally intricately constructed as places of memory within narratives that convey localized knowledge, the key to survival.

The lessons taught by the ancestors live on in memory and in oral stories, disrupting the primacy of the Logos. As Fantine muses on the differences between people, she is reminded of the distinction made a century earlier: "Fur and claws. That's what Moinette taught Marie-Therese, who taught her daughter, Anjanae, who told me, when I was in Azure. The only difference between humans is fur and claws and skin. Same blood inside" (206). Just like in the first volume, the second volume of the trilogy also presents a vision in which animality is an intrinsic part of humanity, where the distinction between them belongs to the contested official narrative, deemed void by the lived experiences of the inhabitants of the hinterlands represented in the novel. A more pertinent distinction is made on the basis of one's attachment to place, even though – or perhaps precisely because – such an attachment is never granted an official status. The protagonists of Straight's novels lose their farms because of racist laws, or despite the legal recognition of their ownership. Yet, even if the legal bonds are broken, the attachment remains in place, in this way subverting the legal narrative dividing places into pieces of property owned by subjects of the law and thus transforming these places into hinterlands: places neither urban nor rural, neither privately owned nor communal, neither here nor there.

Yet the identification with a place is a complex matter, with geography being only its most obvious surface level. The persistence of these internalized landscapes is guaranteed by emotional connections within the community, and it is strengthened by the stories passed on from one generation to the next. Fantine, the protagonist of *Take One Candle*, thinks of her ancestors from Louisiana as immigrants whose original culture is preserved with communal effort: "They came to California and re-created their villages or towns, like everyone else. ... we carried around our individual villages, and what our parents gave us – their caution and fear and anger and vigilance and stories" (20). Food, music, and language bind communities together, just as memory does, to the point that it becomes impossible to distinguish between people and places; and as Fantine reminisces about her childhood and recalls the lessons in loyalty taught in the family, she must come to terms with her own abandonment of the places of her childhood.

Fantine's profession enables her to see parallels between her Californian community and other places in the world. She describes a mountain village in Switzerland: "All the houses were dark old wood, and they had names carved into the balconies. Each house had a name. ... Names of flowers, or trees, or a stream nearby. It was like here. All families" (129). She assumes a global perspective to see the local communities, which makes it possible for her to compare her unique childhood spaces with foreign lands. The individual houses are identified by a family name, which in a way turns the building into another member of the family: the place and the humans inhabiting it merge into one, further stressing the continuity suggested between culturally and geographically different parts of the world.

Just as there is an identification suggested between places and their inhabitants, and affinity between different global locations, in the same unifying fashion the narrator makes the connection between labour in different parts of the world: "The women tying sheaves of wheat in France. The gleaners, following the potato harvest in England. The women carrying baskets of peppers on their heads down the mountain trails of Bolivia. Glorette and me, holding the cut cane like batons" (221). Not only is the connection between various labourers established in this way, but it also suggests that the products of human work cannot and should not be separated from the producers, even if the product seems displaced from its origin through the global network of commerce in the Capitalocene. Straight's narrative suggests returning to these primary identifications.

These parallels and identifications are taken one step further. Just like *Take One Candle* establishes a connection between a product and its producer, in a similar manner it establishes a link between people struggling to survive and other animals with the same preoccupation. As one character explains to a child about shrimp: "He got eyes, too. Just like you. Think about what he see before your papa catch him up. See the water all around him, but somethin in there we don't know. Some food for him, too, oui?" (88). Crustacean or mammal, including human, all animals have their needs and live in their habitats that may not be accessible to other animals of different faculties. Jakob von Uexküll names them Umwelten, giving an example of a tick that reacts to warmth and blood. A realization of differing perceptions of the world implies an awareness of common fragility, a condition specific to all forms of life.

This fragility, the precariousness of the very fact of life, characteristic of human and nonhuman animals alike, is represented through the specific manner of speaking about one's place of residence: "We never said, 'Where do you live?' as that implied a permanence that hardly anyone had. Where do you stay? Right now, for a month, a year, a few minutes? Where have you perched for this moment, until times got better or worse?" (2010, 94). Being perched is ambiguous, as it implies a bird-like situation of impermanence and migrancy, of being in flight, hunted, and in need of a safe haven; but a perch might also imply a place where one hides from danger, so a safe place, if only for a while. Such ambiguity reveals the precariousness of life and highlights human–nonhuman continuity, paralleling the urban–rural dichotomy disruption. The undermining of these binary categories will also be present in the final volume of the Rio Seco trilogy.

The third volume of the trilogy, *Between Heaven and Here* (2012), narrates the story with the protagonists the readers know from the second volume, this time, however, focuses on Fantine's childhood friend, Glorette, a drug addict and a prostitute whose death prompts the members of the community to examine their loyalty and expose its limits. Each volume of the trilogy presents increasingly urbanized, more densely populated areas – Neel's "near hinterlands" – but in each, the key to survival in a hostile environment lies in coexistence with other species. The environment Straight portrays in the novel is fictitious, yet recognizably based on the greater Los Angeles area. Andy Merrifield identifies the paradoxes characteristic of the place, saying,

> Incredibly, the quintessential stretched out, decentered, and dissociated city of Los Angeles is now America's densest metropolis, with the largest expanse of areas with over 10,000 people per square mile, nudging ahead of New York. Once-decentered suburban forms have recentered into new centers; polycentric forms have sprouted new community coalitions (and not only rich, reactionary NIMBY types). (140 n11)

Straight's characters are destitute and disempowered, facing the everyday effects of systemic racism. Theirs are the non-places of rental apartment buildings, vacant parking lots, long stretches of highways with overpasses leading off to more of the same non-descript space devoid of clear characteristics. An appreciation of the natural elements of their environments could hardly be expected from characters struggling to survive in such a context, yet it is precisely the appreciation of the small natural elements intermingling with the ambiguous, not-quite-urban landscape that becomes a precious gift. Glorette shows her son, Victor, the full moon behind the palm tree fronds and she calls it: "The palm tree sparkler. Better than fireworks. ... *You could have it every month, baby. Just look. ... You always got a moon, right here, and you always got a palm tree, baby. Can't nobody ever change that.*" She performs a trick with the light which to the child seems like magic: "She put her fingers like visors over his eyes, to block out the apartment lights, and all he saw was the courtyard palm tree, full moon behind it, the fronds tossing in the wind, their fringes throwing off silver fire" (234). Nature does not exist as a product or a collection of goods; and as Straight's narrative disrupts the characterization of nature, along the lines of the Capitalocene's cheapening of it and its perception solely in terms of the utilitarian function it might play, it also disrupts the distinctions between the urban and the rural zones, making them impossible to distinguish. Straight's use of natural imagery is a move towards a more nuanced presentation of the unequal distribution of resources and a suggestion that an understanding of the world that is not based on material value attached to goods and places is, in fact, possible.

What parallels the disruptions between the urban–rural dichotomy and the natural and non-utilitarian is the attempted abolishment of the distinctions between humans and nonhumans. There is a subtle equivalence suggested between them; for example, birds competing: "two mockingbirds fought over their territory by singing, each song more elaborate and frenzied than the next" (2012, 72) are mirrored by boys fighting: "it's like the crows in the pecan grove by Sarrat, all the yelling, but not lifting up to the sky" (2012, 167). The comparison between birds and humans suggests a deeper relationship between the human and nonhuman animals, one of crucial intermingling and coexistence in an equally indivisible hinterland.

The possible consequence of such a democratic view of human–nonhuman continuity is a broadened understanding of the role that humans perform, dethroned from their anthropocentric position as the rulers of the natural world. The choice that Straight makes in her novelistic representations of animals is a political one; as Dominic LaCapra asserts, "the questioning of a decisive criterion separating the human from the animal or even from the rest of nature has widespread ramifications, indicating the need for a major paradigm shift in the relations of the human, the animal, and nature in general" (189). To cast doubt on the supposedly fixed distinguishing lines between the categories of human and nonhuman, then, means to launch an interrogation into the distribution of resources, and into the discursive power enabling a particular viewpoint, that translates into sustainability or the lack thereof. Straight's prose suggests that writing about nature in a way that suggests its inseparability from urban spaces is a political act.

Such an awareness of the political dimension manifests itself in a discussion of the ills plaguing the community Straight portrays, and it points again to the common vulnerability of human and nonhuman animals. In a direct textual reference to the previous volume of the trilogy, the characters discuss the precariousness of their existence as reflected in the verbs they use. When asked, "Where you stay now?" Victor answers, "Where do you *live* is a standard construction. Because most white people *live* somewhere. But we always say where do you *stay*. Because historically we're used to being there just for a brief time" (91). Such parallels between humans and nonhumans enhance the sense of danger pervasive in the novel.

This ominous atmosphere is amplified with the use of imagery that concerns a murder of crows, who are presented as the rightful inhabitants of the place: "A huge flock of crows lived in the pecan grove … . The birds had been there for decades, according to the old Mexican men who lived in the next grove" (2012, 145). The characters note that the crows are dying, as are the young men of the community who turn to illegal actions that imperil their existence: "The crow lay dead on the patio beside the washline. Another baby. Furry with baby feathers, puffed out like a piece of black boa from some old costume, the small black feet curled like ink writing" (2012, 133). The apparent affection extends not only to the dying baby birds, but also to the older members of the flock, whose qualities are worthy of reflection: "Another crow lay dead in the vacant lot. Recently dead – his feathers still had the glossy purple and gold sheen of movement and flight and disdain" (2012, 145). The descriptions of birds carefully elude an anthropomorphic presentation, thus avoiding the trap of representing nonhuman animals as existing for the human, either as a product or as the abject other. The narrative comes close to magic realism in its portrayal of the mysterious bird deaths, but never actually crosses the line; rather, it explains the plague in strictly medical terms: "West Nile virus ... West Nile – something in the air, or in the blood, that came all the way from Africa to Southern California" (133). It would be too much of a shorthand to assume that Straight wants the reader to draw a parallel between the crows and African Americans, with the virus that causes the deaths of young men, possibly being the effects of racism; rather, the narrative invites us to see the intricate connections between the natural world, the inhabitants of the same biosphere, and the common vulnerability of human and nonhuman animals.

Humans and nonhumans compete for land and resources; for one character who operates an unofficial parking lot, "The crows were the biggest problem so far," as their droppings ruin the hoods of the cars parked there. But the birds are appreciated for their intelligence: "Huddling in the trees, crows were the first to get pecans every year, smart enough to drop them on the street, wait for cars to smash the hulls so they could pick out the raw soft meat" (2012, 219). Just like the birds use the encroaching civilization with its machines and its seizing of land, the disenfranchised and marginalized humans must learn strategies to survive in the unfavourable circumstances, with the birds possibly having a lesson in adaptation to teach them. There is a crucial parallel between the human and nonhuman characters: both groups inhabit spaces designated as the "near hinterlands" – places close to the centre of the modern megacity, like L.A., yet possessing mixed characteristics of a suburban sprawl. Adaptability to new places is required of both humans and nonhumans; the birds' intelligence and perseverance are as admirable as the humans'.

Ancestors are a more obvious source of knowledge about surviving in a hostile environment, though just like in the previous volumes, also in the third part of the trilogy it comes from two sources: animal and ancestral.

In the first volume, Moinette thinks about her skin as hide and her hair as fur; in the third volume, Glorette considers her nails and calls them "Claws. For animals. But now only women were supposed to fight with them. ... Her claws. ... The ones Victor said were designed differently from apes and chimps, and different from cats and dogs. ...*I think they're just leftover,* he'd say. *From something else*" (2012, 198, emphasis in the original). The character's sense of helplessness expressed through the comparison between human nails and animal claws, which exposes the inadequacy of human defences, derives from her double marginalization, a gendered and raced one. It also runs along one of the narrative and thematic arches binding the three parts together, the tie between human and nonhuman animals providing a prominent connection for the parts of the trilogy.

Straight's short, focused, and place-specific descriptions of flora and fauna are interspersed throughout the narrative to such a degree that they cannot be seen in separation from the narrative itself (she rarely devotes a whole paragraph to those observations, giving preference to one-sentence statements, intermingling them with other elements of the narration). The natural world exists intertwined with the world of human affairs, and not for the latter's benefit, to the point that it is impossible to draw a dividing line between them. It is a view suggesting a sustainability that goes well beyond the colonial (and anthropocentric) view commensurate with a plantation economy based on exploitation and a reduction to products of all the elements of the natural world, including humans.

The struggle of the disempowered communities is represented against the backdrop of the hinterlands that comprise places transformed from natural to urban to what can no longer be categorized as either one or the other. Merrifield turns to theorists such as Roger Keil to highlight the fact that "these suburban borderlands and edge-city peripheries are now central in a congealed and legitimate urban form of the future. It is not that sprawl is good: it is that it is here to stay, and not all bad, and it is also the life form in which ecological struggles must now unfold" (140 n11). These global processes are accompanied by the Sixth Great Extinction, and are an indication of the fused discriminatory practices that inform the Anthropocene or the Plantationocene.

Straight's fiction sketches links between the produce (such as cane sugar) and the producer, and these links parallel one between different places: those considered centres of commerce and business and those traditionally perceived as margins; their intermingling results in global hinterlands. People inhabiting those spaces, excluded because of their race, gender, or class, are a testament to the impossibility of distinguishing between them. Their very existence undermines clear-cut divisions.

The characters in Straight's two latter volumes of the Rio Seco trilogy travel the world and go back to their ancestral places; their travels sketch an analogy between the oppressive and exploitative character of both the plantation economy and today's late capitalism. By drawing these parallels, Straight's fiction makes an interesting proposition: to go beyond these equally oppressive systems, alliances must be built, between humans – going beyond the blood-line and immediate family – and between nonhumans – claiming kinship across species lines. These alliances happen in places designated as far and near hinterlands, and their ambiguous, mixed character is a perfect backdrop for possible post-anthropocentric connections.

Works Cited

Braidotti, Rosi. *The Posthuman*. Polity, 2013.
Keil, Roger. "Frontiers of Urban Political Ecology." *Urban Constellations*. Ed. Matthew Gandy. Jovis Verlag GmbH, 2011, pp. 26–29.
LaCapra, Dominick. *History and Its Limits: Human, Animal, Violen*ce. Cornell UP, 2009.
Merrifield, Andy. *The Politics of the Encounter: Urban Theory and Protest under Planetary Urbanization*. The University of Georgia Press, 2013.
Moore, Jason W., ed. An*thropocene or Capitalocene? Nature, History, and the Crisis of Capitalism*. PM Press, 2016.
Neel, Phil A. *Hinterland: America's New Landscape of Class and Conflict*. Reaktion, 2018.
Robinson, Jennifer. *Ordinary Cities: Between Modernity and Development*. Routledge, 2006.
Straight, Susan. *A Million Nightingales*. Anchor, 2006. Kindle version.
Straight, Susan. *Take One Candle Light a Room*. Pantheon, 2010.
Straight, Susan. *Between Heaven and Here*. McSweeney, 2012.
Uexküll, Jakob von. *A Foray into the Worlds of Animals and Humans with A Theory of Meaning*. U of Minnesota P, 2010.

Part III

Regenerative and nostalgic hinterlands

9 (Re)constructing identity along the road through the Chinese hinterland

Gao Xingjian's *Soul Mountain* and Ma Jian's *Red Dust*

Raffael Weger

Introduction

The term *hinterland* was originally coined in German colonial discourses[1] and is nowadays often understood in economic terms as "non city landscapes that support urban life" (Brenner and Katsikis 24). In this article, I will expand upon this narrow definition by looking at two Chinese novels – *Soul Mountain* (1990/2000) and *Red Dust* (2001) – written by two urban intellectuals formerly living in Beijing, Gao Xingjian (高行健, 1940–) and Ma Jian (马建, 1953–), and the way they approach and construct the Chinese hinterland in their autofictional novels. As both authors left the capital due to political persecution and subsequently travelled through the southern and western hinterlands, the power relations between the urban political centre and the rural political periphery will be of special interest to me. Additionally, as both writers were not only seeking refuge, but were also searching for themselves, attempting a reconstruction of their Han Chinese identity, I will also focus on the way the hinterland is being turned into the symbol of a cultural Other, which enables a contrastive redefinition of the self.

In the ancient Chinese compilation commonly known as the *Zhuangzi*,[2] we find a story about the homonymous philosopher Zhuangzi (c. 369–286 BCE) who is visited by two high-ranking officials from the kingdom of Chu while fishing somewhere in the countryside. They deliver a message from the king, inviting Zhuangzi to come to the capital, the centre of political power, to take "charge of all within [the king's] territories". Seemingly unimpressed, Zhuangzi responds: "I have heard that in Chu there is a spirit-like tortoise-shell, the wearer of which died 3000 years ago, and which the king keeps, in his ancestral temple, in a hamper covered with a cloth. Was it better for the tortoise to die, and leave its shell to be thus honoured? Or would it have been better for it to live, and keep on dragging its tail through the mud?" Without hesitation, both officials

DOI: 10.4324/9781032617732-13

agree, "It would have been better for it to live, and draw its tail after it over the mud". This in turn leads to Zhuangzi's final refusal: "Go your ways. I will keep on drawing my tail after me through the mud" (Zhuangzi).[3]

This story touches upon both aspects of the Chinese hinterland that I have already mentioned in my brief introduction: the question of the politization of the hinterland and its cultural status. Through the writings of the grand historian Sima Qian (c. 145–86 BCE), we know that Zhuangzi loathed politics and – contrary to what is known about his famous contemporaries Kongzi (c. 551–479 BCE) and Mengzi (372–289 BCE) – refused to participate in the political power struggles of his time (Wohlfahrt 16). Within the aforementioned story, this refusal is not merely represented by his declining the king's request but also, and more importantly, by his remaining in the economic and what could be called the "political hinterland", implying its status as the periphery of power. As Zhuangzi rejects the offer, he also refuses to accompany the two officials to the capital, the *de facto* centre of power. It thus becomes clear that in this story a distinct relationship exists between geographical space and political power, a fact that still held true for Mao-era China.[4] The CCP had a long history as a rural guerrilla movement before it finally took control in 1949. Its original powerbase mostly consisted of peasants (Brown 1–2), and in 1949 only around 10% of China's population was living in cities (Randelovic 228). Nevertheless, after 1949 and in defiance of its rural roots, the CCP quickly developed a strong urban bias (Whyte 8–9; Brown 4, 6). Under the auspices of a socialist planned economy, this led not only to a rapid growth in urban population, but also to a massive disparity in wealth distribution between the densely populated and highly industrialized coastal areas in the east and southeast of China and the much less densely populated and more agrarian southern and western hinterlands (Miller 97–98, 104).[5] Paired with my interpretation of the story recounted above, this modern urban bias of China's ruling party suggests that, in contemporary China at least, the hinterland should be much less politicized than urban spaces. As will be shown during my analysis, however, this is not at all the case.

The second defining characteristic of the Chinese hinterland I want to highlight is its promise of the possibility of an authentic life and – often caused by this assumption – its perceived status of untouched cultural authenticity. When Zhuangzi denies the king's request, he not only shows his disdain for political accolades, but also presents political life as the direct opposite of what could be called an "authentic" or "natural" way of living. As Zhuangzi seems to imply, what could be more natural to a tortoise than dragging its tail through the mud? By refusing the king's offer, he thus chooses – what to him seems to be – the more natural way of living, one that has not yet been corrupted by the follies of politics. Continuing along such lines, the Chinese hinterland becomes not only the spatial opposite of the thoroughly politicized urban metropolis, but potentially also a kind of refuge and a place of healing for those trying to escape their existence as a *homo politicus.*

As mentioned above, due to internal migration, urban populations kept growing rapidly after 1949. For many urban migrants, however, their rurally located ancestral homes continued to be of great significance (Brown 5–6). This follows a tradition which Lu Hanchao found among intellectuals, politicians, and traders in the early twentieth century. Namely, most of those who moved from the countryside to bigger cities still adhered to two "deep-rooted cultural value[s]": "to bring glory to one's ancestry" and "to return to one's hometown with honor" (37). In many ways, these sentiments survived even after the takeover of the CCP, as can be seen by the fact that two very high-ranking officials, Peng Dehuai (1889–1974) and Liu Shaoqi (1898–1969), "when they were in serious political troubles with Mao and were on the verge of being purged, asked to return to their small hometown as a solution to the discord" (46). Although neither was granted their request, this shows that while the CCP claimed to have broken with traditional culture, in times of crisis even two "veteran Communists ... did not reject the back-to-hometown tradition" (47).

This fact reinforces the aforementioned notion of the hinterland functioning as a space outside of, or at least on the edge of the realm of politics, and in a way as a place of refuge, recovery, and healing (46). Additionally, due to their close ties with their former rural lives, many who moved to the city during the course of the twentieth century developed a form of nostalgia for the perceived beauty and simplicity of the countryside (40).[6] At the same time, they projected a number of negative attributes onto their new urban habitat, linking it with "impotence and death".[7] It is due to these contrastive views that the hinterland became a template for literary projects of individual and collective identity (re)construction. Such projects often focused on concepts such as "local identities, belonging, social homogeneity, traditional family and lifestyles, local ways of production, regional food, nature, etc." (Oltmanns 61), all of which play an important role in the attempted reconstruction of identity we see in Gao's and Ma's novels.

Going back to the roots – the Chinese south as the cradle of Han culture

The early 1980s marked an important break in the history of the PRC. After nearly three decades of political upheaval during the Mao era, such as the Great Leap Forward or the Cultural Revolution, which caused massive traumata for many people, the country experienced a brief period of liberalization when Deng Xiaoping (1904–1997) introduced the Reform and Opening policies in 1978. This meant a shift in the political focus from a purely ideological leadership to an emphasis on modernizing the country through economic buildup and went hand in hand with an opening up of the country's borders – not only for foreign goods and investments, but also for new ideas and thoughts – initiating a period of relative freedom. This in turn also led to new literary experimentation and the possibility for writers to again voice their personal opinions – at least to a certain degree – in their fictional writing, a novelty after nearly four decades of state-mandated Socialist Realism (Carrico 107). However, this period was (only) short-lived, as at the end of 1983 the Campaign against Spiritual Pollution was initiated. The main goal of this campaign was to curb Western-inspired liberal ideas among the Chinese populace – especially among intellectuals (112) – and to reinforce the notion that "culture must henceforth serve economic necessity and the project of modernizing the country in order to contribute to the renaissance and glorification of the nation" (Zhang 26).

For many authors whose writing didn't serve the political mainstream, this meant official criticism, a ban on their works, and sometimes political persecution and punishment (Gold 958, 970–72; Wang 1986, 50–51, 58–59). Although the campaign didn't last very long – it was terminated only two months after its official initiation because the uncertain political climate deterred international businesses, thus threatening the "official vision of reform-era material civilization" (Carrico 115) – it clearly signalled to many intellectuals that the political landscape under Deng had not changed as drastically as they had wished for and that their artistic position was once again a very precarious one.[8] This in turn caused many intellectuals to temporarily leave their urban homes and seek refuge from political persecution somewhere in the vast Chinese hinterland. Among them were Gao Xingjian and Ma Jian, who both started their respective journeys towards the end of 1983 after the initiation of the Campaign against Spiritual Pollution.

At that time, Gao was already a well-known novelist, essayist, playwright, and painter. His writing was heavily influenced by Western authors and his style was often called modernist. Naturally, this strong Western influence became the focus of criticism against him during the Campaign against Spiritual Pollution, with one official calling one of his plays, *Che Zhan* (Bus Stop), "the most pernicious work since the establishment of the People's Republic" (FitzGerald 580). Furthermore, there were rumours that Gao was to be sent to the notorious prison farms of Qinghai province (Lee viii). Alongside these political reasons, there were also personal motives for Gao's flight to China's southern hinterland. Having been diagnosed with lung cancer, only to find out soon after that it had been a misdiagnosis, Gao felt like he had been given a second chance. His flight to the countryside, as the narrator in *Soul Mountain* argues, therefore also had the purpose of finding an "authentic life" (12), something that for him didn't seem to exist in the big cities.

All in all, Gao undertook three separate trips between 1983 and 1984, the longest of which was a journey of around 15,000 kilometres. It is very telling that all three trips took him along the Yangzi River and thus through southern China, as in one of his essays, "Literature and Metaphysics: About *Soul Mountain*", Gao argues that the Chinese civilization derives from two major sources: the "Central Plains culture of the Yellow River Basin" in northern China and the "Yangtze River culture" in the south (Gao 2007, 99). As Gao explains, he feels much more drawn to the south, which he sees as the cradle of modern Han culture (101). This, according to Laurence Schneider, is not a new idea, but has in fact existed for a long time (Major and Cook 10, 14–15). Additionally, from the third century CE onwards, this image was infused with the notion of the Yangzi River functioning as a moat, protecting Han culture from northern barbarians (Schneider 60). However, a conflicting image had always existed in parallel to this, namely that of the south as a forbidding place of political exile: "Being in the South meant being away from the metropolitan centres of power; the presence of the South's tribal people and its primitive ruggedness meant the absence of civilized high culture" (13). This in turn led to yet another depiction of the south: its association "with those who dissent, those who protest" (95). The south thus became not only a place of forced exile, but also a place of refuge for those who did not agree with contemporary politics and willingly went into self-exile. In modern times, the south is therefore often "considered to have an innovative, nonconforming, and revolutionary spirit" (14).[9]

Gao's flight into the Chinese south is both a search for political refuge and an exploration of the seemingly still "authentic" remnants of a culture which he sees himself as a product of (Gao 2007, 103). As such, the main topic of *Soul Mountain* is as much an attempted reconstruction of an individual identity as it is that of a collective Han identity through the collecting and retelling of myths and legends, customs and practices, folk songs, and so on. Stylistically, this double focus is reflected through the use of several protagonists, among them an "I" and a "you". Whereas "I" travels the real world, "you" finds himself on a spiritual journey to the eponymous Soul Mountain. For Gao, the two narrators are both different perceptions of the same subject, thus providing us with different approaches to reconstructing a new identity (95–96). Additionally, the pronoun "you" can also be seen as directly addressing the reader, taking them along for the journey through the hinterland.

Ma Jian's reason for leaving Beijing in late 1983 was equally twofold. During the Campaign against Spiritual Pollution, as officials had found some of his paintings and writings to be unsuitable, he was detained for a month. Once free again, he decided to leave Beijing behind, both to prevent further persecution and, having felt stifled in his artistic creativity by the censoring political reality that ruled urban lives, to also find creative and spiritual liberation. Just like in Gao's case, this search led him back to his perceived roots as becomes clear when the I-narrator, who, like the author, is also called Ma Jian, states: "When I step onto the high plateau of northern Shaanxi I feel I am walking towards my ancestors' heart. ... The fertile banks of the Yellow River here have been cultivated for over eight thousand years. I have come in search of my roots" (Ma 187). Although Ma's three-year journey takes him not only north and south, but also all the way west and even east to the new economic centres of a booming China, the underlying aim of his trip is (therefore) the same as in Gao's case: an exploration of the origins of Han culture and a subsequent reconstruction of his own identity.

While both Gao and Ma thus engage with questions of individual identity, they also describe in detail their encounters and experiences during their journeys, often contrasting them with their urban, Han intellectual perspective. In this way, they simultaneously discover and (re) construct the Chinese hinterland, subsequently using it for personal reflections. This approach often borders on what David Der-Wei Wang calls "imaginary nostalgia", a type of writing he claims is typical for the native soil literature of the early twentieth century and the root-searching movement in the 1980s. He defines this type of nostalgia as "not so much ... a representational effort to enliven the irretrievable past as ... a creation of an imaginary past on behalf of the present" (107).[10] In other words, the past is imagined in such a way that it can function as a template for identity construction in the present.

Whereas Wang uses the term with regard to authors who originally stemmed from the countryside and only later moved to the city, therefore being able to write about the hinterland from the position of ones who had once actually lived in it, I believe it can be similarly used for those authors who have spent their whole life in urban metropolises and who imagine the rural space as the Other through which they define themselves. While the writers whose works Wang analyses write from a position of geo-graphical and temporal distance, Gao's and Ma's distance is more of a cultural one, originating from the fact that they are only able to experience the hinterland from the position of an outsider. Everything they see is influenced by the perspective of an urban Han intellectual (Jian 113), or in other words: "Their imagination plays just as much a role as their lived experience" (Wang 1993, 109).

As the hinterland that both authors imagine is a multifaceted one, I have divided the following analysis of their novels into three different parts, each focusing on a different aspect of their socio-spatial construction of the hinterland. First, I will pay closer attention to the foregrounding of natural sights – either as places of pristine beauty or as witnesses of human destruction. Following this, I will focus on the construction of rural space through human relations. Finally, I will analyze how both authors deal with local histories and traditions which, in their quest for "authenticity", is reminiscent of root-searching literature, implying the literary construction of an ideal, not an actual space.

Inscribed landscapes

Two short phrases help explain the shift in the relationship with nature that took place during the Mao era. Traditionally it had been characterized by the Confucian notion 天人合一 (*Tian Ren Heyi*), meaning "Harmony between the Heavens and Humankind". These characters were replaced during the Mao era by four different ones: 人定胜天 (*Ren Ding Sheng Tian*), meaning "Man Must Conquer Nature" (Shapiro 9). Thus, whereas humanity had traditionally been seen as a part of nature, under Mao's rule nature became an enemy that had to be defeated and whose powers had to be harnessed for China's benefit.[11] Be it the construction of heavy industry from the early 1950s on, widespread irrigation projects during the Great Leap Forward, or massive, "[c]entrally launched earth-transforming campaigns" during the Cultural Revolution – all throughout Mao's reign enormous destruction of natural landscapes took place (2–3). Meanwhile, "[t]rained scientists who uttered words of dissent or caution were often exiled or persecuted to death" and "traditional grass-roots practices concerning the physical world" were suppressed by officials (2–3).

This is probably one of the main reasons why, as Thomas Moran notes, it was not common for Chinese authors in the eighties to write about nature (Moran 212). The fact that both Ma, and to a larger extent Gao, make the environment one of their main foci in their novels is thus especially noteworthy.[12] What we find is a return to the Confucian notion of "Harmony between the Heavens and Humankind" (210), which guides their respective search for "virgin wilderness", "primeval forest", and a "world that belongs to wild animals" (Gao 2000, 2, 28, 38). However, rather than pristine nature, what both narrators actually find are mostly "inscribed landscapes" (Moran 211), places that have been inscribed with the history of the PRC, functioning as memorials to earlier political movements as well as testimonies of current economic reforms. As Ma's narrator follows the paths taken by a famous Tang poet, for example, he notes:

> When the poet Li Bai travelled down this stretch of the river during the Tang Dynasty, he wrote of coloured clouds above the Yangzi and monkeys wailing from the banks. Today the monkeys have been replaced by fertilizer plants and cement factories that pollute the river with yellow waste. Where the green slopes have been cut away, the earth shines like raw pigskin. (161–62)[13]

Likewise, Gao's narrator encounters many forests that according to the locals had once been so thick that you couldn't see the sun, but have nowadays been reduced to mere reminders of their former grandeur if they have not vanished completely.[14] As he visits a nature reserve in Shennongjia for example, an area that once was home to a vast expanse of virgin forest, he learns that in 1966 a highway was built through it, which has since been used to supply the state with 900,000 cubic meters of timber from the area every year (362). The recurring picture of deforestation is mirrored by lakes that have been drained to a fraction of their original size as well as rivers that have been polluted to such a degree that nothing is able to live in them anymore (48, 319, 344, 471).

As the I-narrator travels to Lake Caohai, he learns that not only were the hills surrounding it completely deforested within the past 10 to 20 years, but during the Cultural Revolution the county revolutionary committee also implemented a new initiative with the goal of draining off the water and converting the area into fields. To do so, they mobilized 100,000 civilian workers, who dug drainage channels and erected retaining walls. However, most of the land remained non-arable swampland. Furthermore, this interference caused a breakdown of the local climate, leading to increasingly cold winters and severe droughts in spring. Earlier in the 1950s, when a Shanghainese biologist with an overseas PhD travelled to Caohai to launch a breeding programme to restore parts of the local ecosystem, he was beaten to death by local poachers. The culprits walked away unscathed, showing the lack of appreciation both the local population and the officials had for intellectuals who in their concern for the environment interfered with their projects and businesses (108–9).

One of *Soul Mountain's* especially telling chapters deals with the narrator's visit to a remote panda observation compound in Sichuan in search of primeval forest. The workers he encounters there have neither access to newspapers nor radios: "Ronald Reagan, the economic reforms, inflation, the eradication of spiritual pollution, … etcetera, etcetera, etcetera – that noisy world is left to the cities" (37). And yet, isolated as they may seem to be, even these men can't completely escape the implications of politics, as old trees in the surrounding areas are being cut down and rare animals are being hunted and killed – all in the name of economic development. In fact, as it turns out, any sentiment of virgin, authentic nature in this remote area is only an illusion. As one of the workers explains to the narrator: "They've cut down every tree that can be sold for timber. ... Strictly speaking, there are no primary forests here. At most, these would be secondary growth forests" (47). According to Thomas Moran, seemingly primeval forests such as this one take on several important functions within the novel. Not only do they signify "the degraded state of nature as a whole", but they also carry "the novel's national allegory" (208), thus mirroring the overall state of the country and directly making visible the political campaigns which have marked both urban areas and the hinterland.

These examples clearly show that in contemporary China, the distance between the urban centres of power and the hinterland has been drastically reduced. Contrary to what J. Gerard Dollar says, Gao's narrator in leaving the capital is in fact not successful in "distancing himself from Beijing, the site of personal trauma as well as social and political discontent" (415). In other parts of *Soul Mountain* and *Red Dust,* nature becomes a symbol of the narrators' failure to create a new identity for themselves. In this regard, the futility and ultimate absurdity of their search for virgin wilderness becomes most clear when they finally manage to find a stretch of untouched nature. In the case of Gao, this comes in the form of one of the last primeval forests high up in the mountains, while in the case of Ma it is the Ordos desert in the north of China. Both get lost in their respective locations, the latter almost dying of thirst and only getting rescued in the last moment by an unknown saviour, the former never making it out of the forest at all – at least we never learn how he found his way out, although in later chapters we do encounter him in new locations. Each of these situations and the narrators' near-death experiences mirror the continual frustration of their efforts to find a new way of self-understanding. Instead, "authentic", virgin nature turns out to be as fearsome an enemy as the political system they are running from. As Ma's narrator states at one point: "[N]ow I know that nature is as cruel and heartless as the cities I ran away from" (141).

Politicized human relationships

As mentioned above, in the case of both authors/narrators it was, to a large extent, the political situation which drove them away from Beijing. Yet their respective flight into the countryside did not bring with it the desired depoliticization of their lives. Instead, even while travelling through remote areas of the hinterland, they are again and again confronted with the fact that in the 1980s, politics have, against their explicit urban bias, not solely limited themselves to urban areas, but have penetrated almost every corner of the country and every aspect of life of the rural population, which still numbered roughly 80% of the nation (Kennedy 294).

One recurring marker of this politization is the repeated highlighting of the fact that travelling through China at that time was illegal. In the case of both narrators, this was not so much due to their being politically persecuted, but rather it was a consequence of the *hukou* or household registration system. According to Martin King Whyte, although such a system had existed for centuries (7), it was only after the CCP's takeover that the party started to use this system to control rural-urban mobility. Between 1953 and 1958, all citizens were classified as either "urban" (with further subdivisions according to the level of city they lived in) or "agricultural". These classifications, which were inherited at birth, governed many aspects of a citizen's life. While "all voluntary, individually initiated migration to urban areas" was essentially prohibited (11), an urban classification "guaranteed food rations, housing, health care, and education to city residents" among other benefits (Brown 3–4). In contrast, holders of an agricultural *hukou* "were outside of the state budget, and generally only received such compensation and benefits as their own labors and their local communities could provide" (Whyte 9, 12). Although these regulations have been somewhat softened since, they continue to exist today (15) and were certainly still very much in effect in the 1980s, as can be seen in both novels.

During their trips through the Chinese hinterland, both narrators' identities are regularly checked by officials, the local police, hotel receptionists, bus conductors, and other personnel, so they have no option but to use fake IDs and forged official letters of introduction from their former work units or other institutions to be able to travel and find accommodation (Gao 2000, 223, 260; Ma 63). And yet, their fake credentials still often arouse suspicion. For example, when Gao's narrator tries to pose as a journalist from Beijing, he realizes that "reporters sent by the central government authorities have a certain style. But I have neither a county interpreter nor a special jeep to take me around" (251). Furthermore, even some of the narrators' friends and acquaintances refuse to host them because, given their precarious political status, they fear the consequences that personal contact with them might have for their own life. In *Red Dust,* soon after Ma Jian gives a lecture at Kunming University, the students warn him that there is a warrant for his arrest given out by the university's propaganda department. Fleeing to another city thereafter, he again can't stay for long. When being told by the local writers' association to stay away from Ma Jian while his case is still being investigated, the poet who hosts him also begs him to leave his house (263). Even in the hinterland, the political periphery, the narrators suffer from the indirect consequences of political persecution.

A political shadow has not only been cast upon their own lives, however, but it also haunts many of the individuals they meet. It is thus very common that when new acquaintances are described, we first learn about the implications that political movements have had on their lives. Ma tells of a poet friend whose mother was beaten to death during the Cultural Revolution and an acquaintance whose father lost his mind during the same period due to being rectified so severely (19, 26). Likewise, in *Soul Mountain* we get to know a man who one day "offended the branch party secretary of the hospital and was expelled from the party, branded a rightist element and sent to work in the fields in the country" (278). Others are suffering from the CCP's one-child policy, the widespread corruption, or are being forced to give up their traditional nomadic lifestyle and move to the city (Gao 2000, 497; Ma 86, 106, 183). Additionally, wherever the narrators go, they encounter political symbols such as larger-than-life Mao faces staring at them from posters, propaganda songs blaring from loudspeakers even in the remotest of villages, and banners propagating new political campaigns (Gao 2000, 366; Ma 64, 82, 305). The powerful grip that the Party has over citizens' lives indeed becomes clear when Ma, during his visit to a small town, writes: "Sons of men killed by the Party work for the Public Security Bureau. Families destroyed by Mao Zedong hang posters of him on their walls" (196).

Another especially telling scene takes place when Gao's narrator accompanies an old peasant to his house in a very remote village to listen to him perform old Daoist rituals and songs which have been forbidden due to being labelled as superstitious practices. After only a few songs the man's son arrives and, in his position as village head, puts an end to the illegal goings-on. This scene again clearly shows that politics have even invaded the private realm of the family (287, 297–98). Additionally, it highlights the still ongoing struggle that followers of old traditions face in a political climate which, for a long time, saw the abolishment of ancient traditions as one of the most important factors along the way to modernization. This latter point is essential for the last aspect I will look at, as it is exactly those ancient traditions the two narrators turn to in their search for a new identity.

Root-searching and cultural alienation

As mentioned above, the liberalizing effects of the reforms in the eighties led to a wider variety of literary movements and genres, one of which was the so-called "root-searching literature". The representatives of this kind of literature saw rural areas as the cradle of Chinese culture and thus turned to those areas – at least in their literary works – in search of old traditions and values. These represented for them a possible template for reconstructing their cultural identities and thus a way out of the historical traumata they had experienced during the Cultural Revolution – which in part had the goal of eliminating any old traditions and values – and other prior political movements (Yeung 80). In many regards, both *Soul Mountain* and *Red Dust* can be counted as belonging to this literary movement as their narrators too are visiting different minority cultures, recording songs and stories they are being told, and commenting on the traditions and values they learn about (Moran 209). In this regard, the nature that both are looking for in the Chinese hinterland must be understood not only as the Chinese flora and fauna but also as a kind of authentic, virgin nature of humankind or rather of "authentic" Chinese culture, whose remnants they hope to find in the minority communities they come across.[15] With this, their descriptions of their journeys also represent a break with orthodox history insofar as they deviate from a representation of "real life" as it is supposed to be depicted in Socialist Realism (Kong 133).

Their focus on an "authentic life" and the roots of Chinese culture is, however, not unproblematic. As mentioned above, in one of his essays, Gao states: "I look at Han culture in this way because I am a product of this culture" (Gao 2007, 103) – Han being the largest of China's 56 officially recognized ethnic groups, accounting for more than 90% of the whole population (McLaren 459). This self-identification is doubly problematic: on the one hand, because the equation of the dominant Han culture with Chinese culture *per se* is at best questionable, and on the other hand because, as it has often been argued, considerable diversity exists even within the population known as Han Chinese. This diversity is being rendered invisible by the propagation of a monolithic Han Chinese identity (McLaren and Zhang 20). By comparing Han Chinese culture to the native cultures they encounter, while on the surface celebrating a "cultural form of biodiversity" (Dollar 415), Gao's and Ma's novels thus simultaneously put the two in direct opposition, thereby reinforcing the binary understanding of a dominant Han Chinese culture versus ethnic minority cultures as propagated by the central government.

Neither narrator ever manages to fully abandon his perspective of a male Han intellectual who has spent most of his life in Beijing, the political centre. In the case of Gao, this is reflected by the fact that he repeatedly talks about "primitive civilization", "primitive peoples", or "primitive lives" and contrasts their "leisurely and carefree" lifestyle with the "meaningless ritual of city people" (1). According to the narrator, these "simple people" are not perplexed by the question of the meaning of life, do not suffer from an identity crisis, and are hence free of existential anxiety. He explains this by stating that they have a lower level of self-consciousness and differentiation, and thus a lower level of existential awareness (Gao 2000, 202; Jian 111, 113; Luo 295). All of this seems to expose the latent superiority complex of an intellectual towards "common" people, as well as a greater sense of power and legitimacy of a Han intellectual towards ethnic minorities, finally culminating in the narrator stating, during a visit to a mountain hamlet, that "the generations of villagers who have lived here since don't know the history of the place, don't know about themselves" (42). This seems to imply that a "self-conscious being" like himself is needed to witness and explore ethnic histories and cultures, thus taking any agency to create their own histories away from the local people.[16] By doing so, he turns them into a cultural Other that is not studied for the sake of itself but rather to reinforce the narrator's self-perception, a culturalist position that is typical of many root-searching authors (Zhang 26). The absurdity of this exoticizing perspective of an urban intellectual becomes obvious in a conversation the narrator has with a *bimo*, a sort of priest or shaman, who he asks about Yi's former cruel practices of lynching and torture. When the man rhetorically asks him if it has not been the same with the Han people, especially during the Cultural Revolution, the narrator can only admit that this is in fact the case, thus for a moment losing his position of perceived superiority (123).

Even though Ma Jian's narrator never uses the word "primitive", his approach towards ethnic minority communities is equally that of a Han intellectual. He too often expatiates upon their local histories and myths and at one point helps a friend build an artificial minority village in one corner of a park in Guangzhou where city people can come to observe their traditional garments and dances (216–20). The goal of this project, however, doesn't seem to be the promotion of a better mutual understanding, but rather the possibility for city people to observe a non-Han native Other.

And yet, while neither Gao's nor Ma's approaches are unproblematic, they must still, at least partly, be seen as an opposition to the central government, because of the active discussion of minority cultures and a recording of their local histories and myths, which have often contradicted and thus been elided by the monolithic version of history created by the Party, was virtually non-existent in the three decades of CCP rule before the 1980s (Zhang 26; McLaren and Zhang 20, 23). By foregrounding an attempt at reconstructing their own identity outside of their original communities, both authors furthermore stray away from the trend of root-searching literature to reinforce the dominant culture through a detour via minority cultures, ultimately serving root-searching authors as a way back into the collective community (Zhang 26). Neither the narrator nor the author ultimately succeeded in reconciling himself with the collective community, an outcome that is normally defining for root-searching literature. Whereas in root-searching literature the "ego is being socialised", both narrators feel increasingly alienated from the collective they are supposedly a part of (Yeung 83).[17] At the same time, however, they are also unable to find a new place and identity for themselves among the minority cultures they visit in the Chinese hinterland.

Conclusion

As has become clear through the course of my analysis, not only an economic relationship but also a cultural one exists between the metropolis and its hinterland, as the hinterland becomes a potential template for a contrastive reconstruction of individual urban and collective identities. This simple urban-rural binary is being called into question; however, as in regard to a politization of life, both novels show clearly that a big difference between life in urban areas and in the hinterland does not in fact exist. This might also be the reason why both narratives end with "spiritual loss, a disillusioned 'coming down' from the high mountains and remote grasslands" (Dollar 419). Neither narrator – and because of the autofictional nature of both novels it must also be assumed neither author – ultimately succeeds in leaving the urban political centre and its implications behind and in constructing a new identity for themselves. Indeed, we find in both novels scenes in which the narrators declare their wish to leave the rural areas they reside in and return to the big city, its conveniences, and its promise of human society (Gao, 2007, 222; Ma 324). Still, their overall alienation both from their former urban lives and the alternatives they get to experience along the way proves to be permanent, and both authors thus found it impossible to return to their old lives in the capital. In retrospect, their travels through the Chinese hinterland therefore functioned as a preamble for their next journeys. Since the only solution to the impossibility of forming a new identity for themselves in the Chinese hinterland seemed to lie in continued flight, they both left China once and for all soon after returning to Beijing. From 1985–1986, Gao Xingjian worked and lived in Germany and in 1987 he moved to Paris. After criticizing the CCP publicly in the wake of the Tian'anmen massacre, he applied for political asylum in France and in 1998 he was officially granted French citizenship. Ma Jian left mainland China in 1986 to go to Hong Kong, which then still belonged to Great Britain, and later moved onwards to Germany and from there to London, where he still lives today.

Notes

1 During the research for this article, I found that most authors are using the term *hinterland* without further defining it or reflecting upon its origins. While the scope of this article does not allow for a thorough discussion of the term's problematic past, I still find it important to make this link visible and hope that in the future further research will be done on its imperialistic connotations. For one of the few already existing discussions on this, see Matthew Unangst.

2 The *Zhuangzi*, along with the *Daodejing*, constitute the two foundational texts of so-called philosophical Daoism. Although the multitude of stories that make up the body of the *Zhuangzi* are often attributed to the legendary Chinese philosopher Zhuangzi, it is unclear whether they were in fact written by a single person or several people.

3 The story under discussion is part of "The Floods of Autumn" section of the "Outer Chapters".

4 As Jeremy Brown states: "The city was the locus of economic and political power in Mao-era China". And further, "People "at the top" lived in cities and prioritized them over villages". Jeremy Brown, *City Versus Countryside in Mao's China. Negotiating the Divide* (New York: Cambridge University Press, 2012), 4, 6.

5 As Miller further elaborates: "There are eighteen provinces in the officially designated central and western regions, which account for 55% of national population but only 27% of GDP" (106).

6 While such views were often expressed in early twentieth-century literature, we find similar sentiments in the writings of many authors from the 1980s onwards; most famously among them the 2012 winner of the Nobel Prize for Literature Mo Yan.

7 This is reminiscent of what Kam Louie says about the relationship between migrants who settled in new home countries and their places of origin: "It is common for migrants to hold to the belief that though they have changed, their homelands do not; that the homeland still has true values and simplicity of life while the adopted country is too modern, too chaotic or too wealthy for the good of its citizens" (12).

8 The symbolic power of the campaign might have been further reinforced by the fact that 1983 also saw "more serious government reaction [to crime] than ever before since the early days of the People's Republic" (Mackerras 178). For example, in July 1983, "the police began a massive sweep, rounding up thousands of criminals in one night in major cities. After quick trials and public denunciations, many were put in trucks and, in the age-old Chinese fashion, paraded through the streets before being executed, to teach a harsh lesson to the spectators" (Gold 950).

9 The prototypical expression and one of the main historical literary reference points of this perspective is the *Zhuangzi*, which I quoted at the beginning of this chapter (Schneider 97).

10 See also, David Der-Wei Wang: "They reconstruct the past in terms of the present; and they see in the present a residue of the past" (110).
11 As Judith Shapiro further explains, political campaigns during the Mao era were "often accompanied by the use of military imagery. Official discourse was filled with references to a 'war against nature.' Nature was to be 'conquered.' Wheat was to be sown by 'shock attack.' 'Shock troops' reclaimed the grasslands. 'Victories' were won against flood and drought. Insects, rodents, and sparrows were 'wiped out.' This polarizing, adversarial language captures the core dynamic of environmental degradation of the era" (3–4).
12 See also, Luo: "Gao is perhaps one of the first Chinese writers to express ecological concern in his writing" (294).
13 When passing through a small town, Ma's narrator further notes: "All the cyclists wore face masks to protect them from the pollution. There are so many factories here, the town is shrouded in soot" (68).
14 As Judith Shapiro explains, there were "three great cuttings" in the history of China: during the Great Leap Forward, during the Cultural Revolution, and when land was redistributed during the economic reforms (80).
15 In one episode, for example, when hearing the marvellous and haunting songs of some quarry workers, Gao's narrator believes that he has finally captured the soul of Han culture (358–61).
16 Gao thus effectively colonizes the Chinese hinterland he travels through: "Hinterlands are at the edge of the places where history takes place, the port cities, oceans, or empires that integrate the hinterland into bigger historical narratives, their inhabitants the recipients of change but without the agency to create their own histories" (Unangst 4).
17 For these reasons, while using techniques and themes typical for root-searching literature, the two novels don't entirely belong to this type of literature.

Works Cited

Brenner, Neil, and Nikos Katsikis. "Operational Landscapes: Hinterlands of the Capitalocene." *Architectural Design*, vol. 90, no. 1, 2020, pp. 22–31.
Brown, Jeremy. *City Versus Countryside in Mao's China. Negotiating the Divide.* Cambridge University Press, 2012.
Carrico, Kevin. "Eliminating Spiritual Pollution: A Genealogy of Closed Political Thought in China's Era of Opening." *The China Journal*, vol. 78, no. 1, 2017, pp. 100–119.
Dollar, J. Gerard. "In Wildness is the Preservation of China: Henry Thoreau, Gao Xingjian, and Jiang Rong." *Neohelicon*, vol. 36, no. 2, 2009, pp. 411–419.
FitzGerald, Carolyn. "Gao Xingjian and Soul Mountain." *Routledge Handbook of Modern Chinese Literature*. Eds. Gu Ming Dong and Feng Tao. Routledge, 2018, pp. 580–591.
Gao, Xingjian. *Soul Mountain*. Translated by Mabel Lee. HarperCollins, 2000.
Gao, Xingjian. *The Case for Literature*. Translated by Mabel Lee. Yale University Press, 2007.
Gold, Thomas B. "'Just in Time!': China Battles Spiritual Pollution on the Eve of 1984." *Asian Survey*, vol. 24, no. 9, 1984, pp. 947–974.

Jian, Ming. "Life's Unattainable Goal and Actualized Meaning: Existential Anxiety and Zen Tranquility in Gao Xingjian's *Soul Mountain.*" *Chinese Literature: Essays, Articles, Reviews*, vol. 31, 2009, pp. 97–120.

Kennedy, John James. "Rural China: Reform and Resistance." *Politics in China: An Introduction*. Ed. William A. Joseph. Oxford University Press, 2014, pp. 293–319.

Kong, Shuyu. "Ma Jian and Gao Xingjian: Intellectual Nomadism and Exilic Consciousness in Sinophone Literature." *Canadian Review of Comparative Literature / Revue Canadienne de Littérature Comparée*, vol. 41, no. 2, 2014, pp. 126–146.

Lee, Mabel. "Introduction." *Soul Mountain*. by Gao Xingjian. HarperCollins, 2000, pp. v-xi.

Louie, Kam. "Returnee Scholars: Ouyang Yu, the Displaced Poet and the Sea Turtle." *New Zealand Journal of Asian Studies*, vol. 8, no. 1, 2006, pp. 1–16.

Lu, Hanchao. "Small-Town China: A Historical Perspective on Rural-Urban Relations." *One Country, Two Societies: Rural-Urban Inequality in Contemporary China*. Ed. Martin King Whyte. Harvard University Press, 2010, pp. 29–54.

Luo, Shao-Pin. "Magic Mountain and Sacred Script: A Bakhtinian Reading of the Novels of Gao Xingjian." *Critique*, vol. 46, no. 3, 2005, pp. 283–300.

Ma, Jian. *Red Dust*. Translated by Flora Drew. Vintage-Random House, 2002.

Mackerras, Colin. "'Party Consolidation' and the Attack on 'Spiritual Pollution'." *The Australian Journal of Chinese Affairs*, vol. 11, no. 11, 1984, pp. 175–186.

Major, John S., and Constance A. Cook. *Ancient China: A History*. Routledge, 2016.

McLaren, Anne E. "Eco-sites, Song Traditions and Cultural Heritage in the Lower Yangzi Delta." *Asian Studies Review*, vol. 35, no. 4, 2011, pp. 457–475.

McLaren, Anne E., and Emily Yu Zhang. "Recreating 'Traditional' Folk Epics in Contemporary China. The Politics of Textual Transmission." *Asian Ethnology*, vol. 76, no. 1, 2017, pp. 19–41.

Miller, Tom. *China's Urban Billion: The Story Behind the Biggest Migration in Human History*. Zed Books, 2012.

Moran, Thomas. "Lost in the Woods: Nature in 'Soul Mountain'." *Modern Chinese Literature and Culture*, vol. 14, no. 2, 2002, pp. 207–236.

Oltmanns, Claudia. "Rurality in a Society of Cities." *Ruralism. The Future of Villages and Small Towns in an Urbanizing World*. Eds. Vanessa Miriam Carlow and Institute for Sustainable Urbanism ISU. Jovis, 2016, pp. 56–63.

Randelovic, Ruta. "Urbanizing Shanghai's Suburban Farmland." *Ruralism. The Future of Villages and Small Towns in an* Urbanizing *World*. Eds. Vanessa Miriam Carlow and Institute for Sustainable Urbanism ISU, Jovis, 2016, pp. 228–241.

Schneider, Laurence A. *A Madman of Ch'u*. University of California Press, 1980.

Shapiro, Judith. *Mao's War against Nature: Politics and the Environment in Revolutionary China*. Cambridge University Press, 2001.

Unangst, Matthew. "*Hinterland*: The Political History of a Geographic Category from the Scramble for Africa to Afro-Asian Solidarity." *Journal of Global History*, vol. 17, no. 3, 2021, pp. 1–19.

Wang, David Der-Wei. "Imaginary Nostalgia: Shen Congwen, Song Zelai, Mo Yan, and Li Yongping." *From May Fourth to June Fourth. Fiction and Film in Twentieth-Century China*. Eds. Ellen Widmer and David Der-Wei Wang. Harvard University Press, 1993, pp. 107–132.

Wang, Shu-Shin. "The Rise and Fall of the Campaign against Spiritual Pollution in the People's Republic of China." *Asian Affairs: An American Review*, vol. 13, no. 1, 1986, pp. 47–62.

Whyte, Martin King. "The Paradoxes of Rural-Urban Inequality in Contemporary China." *One Country, Two Societies: Rural-Urban Inequality in Contemporary China*. Ed. Martin King Whyte. Harvard University Press, 2010, pp. 1–28.

Wohlfahrt, Günter. "Introduction." *Zhuangzi*, by Zhuangzi. Ed. Günter Wohlfahrt. Reclam, 2003, pp. 9–34.

Yeung, Jessica. *Ink Dances in Limbo: Gao Xingjian's Writing as Cultural Translation*. Hong Kong University Press, 2008.

Zhang, Yinde. "Gao Xingjian: Fiction and Forbidden Memory." *China Perspectives*, vol. 82, no. 2, 2010, pp. 25–33.

Zhuangzi. "The Writings of Chuang Tzu." *Chinese Text Project*. translated by James Legge. www.ctext.org/zhuangzi. Accessed 4 Oct. 2022.

10 Chenkalchoola

Reconfiguring the social imaginary of an Indian hinterland

S. M. Mithuna and Maya Vinai

Introduction

Chenkalchoola, located in the Thiruvananthapuram district in Kerala, the southernmost state of the Indian subcontinent, is a geographical region that functions as a hinterland, despite existing close to the urban core. In fact, its proximity to Thiruvananthapuram Central Railway Station and Thampanoor bus station has made Chenkalchoola the final destination for excluded and ostracized people from rural and urban areas of Kerala, mediating the formation of this community (Figure 10.1). Its peculiarity is not determined by exclusion or marginalization based on caste, class, race, ethnicity, or creed, something that is common in many other parts of India. Life within this singular space can be described in terms of hybridity, non-normativity, and cultural ambivalence. Over several decades, people who once belonged to fixed categories but were cast out for executing their free will have come to Chenkalchoola and gradually formed a *communitas* that is separate from the rest of society. Yet, in the rest of Kerala's social imaginary, it functions as a slum, an abode of criminals, and a cradle of violence.

This paper probes into the shifting perspectives on life in Chenkalchoola, as depicted in the memoir *Chenkalchoolayile Ente Jeevitham (My Life in Chenkalchoola*, 2014), written by S. Dhanuja Kumari, who grew up and continues to live in Chenkalchoola. By poignantly capturing the lives of three generations in Chenkalchoola from an insider's perspective, the book undermines the perception of Chenkalchoola as a slum, an abode of criminals, and a cradle of violence in Kerala's social imaginary. In the polyphonic world of the text, Chenkalchoola comes across as a structureless community founded on heterogeneity. Using the concept of the "hinterland" enables us to bring out the ways in which Dhanuja connects theory and practice, the personal and the political, the local and the universal, and how she re-imagines the history, culture, and future of Chenkalchoola. We relate the idea of the hinterland to the age-old Indian caste system and the modern

DOI: 10.4324/9781032617732-14

Figure 10.1 Entrance to Chenkalchoola. (Copyright Lekshmi Nath. Permission by the Author).

governmental project called the Reservation System, so as to trace the way in which "belonging" becomes a political issue for the inhabitants of Chenkalchoola. Drawing on Robert Park and Ernest Burgess' idea of the transitional zone, William Cronon's views on individualism and economic forces, and Raymond Williams' problematization of the rural/urban divide, we first discuss Chenkalchoola as a geographical and social space, and then go on to explore how Dhanuja's writing about it enriches the understanding of the term "hinterland".

Outsider and insider perspectives on Chenkalchoola

Located near the urban core (Figure 10.2), Chenkalchoola is a densely populated district sprawling over 12.6 acres of land. Its evolution as a geopolitical location and as a community was heavily influenced by the adjacent railway and bus transportation hubs. In contrast to the real estate in Kerala, most of which is privately owned and hereditary, Chenkalchoola does not belong to any group of individuals. Any outsider who reaches the community is offered accommodation and access to its resources. In many parts of rural and urban India, social exclusion, marginalization, and untouchability have been normalized and are ubiquitous. Caste, class, race, and ethnicity are predictors of marginalization suffered by a considerable section of Indian society. But the peculiarity of Chenkalchoola is that the exclusion faced by its people emerges from their association with the place, rather than from hereditary determinants.

Chenkalchoola has not been perceived as an ideal space to live in. Existing studies on Chenkalchoola highlight problems posed by its architectural space, particularly the housing. We may infer from those studies that as people settled in Chenkalchoola over the period of many decades, the makeshift housing, which lacked sanitation and did not meet safety standards, grew very dense. In *Trivandrum City: Report of a Household Survey* (1975) by P. K. B. Nayar and G. Narayana Pillai, Chenkalchoola is identified as one of the eight slum areas in Trivandrum. The report highlights the frequent flooding of the eastern part of the area during heavy downpours. During such times, the residents have to move to the nearby Model School building and camp there until the water recedes (25–29). The local government has attempted a top-down solution to these problems. In *Laurie Baker: A Model for Sustainable Agricultural Design* (2015), Saurabh Tewari mentions Chenkalchoola's Slum Rehabilitation Project. Whereas engineers and architects usually opt for "a repetition-based mass production culture", in this case, they proposed building "beautiful exposed brick row houses" without any noticeable connotations of a slum (5). Yet, as S. R. Praveen explains in the article "Living under a Cloud of Alienation", "despite the lure of new flats, all of [the residents] say that they are not ready to leave the land which has been home to them for several generations" (n.p.). Also, Nayar and Pillai note the inhabitants' strong opposition to the housing renewal project which, they believe, will turn them from free occupants of land and property into

Figure 10.2 Chenkalchoola. (Copyright Lekshmi Nath. Permission by the Author).

tenants. Having no fixed income, the residents would find it difficult to pay the rent. Paradoxically, redevelopment also limits access to food. For instance, in *Digital Economics at Global Margins* (2019), Mark Graham notes that when the population decreases, many of the ration shops, which provide subsidized products for consumers in "slum" areas, lose customers, become unprofitable, and are closed down (162).

Sociological and ethnographic studies do throw light on Chenkalchoola, but most tend to focus on sanitation and housing, overlooking local subjective perspectives and the collective views of its people. Largely ignored by scholars, architects, and the Kerala authorities alike, the people of Chenkalchoola have continuously had to struggle for recognition (Figures 10.3 and 10.4). Subjective views are often most fully expressed through the medium of creative writing, but there is a dearth of literary representations of Chenkalchoola, particularly by cultural insiders; Dhanuja's *My Life in Chenkalchoola* is a notable exception. We believe that looking at Chenkalchoola from a literary and cultural studies perspective contributes to the understanding of its significance as an urban hinterland, a unique community hospitable to those who are unwelcome in both rural India and the more urbanized sections of cities like Thiruvananthapuram.

A question of naming

Etymologically, *chenkalchoola* signifies a site for baking red bricks. From the mid-nineteenth century onwards, Chenkalchoola served as a source of labour and raw materials for the construction of mostly government buildings in Thiruvananthapuram, the capital of the state of Kerala, a fact that remains largely unknown and unappreciated. Today, Chenkalchoola is perceived by Keralites as little more than a slum. While labour flows from Chenkalchoola into various unorganized sectors in the city, an invisible contour line exists, demarcating the district and preventing deeper interaction between people living inside and outside Chenkalchoola.

Interestingly, the place has been called a "colony" in Kerala's public and private discourse. Just as the white imperial administrators called India a "colony", today the Indian residents of Kerala use this problematic term, signifying absolute otherness, to define Chenkalchoola. Yet in the colonial era, Indians also used the word "colonies" to name the zones where the affluent British people lived – zones inaccessible to people from the lower strata of Indian society. In a paradoxical manner, then, this nomenclature functions as a parody of the practice of naming the colonizers *vellakaranmar* (the white other) in the local language, Malayalam, during the colonial era. Today, the name "colony" defines Chenkalchoola as the obvious other, establishing a clear social and cultural divide between life in Chenkalchoola and that outside it. Experiencing social segregation from different quarters, the people living there are forced to question the dilemma of the conflict between social stigmas and their communal identity.

Figure 10.3 Houses in Chenkalchoola. (Copyright Lekshmi Nath. Permission by
the Author).

An Indian hinterland

How did Chenkalchoola become a hinterland? Adapting the concept
of hinterland to the Indian context, we use it to mean the abode of
people who have encountered and/or continue to encounter different

Figure 10.4 Houses in Chenkalchoola. (Copyright Lekshmi Nath. Permission by the Author).

forms of ostracism, marginalization, and discrimination. Like other hinterlands, Chenkalchoola has been undergoing dynamic transformation, one effect of which is its hybrid culture. What informs our study is the resistance of its people against the social injustices they encounter, and the numerous ways in which the local identity of the younger generations has been strengthened by their parents' and grandparents' struggle against stereotyping, alienation, and marginalization. It is worth noting that the marginalization faced by the people of Chenkalchoola is not determined by conventional Indian exclusionist paradigms like caste, class, race, or ethnicity. Paradoxically, it is determined by the locus itself, the habitat, the home to which they belong, and the place name which dominates their social identity (Figure 10.5). Ironically, then, it is not estrangement but "belonging" that causes their marginalization.

The twin definitions of the hinterland proposed by Emma Doolan best explain this connection between a multivalent concept and its application to the land and the community inhabiting it. She first considers the hinterland as "an underdeveloped or rural area locked into an economic relationship with an urban center" and then points out the term's association with "interior life and the psychological", relating them to "intellectual" and "political" hinterlands, which are said to be embedded in the "metaphorical land" that forms the spatial framework for the "knowledges and convictions" (177) that foster generation and growth. The necessity of merging the two ideas becomes more acute as a result of the shift in self-perception of the people of Chenkalchoola. Whereas they initially saw themselves as belonging to an unattended and unfettered place in a secluded social location, now they self-consciously belong to a democratic collectivity. The shift from the earlier perception to one that involves the recognition of agency leads us to define Chenkalchoola as a hinterland. The *hinterland* would then be a term that could be reclaimed as a stable signifier of a continuum between fragmented voices from the people's past and efforts at education, liberation, and emancipation in the present. Besides, considering the hinterland as a "region of contrast" (Doolan 176) and its people as representing the intertwined existence of "opposition and transgression of the boundaries" (176), the possibility of detecting "otherness" encountered by them within institutions of the trans-hinterland spaces such as school, college, court, and finally, political representation, would need to rely on existing testimonies or experiential discourse. In fact, wherever the realization of collective identity occurs and whenever the inevitability of communal harmony is validated from within, the elimination of stigmas is fuelled and intensified. Still, the fact remains that the spirit and strength for finding a joint identity and collective voice came the hard way for the people of Chenkalchoola, after a century of fighting marginalization.

Figure 10.5 Habitat determining identity in Chenkalchoola. (Copyright Lekshmi
Nath. Permission by the Author).

Communitas within the transitional zone

Why Chenkalchoola became such a stereotyped place becomes clearer if we look at the idea of the transitional zone of a city in relation to it. In their study, *The City* (1925), Robert Park and Ernest Burgess imagined the city as a series of concentric circles. Among the five zones, including the central business zone, the residential zone, and the commuter zone, there is the transitional zone characterized by "population flux, conflict, breakdown of traditional beliefs, norms and values" (178). Although Park and Burgess' concentric model is no longer applicable to most Western cities, we find that it remains useful for thinking about Indian states like Kerala, which have had a different history of development. Chenkalchoola fits into the geographical and ideological parameters governing the concept of the transitional zone. Population flux remains a basic characteristic of this space, as Chenkalchoola cannot be seen as the abode of a fixed number of family units. People have the social freedom to arrive here from different parts of Kerala. Migrants settle in this somewhat disorganized space, and while for some of them, it functions only as a temporary asylum, others stay there for good. Among them are people who once belonged to the fixed categories of caste, class, race, and ethnicity, and who followed traditional values. If they chose alternative lifeways and went against the dominant traditional cultural values, engaging in what was considered transgressive behaviour, such as inter-caste marriage or pregnancy outside of wedlock, they were ostracized by their families. Coming from different backgrounds, these outcasts moved to the transitional zone at different times and exist together as a *communitas*. Victor Turner used the Latin term *communitas* to signify a social relationship that emerges from an "area of common living" (360). He observed that in a *communitas*, each individual's life experiences contain "alternating exposure to structure, communitas, state and transitions" (361). The people of Chenkalchoola have never turned into a closed homogenous group, forming instead a hybrid community. In such a social environment, however, the proliferation of conflict – a feature of transitional zones – is inevitable. Just like mutual dependency, conflict emerging from heterogeneity becomes a necessity for the communal development of free-willed individuals. Within the logic of the transitional zone, Chenkalchoola's case reminds us that incorporating the major tenet of India's societal setup, the caste system, into a constructive discussion in a metatheoretical fashion complicates the Western paradigms, as observed in the next section.

The hinterland and the Indian caste system

We want to relate the concept of the hinterland to the ambiguities pervading the Indian caste structure, which exists both as a knowledge system and a social reality. Here, the concept of the transitional zone needs to be organically restructured in a temporal dimension, so as to trace the transition of successive generations of a set of othered people. During the Vedic Age of Indian history, society was stratified into four *varnas* or categories, characterized by a clear-cut hierarchy. This categorization was sanctioned by the ancient Indian scriptures and validated by its association with the concept of *dharma* (duty to God) in the nomenclature *varnasramadharma* (practicing caste as a form of duty or obligation). The varnas were *Brahmin* (priests), *Kshatriya* (warriors), *Vaishya* (traders), and *Sudra* (servants to the other three castes). Occupying the lowest position in the hierarchy were the "others", who existed as nameless or unidentified human beings occupying the hinterlands of Indian society. With the passage of time, this age-old classification underwent many changes and reshufflings. In the post-independence phase of Indian history, a radical shift occurred in these hierarchical positions. The "others" were repositioned through a governmental project called the Reservation System, introduced and implemented by Dr. B. R. Ambedkar, the creator/writer/maker of the Indian Constitution. In the Constitution, Indian citizens are categorized into "scheduled castes" and "scheduled tribes". Their members have the right to apply for reservations in government educational institutions and government jobs, as well as to receive subsidized grocery products, allocated through various state governments. Articles 330 and 332 of the Indian Constitution provide for the reservation of seats in favour of the scheduled castes and scheduled tribes in the House of the People/Lok Sabha, at the Centre and in the Legislative Assemblies of the State. Thus, social mobility has been constitutionally promised in India.

Unsurprisingly, most of the people living in Chenkalchoola do not belong to any particular caste or tribe. Many of them cannot trace their family lineages, as their parents and grandparents violated caste norms and, consequently, could not return to their previous positions within mainstream society. Thus, none of the aforementioned reservations are accessible to most of them. Since "belonging" to the "schedule" remains the primary criterion for receiving government benefits, including access to food, health care, education, and livelihood, those who have destabilized the very notion of caste and tribe remain in the hinterland characterized by poverty and alienation. Not many policymakers in India recognize the fact that the Reservation System, supposed to have had an enormously constructive effect on society, automatically closes the doors to those who are most in need of its benefits.

A literary representation of Chenkalchoola

So far, only one resident, S. Dhanuja Kumari, has written autobiograph-
ically about life in Chenkalchoola. The famous Malayalam poet
Vijila Chirappad assisted her in compiling her real-life experiences
into a memoir titled *Chenkalchoolayile Ente Jeevitham* (*My Life in
Chenkalchoola*), published in 2014. Being the only published autobiographical voice, the narrator serves as a representative of all the people
of Chenkalchoola, and her dreams, hopes, and aspirations can be read as
representing those of the community. The narrator states in the opening
section that Chenkalchoola's sociocultural context is of paramount
importance in interpreting the lives of people in this community.

> When you hear the name *chenkalchoola*, what immediately comes to
> mind is the image of a filthy place ... breeding ground of criminals,
> alcoholics, unlawful activities and internal dissonance ... I was born
> and raised in this very place. This book is a record of the survival of
> its people ... despite the fact that it has been trampled by the growing
> city ... weighed down amidst urban development.[1] (Dhanuja 11)

The agonies the narrator has endured are described with deep insight in
this nonlinear narrative, which helps to throw light on the multiple
crossroads of memory and both individual and collective experience.
Dhanuja's writing stands for the collective voice of the community insofar
as her memories reflect shared suffering. As observed above, poverty,
governmental neglect, and lack of basic amenities have made the people of
Choola stand together. Multiple unsubordinated voices, representing
diverse perspectives, can be found within Dhanuja's narrative, including
those of artists, "coolie" workers, housemaids, watchmen, sweepers, and
many others. The text is a polyphonic universe where the narrator ar-
ticulates an all-encompassing perspective, exploring the relationship
between the hinterland and the individuals living in it, along with its
embodiment in their lives. From an empathetic standpoint, Dhanuja
chronicles the lives of those familiar to her and those known to her
through her parents' shared memories. Through her narration, we have
access to the lives of Podichi, Dileep, Ajitha, Stephen, Laila, Dhanuja's
husband, Sajeesh, and their two sons, Niteesh and Sudheesh. She vividly
portrays their pariah existence in a social world looked at with contempt
by many outsiders. As we navigate the different experiential narrations,
we encounter internal and external conflicts.

When we think of the hinterland as a "shifting terrain" and the "land
behind" the city (Doolan 176), the political nature of each form of resistance becomes clear through the translation and rendition of true stories

and the fusing of each of the narrated experiences with seemingly hypo-
thetical yet inherently political questions. Dhanuja has chosen non-
fictional autobiography as the medium for retrospective self-expression.
The choice of non-fictional autobiography over fiction in itself signifies the
rootedness of her everyday experience. Moreover, she connects most of
the painful as well as hopeful life experiences with news reports from the
same periods, highlighting the attention given by the media to the hinterland over the decades. These include reports, printed in rectangular
boxes, decrying the criminal instincts of Chenkalchoola's youth, as well as
articles celebrating their artistic potential. The two following sections
consider these seemingly oppositional identities in relation to Dhanuja's
narration of her partner's and son's struggles in mainstream society.

Criminalization and stereotyping by outsiders

A survey conducted by the School of Global Affairs, Kings College
London, titled *(Dis)Connected Infrastructure and Violence Against
Women (VAW)*, notes that Chenkalchoola "is a big problem area" (20). A
respondent says: "It is not that I am scared when I go there, but that is an
area where a lot of crimes happen. Once a woman was taken away to a
building terrace and gang raped by 7–8 men. The entire area is extremely
unsafe. Goondas and even women consume alcohol there" (20). Though
the above lines appear in one of the most trusted sources of the academic
world, the authors' limited concern with Chenkalchoola's relation to the
already existing scenario of separatism does not escape our attention. Not
one, but several alternative versions of mostly authoritarian abuse and
criminalization of individuals are provided by Dhanuja.

Sajeesh, her partner, a *chenda* (Indian musical instrument) artist, encounters torture at a police station one night. The police strip Sajeesh
naked and humiliate him. The police officials assume he has a criminal
background, knowing that he belongs to Chenkalchoola. This incident
follows his arrest for smoking a cigarette in a public place at night. The
same man holds a record in Kerala for playing *chenda* continuously for 48
hours. There is also the case of Dileep, an orphaned boy arrested for a
petty offense, who becomes paralyzed, and is later moved to a mental
asylum. "He is from the colony. He had no money to hire a lawyer, fight
the case, and come out" (78). In chapter 21, Dhanuja shares the experience of approaching the passport office on behalf of her elder son when
he is 21 years old. The officials ask repeatedly: "Has no case been ever
registered in his name?" When she retorts, "No", they suspend the
application process and tell Dhanuja and her son that an enquiry has
to be conducted first (84). In the eyes of the police force, living
in Chenkalchoola implies that the son is involved in criminal activities.

Even a young man who has hardly any interactions with people outside his family is treated as a potential criminal. Commenting on this predicament, Dhanuja states: "One need not say a hundred times that one is a criminal. Ten times is enough to make one a criminal. There are other such youth in the colony with whom this has happened" (78).

Thinking about this experiential narration, let us look at how the criminal justice system relates to the people of the hinterland. According to the Chicago School of Sociology, criminals and delinquents are normal individuals whose criminal acts are stimulated by their environment: the ghettos or the slums that emerge at the centre of the metropolis (Brown and Rafter 68). Similarly, labelling theory states that crime is socially constructed, and defining individuals or criminals or labelling them may worsen their criminality. Sociologist Howard Becker famously wrote, "Deviance is not a quality of the act the person commits, but rather a consequence of the application by others of rules and sanctions to the offender" (Becker qtd. in Brown and Rafter 69). Thus, the deviant is one to whom that label has been successfully applied, and deviant behaviour is behaviour that people so label (119). Through an internalization of this stigmatized identity, some youngsters of Choola identify with their deviant status and organize their lives around it. Other identities, such as those of sibling, spouse, or parent, are supplanted by their criminal identities and negative self-perception. Ties with family and other institutions are weakened and all of this builds up pressure for further criminal activities and criminal associations. However, crime is an arbitrarily and re-lationally defined concept. Consequently, the duality of labelling someone a criminal and the existence of actual crime in the hinterland is bound up with its transforming nature. Addressing the linkage between the out-siders' stigmatizing gaze and the attribution of criminality to the insider becomes important in the latter's everyday struggle for survival.

Embracing art as a form of resistance

One of the issues raised by Dhanuja's memoir is the way Indian institutions and flagbearers of traditional art look down upon the artist from the hinterland. While the inhabitants of Chenkalchoola seek experience, accommodation, and recognition from the outside, their individual identity remains locked and attached not to their location but to its stereotyped image. Inhabitants of Chenkalchoola find themselves in vulnerable and traumatic positions when taunted and admonished in public. A shared memory of stereotyping relates to students from Chenkalchoola. Teachers, who are given a place equal to God in the Indian tradition, brand them as "boys from the colony" (51). The most unnerving textual exemplification of stereotyping found in the book is Dhanuja's elder son Niteesh's experience at Kalamandalam. Being a prestigious institution that offers courses on *Kathakali, Mohiniyattam, and Thullal* – the traditional high art forms of Kerala, Kalamandalam is deemed in the social imaginary as preparing its students to be cultural ambassadors of merit.

Dhanuja recounts the first day of Niteesh's university education with grief. "He was asked where he comes from" (60). Not having the practical sense to tell a lie and hold on to the transient ray of hope, Niteesh reluctantly replies: "At Thiruvananthapuram, near Thampanoor, near Housing Board junction, in Chenkalchoola" (60). Studying at Kalamandalam makes him understand the depth of contempt with which outsiders look at Chenkalchoola. On an occasion when he is late in joining the morning class, the teacher slaps him on the face and prevents him from explaining what made him late. "The teachers would also throw canes at him" (60). One teacher yells at Niteesh: "Even if I am made to resign from this job, I won't allow you to stay here. I will break your hand with this cane. I don't care if I get arrested and put in jail for this" (Dhanuja 62). But although he is pressured by the teachers to leave the institution, Niteesh perseveres in pursuing his passion by joining a modern music academy.

Niteesh's experience within Kalamandalam suggests that the more individuals from a marginalized community try to empower themselves by acquiring admission into ostensibly inclusive educational spaces, the more likely they are to encounter discrimination and oppression. We see here the ambivalent relationship between a grassroots artist from the hinterland and representatives of traditional high art, the preserve of those in possession of power in terms of exerting hegemonic control over the "other". In the specific case of Niteesh, the denial of livelihood accompanies the denial of education. Dhanuja compares her son's experience with that of a character named Ekalavya in the Indian epic *Mahabharatha*, where someone who belongs to a hinterland, far away from the city of Hastinpur, approaches a royal teacher, Dronacharya, and implores him to teach him archery. Eventually, Ekalavya is made to chop off his index finger as a gift to the teacher. Like this "othered" mythical student, Niteesh is ostracized and barred from the formal education system by the teachers for the sole reason of belonging to a hinterland, Chenkalchoola. Hence, Dhanuja's evocation of her son's experience in an unreflective and conservative cultural environment, particularly the way he refuses to have his wings clipped by the Kalamandalam teachers, functions as both cathartic and inspirational tropes in the text.

Coda

Dhanuja's memoir presents Chenkalchoola politics without proposing an unrealistic resolution. In recent years, the technical and creative skills of youngsters from Chenkalchoola have been recognized and appreciated to a great extent in the public domain. A YouTube cover song and video made by a group of youngsters from Chenkalchoola, celebrating their social and cultural background, was released recently. The video, with its spectacular camera work and action sequences, resembling those in the original song "Pala Palakkura", received instant widespread acclaim. Moreover, as a direct consequence of the effective implementation of various governmental policies, there has been significant improvement in access to higher education. Dhanuja's expression of her experiences through her creative pursuit best exemplifies women's empowerment in recent times. What we, as researchers discern on the basis of this study, is that it is not a textual and unrealizable hope that people living in Chenkalchoola, looked down upon by the rest of society, could create positive change through their own agency. Choola's future is most likely to be determined by the interaction between the inside and the outside that will break down the social walls, merging the hinterland with the non-hinterland. As Dhanuja's writing testifies, the people of Chenkalchoola are becoming much more assertive in the pursuit of creative writing and art. The author herself stands as a survivor of marginalization, discrimination, and stereotyping, having converted her own and her neighbours' experience into an inspiring and hopeful narrative.

Note

1 All quotations from Dhanuja Kumari's *Chenkalchoolayile Ente Jeevitham* (*My Life in Chenkalchoola*) have been translated by S. M. Mithuna and Dr. Maya Vinai.

Works Cited

Brown, Michelle, and Nicole Rafter. *Criminology Goes to the Movies: Crime Theory and Popular Culture*. New York: New York University Press, 2011.

Cronon, William. *Nature's Metropolis*. New York: Norton, 1991.

Dhanuja Kumari, S. *Chenkalchoolayile Ente Jeevitham* [My Life in Chenkalchoola]. Kollam: Chintha Publishers, 2021.

Doolan, Emma. "Hinterland Gothic: Subtropical Excess in the Literature of South-East Queensland." *eTropic – Special Issue: Tropical Gothic*, vol. 18 no. 1, 2019, pp. 174–191.

Graham, Mark. *Digital Economies at Global Margins*. Cambridge, MA: MIT Press, 2019.

Nayar, P. K. B., and G. Narayana Pillai. *Trivandrum City: Report of a Household Survey*. India, Department of Sociology, University of Kerala, 1975.

Park, Robert E., and Ernest W. Burgess. *The City.* 1925. Chicago: University of Chicago Press, 2019.

Praveen, S. R. "Living Under a Cloud of Alienation." *The Hindu*, 30 March 2015.

Tewari, Saurabh. "Laurie Baker: A Model for Sustainable Architectural Design." *Conference: Cumulus Mumbai 2015: In a Planet of Our Own – A Vision of Sustainability with Focus on Water*, Mumbai, vol. 1, 2015, p. 5.

Turner, Victor. "Liminality and Communitas." *The Ritual Process: Structure and Anti-Structure.* Chicago: Aldine Publishing, 1969.

Williams, Raymond. *The Country and the City.* Oxford: Oxford University Press, 1973.

11 Neither peace nor haven

Sussex as Virginia Woolf's imagined hinterland

Paulina Pająk

Introduction

"Sussex has become the Bloomsbury among English counties", announced in 1927 the *Westminster Gazette*, an influential liberal London daily ("Bloomsbury" 5). Indeed, since the early 1910s, Virginia Woolf and Vanessa Bell had rented houses in East Sussex, followed by other members of the Bloomsbury Group. The Modernists created there hybrid networks, connecting London to several locations in the South Downs and gravitating to a dyadic centre: Monk's House in Rodmell and Charleston near Firle, situated within walking distance of each other. These cultural hubs hid cosmopolitan interiors under the disguise of common cottages and farmhouses, immersed in the landscapes that to their Bloomsbury inhabitants seemed everlasting: while Lydia Lopokova marvelled at the "Eternal Downs" (Lopokova and Keynes 229), Virginia Woolf recorded numerous walks "among those primeval downs" (*D4* 74).[1] In her essay "Evening Over Sussex: Reflections in a Motor Car", Woolf encapsulates Sussex landscape into a single immutable view, "what there was when William came over from France ten centuries ago: a line of cliffs running out to sea" (*E6* 453). In the interwar years, Woolf living – in her own phrase "a betwixt and between life" (*L6* 416), as a Modernist newcomer and local resident in Sussex – witnessed how her imagined unspoilt hinterland was colonized by the suburban growth and industrial developments, becoming transformed into what William Cronon called the "second nature" (56–58).

Drawing on current research on different sites of Modernism(s), new archival sources in Woolf studies, and critical urban theory, this chapter examines Woolf's epistolary exchanges, letter-essays, and fictional works that offer not only the representation of imagined hinterland but also the critique of building developments and industrial sites in Sussex. It provides an overview of the Bloomsbury Group's activities in Sussex, delineates the interwar changes in housing, and discusses some critical

DOI: 10.4324/9781032617732-15

approaches to the transformation of hinterland territories. Then, the chapter explores the experimental textual strategies used by Woolf to capture the impact of urbanization and industrialization on the historical hinterland and landscapes of Sussex. It argues that Woolf gestures toward hybridity and modernist irony while accurately capturing the transformation of hinterland. It also demonstrates that these interwar changes eventually resulted in the creation of the operational landscape of waste – the Beddingham Landfill Site, which caused the demolition of Asheham House, one of the writer's abodes in Sussex that inspired her fiction.

Bloomsbury and Sussex in the interwar years

Not only did the *Westminster Gazette* article reveal the Bloomsbury Group's presence in Sussex, but also it enumerated the members that had already settled in the South Downs: "Leonard and Virginia Woolf are down there for their holidays, not too far away to be able to run up to town to keep an eye on the Hogarth Press… Besides the Woolfs – or Wolves, as they are more generally called – Vanessa Bell, who is Mrs. Woolf's sister, and the Keynes have houses near Lewes" ("Bloomsbury" 5). An anonymous journalist referred therein to the iconic dyad: Monk's House that belonged to the Woolfs (1919–69) and Charleston inhabited by the artists Vanessa Bell and Duncan Grant (1916–78), accompanied by Tilton House leased by the economist John Maynard Keynes and the dancer Lydia Lopokova (1924–77). These cottages and farmhouses with cultivated gardens offered regenerative spaces and activities – from long walks across the downs to bicycling to boules games.

On the basis of Woolf's early journals, Bonnie Kime Scott has demonstrated how the writer's "preference of place gradually moved to the margins of her island, where she favored hills with a prospect of the sea" (123). Surprisingly for her later housing views, Woolf's first residence in Sussex was "not a cottage, but a hideous suburban villa" (*L1* 476). In the years 1912–1919, she rented, with Vanessa Bell, Asheham (spelled also Asham) House in Beddingham, a cottage with impressive views over the downs and the Ouse River. The Woolfs spent their summers there during the first years of their marriage, marked by Virginia's decline in health. Nevertheless, this place inspired (along with its rural legends) Woolf's spectral love story "A Haunted House" and possibly also Pointz Hall in *Between the Acts*. In 1919, the Woolfs settled in Monk's House in the village of Rodmell. In July 1919, Virginia announced to the scholar Janet Case, "the house is an ancient Monk's House, with niches for the holy water, and a great fireplace; but the point of it is the garden … This is going to be the pride of our hearts" (*L2* 379). The "ancient" Monk's

House, in fact, a sixteenth-century cottage, was to remain the Woolfs' home for the rest of their lives.

Bloomsbury's early Sussex years may have resembled Woolf's juvenilia story "A Cockney's Farming Experiences" that pictured the adventures of East Londoners who moved to the country, unaware of such challenges as milking of cows or collecting eggs. The artist Dora Carrington, who then visited Charleston, was appalled by the Bloomsburians' living conditions and ignorance, as she recounted to her friend, painter Christine Kühlenthal: "We lived in the kitchen & cooked & ate there … . They were astounded because I knew which part of the leek to cook!" (Part 1, 1915). However, Carrington was equally impressed by this retreat, as she described it as "a romantic house buried deep down in the highest & most wild downs" (Part 1, 1915) vividly capturing its isolated position. Though all Bloomsbury houses were adjacent to the nearby villages, this secluded character was one of their defining characteristics: Lopokova sent Maynard a "kiss" from her "Tilton planet" (Lopokova and Keynes 228), Woolf referred to Monk's House as an "island", sometimes with wry humour, as when expecting unwelcomed guests in July 1940, she noted: "our island will be invaded" (*D5* 307).

However, this splendid isolation was threatened by the rise of new developments in the neighbourhood. In the 1920s, Woolf was frequently tormented by the visions of nearby buildings, looming over the Monk's House and irreversibly spoiling the vista, which she once described as "the finest view in Sussex: marsh, down, church and pear tree" (*L4* 220–21). A case in point is Woolf's letter, written in August 1921 to the critic Roger Fry, who painted the landscape *South Downs* in Asheham House during WWI (Scott 126): "Then, having become very ambitious about our garden, we hear that the Squire is going to build a villa overlooking it" (*L2* 476). The *Times* manager and owner of a large house in Rodmell, J. M. Allinson (aka the "Squire") remained a constant menace. In May 1927, Woolf sarcastically reported to Vanessa: "The garden is this year a miracle of order. But that damned Allinson, in concert with Durrant, has changed a farmbuilding into a florid surrey villa" (*L3* 381). In July 1928, Woolf declined an invitation to a soiree organized by the designer Sybil Colefax, offering a mock-heroic explanation: "Its angelic of you, but owing to the cursed habits of landowners, we've got to go down to Lewes on the 18th and bid for as much of the Downs as we can afford to save them from the citymen's bungalow, and shan't be back for dinner. And we shall be bankrupt" (*L3* 513). Clearly, the Woolfs' attempts at the preservation of the downs became a demanding task, involving financial sacrifices.

Since interwar Britain witnessed the unprecedented growth of suburbs and plotland developments, Jeremy Burchardt argues that the years

1918–1939 were characterized by "the highest annual loss of rural land to development of any period of British history" (110). Though nowadays, the assessment of these changes in housing varies, as they are seen both as "socially progressive, even liberating" and "environmentally destructive" (Hassan 112), they had been almost unanimously criticized by contemporaries. In the 1930s, the disdain for villas and bungalows, prevailing in suburbs and costal developments, was shared by urbanists, architects, and intellectuals from left to right (Sugg Ryan 52). The changes in the landscape, resulting from unplanned new buildings, were frequently described as "bungaloid growth" (Sugg Ryan 45, 149) or even "bungalow colonies" (Hassan 113).

From the perspective of critical urban studies, these changes epitomize the futility of attempts to separate non-city and city spaces by examining them within an "externalist framework" (Brenner 219). In his *Nature's Metropolis*, Cronon proposed that a symbiotic relationship or a hybrid system emerged between cities and their hinterlands in the nineteenth century (264, *passim*). Recently, Neil Brenner demonstrates further how the "historically inherited hinterlands" have gradually evolved into "operational landscapes", created in the non-city by the transformation of all activities, subordinated then to "capital accumulation" (220). This chapter proposes that the changes in housing and rapid industrial developments brought by the aftermath of WWI in the United Kingdom – observed and captured by Virginia Woolf – could be interpreted as the middle stage of this process, since Sussex became a "terrain of capitalist urbanization" (Brenner 219). In this context, interwar Sussex – with new developments ranging from ribbon housing along roads and bungalows on coastlines to the expansion of suburban areas and industrial sites into the countryside – may have seemed to Woolf like the "far hinterland", defined by Phil A. Neel as a hybrid area beyond the binary non-urban/urban that includes "dispersed" and "cosmopolitan" elements (71).

Urbanization of an "unspoilt" hinterland

Having found nearly all phenomenological "modes of experiencing landscape" of the South Downs in Woolf's diaries, Elisa Kay Sparks connects Woolf's landscape writings to her feminist stance: she argues that by focusing on the ephemeral effects of light on the downs, the writer "undercut the sense of power and domination", associated with the observer's gaze (20, 21). It would be then simplistic to equate Woolf's critique of rapid urbanization in Sussex to Nimbyist attitudes.

Woolf's perceptive observations originated not only in her backyard, but also in her long walks. Since the end of WWI, Woolf's strolls are frequently spoilt by adjacent new buildings, as abundantly proved by the writer's correspondence. In July 1933, she confessed to the composer Ethel Smyth: "Here I walk on the hot downs; but then I see some villa and my gorge rises" (*L5* 209). In May 1936, Woolf ironically opened her letter to the writer Victoria Ocampo: "It was very nice to hear from you, and from such a romantic place, compared with out little suburban country, daily breaking out into a new villa" (*L6* 35). From this epistolary hinterland, Woolf's critique migrated to her journalistic work and hybrid letter-essays that she used as a platform to spread her political and social views in the 1930s.

Though there were several new developments in Sussex that recurred in Woolf's letters and diaries, Peacehaven was one of the most criticized locations. Planned as the garden city by the sea, Peacehaven was established in 1916 on the cliffs between Brighton and Eastbourne, providing initially "a low-density but intrusive development of 650 houses" (Hassan 114). The town was built on the U.S. grid system, without a centre. After a visit to Brighton in September 1927, Woolf observed that in "places like Peacehaven", "[a]ll aesthetic quality is ... destroyed. Only turning & tumbling energy is left" (*D3* 156). In one of her last diary entries, dated February 1941, there is a glimpse of this town in her matter-of-fact remark, "Irritated as usual by the blasphemy of Peacehaven" (*D5* 357). The town quickly became a symbol of "bungalow colonies", used in political polemics by intellectuals and inspiring the formation of preservationists' societies, which wanted to introduce coastal and countryside planning.

In September 1925, Woolf voiced her preservationist concerns about Peacehaven in a brief mock-letter, published in the "Life and Letters" column by "Kappa" in *The Nation and Athenaeum*. It demonstrates her early experiments with the epistolary form and participation in the public debate. The writer uses a framing: the letter is cited by the *Nation* journalist, since the first-person plural pronoun in the title "A Brilliant Englishwoman Writes to Me... " is followed by a text stylized to a letter to newspaper with first-person plural pronouns, e.g., "we ask ourselves" (*E4* 290). The letter opens with an extended dramatic question: "Would it much affect us, we ask ourselves, if a sea monster erected his horrid head off the coast of Sussex and licked up the entire population of Peacehaven and then sank to the bottom of the sea?" – followed with a brief "No" for comic effect (*E4*: 290). The participatory form "we" (problematized later in *Three Guineas*) early establishes a pact between the writer and her readers. The rhetoric relies on series of polysyndeton, as Peacehaven stands for all that is "cheap and greedy and meretricious" (*E4* 290). The actual condition of a town with its "gimcrack red houses and raw roads and meaningless decorations" is ironically juxtaposed with the phrases from advertisements, offering "'constant hot water' and 'inside sanitation' and 'superb views of the sea'" (*E4* 290). Though as Stuart N. Clarke observes, Woolf closely follows here a promotional note published by *The Times* in March 1925 ("Notes"), the letter parodies numerous advertisements of Peacehaven that were published in newspapers across the United Kingdom. For instance, the one-page ad that appeared in *The Bystander* in September 1921, promised that "[t]he restful picturesqueness of Peacehaven will be preserved, and nothing will be allowed to interfere with uninterrupted view of the sea", offering as well "an ample supply of water" and "excellent sanitation" ("Peacehaven" 41).

Woolf closes her letter with an ironic vision of an escape from human civilization into the pastoral one, with its cult of "the first flock of sheep" and "the simplest of shepherds" (*E4*: 290). A similar ending appears in Leonard Woolf's account of Peacehaven, published in his *Autobiography*. On 28 July 1914, Virginia and Leonard were walking – yet unaware that it was the day when WWI broke out – from their Asheham House in Beddingham to the cliffs occupied later by Peacehaven. Leonard Woolf emphasizes that all of the places that they passed remained "unchanged" for hundreds of years: from Itford Farm to the church in Southease to the Ouse valley itself – except for the railway line. At the end of their ramble, the Woolfs saw "the shepherd and his great flock of sheep", yet "no sign of human habitation all the way to the sea" (L. Woolf 103–104). Woolf's nostalgic recollection of the pre-war Sussex landscape is contrasted with the "current state of the downs", as he perceives the establishment of Peacehaven as no less than a "part of destruction of the civilisation, the way of life, which existed in Sussex and vast stretches of England before 1914" (104–105). He finishes his diatribe with the statement, "I am not sure that one should not prefer the civilisation of the sheep" to the unplanned cheap buildings that dominated the area" (105). Both in Virginia's performative letter and Leonard's recollection, there are some traces of an attitude that Mark Hussey aptly describes as "typical of the resistance to change of those who feel their own presence in a rural setting has done nothing to spoil it" (11). Nonetheless, these texts also demonstrate the Woolfs' nostalgic mythologization of pre-war Sussex as unspoilt and immutable hinterland, as well as their perceptive observation of how this land became a terrain of urbanization.

The bungalows and plotlands were indeed increasingly common in the nearby downs. In September 1931, Woolf complained to the writer Vita Sackville-West: "They've sold the Down above the village, and its all to go in plots, and two bungalows are already being run up, and its all ruined for ever and ever … I dont see any point in living here in a suburb of Brighton" (*L4* 380). This fear was not irrational (despite the distance), as the 1931 census showed that Brighton reached 147,000 residents while the population of its conurbation – even a quarter of a million people

(Gilbert 30). Even more problematic was the "blasted villa" built by the "infernal labour candidate" (*L4* 380). Its owner was Frank Rivers Hancock, a pacifist and a conscientious objector, who stood for Lewes constituency in 1931 and 1935 general elections. Since Leonard Woolf was deeply engaged in the work for the Rodmell Labour Party, which met at Monk's House, Virginia sometimes encountered Hancock, as in August 1932: "And the Labour Party is meeting in the drawing room tonight, and I must politely greet the man who built the bungalow" (*L5* 86).

Woolf's letter to Sackville-West has its literary continuation, "The Villa Jones", found by Clara Jones in the writer's 1931 notebook in the Morgan Library in New York. The scholar observes that though this draft letter-essay "'creates in Jones, the villa-owner, a figure who appears to stand for a threateningly mobile middle class, bent on invading the countryside", it may have offered Woolf "an opportunity to parody her own extreme responses to building in Sussex" (Jones 76, 79). Correspondingly, she argues that the villa owner is based on Hancock and named after the phrase "keeping up with the Joneses" (80–81). However, the eponymous title of the essay could also originated in Woolf's animosity towards the writer Enid Bagnold and her husband, Chairman of Reuters, Roderick Jones, whose country house was located in nearby Rottingdean. In June 1930, Woolf admitted to Smyth: "No I don't much like Enid; maybe for knowing the sequel, that she married Jones and has a villa" (*L4* 180, 180n2).

Similarly to her 1925 note on Peacehaven, Woolf structures "Villa Jones" as a parody of a letter to a newspaper. She opens the draft with a journalistic stock phrase, used to express common concerns: "the refrain we catch, {at} from all over England is the same. Its spoilt now. There's building there. The view is {spoilt}" (Woolf, "Villa Jones" 91).[2] Woolf introduces a binary opposition of two groups of new residents in the country: the "unselfish builders", who are "concerned with sanitation & comfort", yet frequently make poor building and design choices due to haste or ignorance, and the "voluntary view spoilers", who situate their houses on slopes and hills, making them visible in the distance – such as Jones, who built his villa "on the very top of the Down" (91, 93). Woolf proposes two solutions: taxes for "view spoilers" and design guidelines for "unselfish builders", discouraging particularly red and white colours. As Jones has demonstrated, these recommendations draw on the publications of the Council for the Preservation of Rural England (82). However, Woolf employs here much more fiery rhetoric than preservationists' societies – she goes as far as to announce: "we consider Jones who has spoilt ten miles of the view for us no better than a robber, a murderer, & a hater of his kind" ("Villa Jones" 93). As this chapter will discuss later, this rhetorical equating of landscape destruction with a crime appears also in Woolf's *Between the Acts*.

Since Woolf's 1931 notebook contains a draft of the essay "A Letter to a Young Poet", published in the "Hogarth Letters" series, the writer may have planned "The Villa Jones" as another contribution to the essayistic endeavours of the Woolfs' press. This may have been one of Woolf's earliest attempts at letter-essays, which – as Alice Wood explains – use the epistolary frame and intimate tone "to address the public as a whole on an issue of collective concern" (80). Woolf as a public intellectual used this hybrid form to enter a journalistic debate on her own terms throughout the 1930s, in such works as the review "All About Books", the "Introductory Letter" to Margaret Llewelyn Davies's *Life As We Have Known It*, *A Letter to a Young Poet*, and finally in *Three Guineas*.

Critique of industrialization and housing policy

By the late 1920s, "the cursed habits of landowners" paled in comparison to the expanding industry: chalk quarries on the rolling hills of the South Downs, accompanied by cement and lime works (Tyson ch. 3). In September 1927, Woolf shared her despair with the writer Lytton Strachey: "They are starting a cement works at Asheham. A railway line runs round the field, and the down behind is nothing but chalk. Isn't it damnable? What is to become of us? Are we to migrate to the South of France? or Rome? or where?" (*L3* 45). In January 1931, Woolf bitterly complained to the writer Molly MacCarthy: "Sussex is a mere swamp, and the devils are putting up electric posts in the middle of our view" (*L4* 285). In August, Woolf bemoaned her spoilt view, writing to Colefax: "My view's entirely ruined – galvanised iron sheds, [Asheham] cement works, bungalows. Gods save us all. Better be in London" (*L4* 364). Woolf's letters demonstrate that she was deeply concerned about the transformation of the local areas and attempted to capture with effective phrases the industrialization observed (literally) from her backyard.

In 1932, Asheham Cement Works was established near the Woolfs' former Sussex abode, Asheham House. In January, Woolf grimly noted: "they have been putting up a great erection of girders on the ban opposite Asheham ... And Anny repeats vague gossip that there is to be a series of factories between Newhaven & Lewes" (*D4* 62). In March, she braced herself for the shock: "True, they are building the vast elephant grey sheds at Asheham, but I intend to see them as Greek temples" (*D4* 85). However, Woolf's correspondence with her confidants did not comply with this ideal of stoic composure, as the sheds spoilt both the views from the Monk's House and the writer's walks. In April, she wrote to Smyth: "My view is ruined for ever. They've put up 3 iron sheds, literally the size of St Pauls and Westminster Abbey on the down which overlooks my marsh. Hence the entire flat is commanded by these glaring monstrosities and all my walks that side, not only the downs ruined: and the view from the terrace: the view I always swore was eternal and incorruptible" (*L5* 39). In Woolf's epistolary narration, the industrialized sheds epitomize the post-war civilization, rapidly destroying the environment: "This is what they call civilisation – and its to produce cement, of which England has already more than she can use: so they'll smash, in a year or two, and there the horror will be forever" (*L5* 40). On the same day, Woolf sent a letter to Sackville-West, informing her about the cement works with yet another hyperbole: "You can't think what horrors – vast galvanised iron sheds, 3 of them, about the size of the Albert Hall, aren't rising right in the middle of my marsh. The terrace is irretrievably ruined" (*L5* 41). Though the size of the sheds diminished with each letter (from 365 feet of St. Paul Cathedral to 135 feet of Albert Hall), their surreal appearance must have been impressive – as visible in the watercolours by Eric Ravilious, who painted them in 1934.[3] The expression that Woolf used to describe the sheds in her letters – "horrors" – may have been inspired by C. E. M. Joad's pamphlet "The Horrors of the Countryside" that offered a satirical critique of housing policies in the country and was published by the Hogarth Press in the series "Day to Day Pamphlets" in 1931.

The cement works continued operating near Rodmell for more than 40 years. In 1937, Virginia sighed: "The Cement works are looking positively sublime in the evening light" (*L6* 134) while in January 1941, she characterized the colour of "the smoke convoluting out of Asheham Cement Works" as "a ruffled pink that absolutely defies description" (*L6* 460). Local newspapers reported that chalk dust covered the area like snow – most picturesquely in 1961, when the road from Beddingham to Newhaven was dubbed a "Little Siberia of Sussex" by *Sussex Express & County Herald* (6). In 1979, the cement works and query were replaced by the Beddingham Landfill Site, which gradual expansion led to the demolition of Asheham House in 1994. Due to risk to groundwater, the site was closed in 2009 and is currently restored to chalk downland. The story of the Woolfs' Asheham House illustrates how the downs were transformed into an industrialized landscape in the Woolfs' lifetime, and then into an operational landscape of waste, as the profits "justified" the use of this unique natural area as a landfill site.

Interestingly, Woolf intertwined the image of a "galvanised iron shed" – epitomizing the cement works in her letters – with the problem of housing in the novel *The Years* (1937), a subversive women saga that tells the stories of the Pargiter family. The eldest Pargiter, Eleanor, works in a philanthropic committee for the housing reform, which holds its meetings in a "galvanised iron shed" (*Y* 441n82:14, 84). Eleanor attempts to provide affordable houses decorated with hopeful sunflower plaques, yet only after a few years, it turns out that the buildings are in poor condition, as "the roof was leaking again; there was a bad smell in the sink" (*Y* 84). The houses' location in Peter Street is not accidental, as since the early twentieth century the street became a building site: its late-seventeenth-century houses, described in the press as "wretched hovels" and "disgrace to humanity", were replaced with new housing (Survey of London 219–29). Throughout *The Years*, Woolf presents inadequate housing policies and emphasizes economic gendered disparities by portraying different levels of women's urban poverty.

The critique of housing policy, though situated within the non-city contexts, recurs in Woolf's final unfinished novel-play *Between the Acts*. One of the central elements of this work is a pageant, written and directed by Miss La Trobe in June 1939 – it mirrors not only Woolf's interest in alternative visions of British cultural history and pageantry revival. Certainly *Between the Acts* was inspired by Woolf's involvement with her local community – as is visible in her correspondence. In 1940, the Rodmell Women's Institute invited Woolf to write a play for her village and she half-mockingly announced to the activist Margaret Llewelyn Davies: "I'm becoming ... an active member of the Women's Institute, who've just asked me to write a play for the villagers to act. And to produce it myself" (*L6* 391). Although the writer did not create such a play, she supported the "village plays; written by the gardener's wife, and the chauffeur's wife; and acted by other villagers" (*L6* 400). On the basis of interwar newspapers and preservationists' publications, Hussey has also established that the conversations held by the pageant audience echo acrimonious disputes that had escalated in the United Kingdom after WW1, oscillating between such topics as "the impact of modernity on rural life and customs", "the development of the countryside", and "the relations between town and country" (2). The researcher suggests that in her attempts to preserve the downs, Woolf may have even tried to contact the architect Patrick Abercrombie, who proposed the idea of national parks in the 1920s (Hussey 10).

Woolf located her fictional pageant in *Between the Acts* on the grounds of Pointz Hall, the house inhabited by the Olivers in a "remote village in the very heart of England" (*BA* 12) – and she took the downs to this heart. She opens her novel-play with aerial perspectives of the South Downs, in which the impact of subsequent civilizations is manifested as "the scars" (*BA* 3). The pageant audience discusses building developments: "'That hideous new house at Pyes Corner! What an eyesore! And those bunga-lows! – have you seen 'em?'" (*BA* 55). The juxtaposition of Pointz Hall, a "whitish house with the grey roof", with the Haineses' "red villa" (*BA* 5) echoes the colour guidelines from "The Villa Jones", in which the persona warned that "[o]f all colours, red & white are the most antipathetic to the ... greens & browns & greys of the fields" (Woolf, "Villa Jones" 91).

The question of preserved (or spoilt) views gains new political significance as the new war unfolded – the novel-play portrays a dispersed society that remains divided in their attitudes towards the cultural heritage and progress. The elder generation of Olivers, Bart, and Lucy, nostalgically admire their view from Pointz Hall (same as described in the 1833 guidebook) and hope that it would "outlive" them. Contrastingly, immersed in the devastating reports from the continent, "bristling with guns, poised with planes", Bart's son, Giles, expects that "[a]t any moment guns would rake that land into furrows; planes splinter Bolney Minster into smithereens and blast the Folly" (*BA* 39), imagining the destruction of the costal landscape in war.

However, Giles, with his contempt for "old foggies", a patriarchal attitude towards his wife, Isa, and homophobic prejudices against William Dodge, problematizes the binary between barbaric militarism and civilized society. Throughout the performance, the audience remains "dispersed", and even the moments of apparent unity are achieved by the exclusion of those who are perceived as strangers or scapegoats. After the mirror scene, in which the pageant audience is exposed, confronted with their own fragmented and dispersed images, an anonymous voice warns: "Consider the gun slayers, bomb droppers here or there. They do openly what we do slyly. Take for example (here the megaphone adopted a colloquial, conversational tone) Mr. M's bungalow. A view spoilt for ever. That's murder" (*BA* 134). The paradoxical equation of a spoilt landscape with a murder echoes the rhetorical arch from "The Villa Jones" and becomes intertwined with the extreme destruction brought by the war. Simultaneously, the "colloquial, conversational tone" adopted by the megaphone reminds how consciously Woolf drew on the private letter form in her letter-essays and fiction, fully aware of the propagandist aspects of this form.

In *Between the Acts*, Woolf connects ordinary acts of violence in a dispersed community – using the view-spoiling bungalow among her examples – to the massive destruction brought by war. Inspired by the Sussex landscapes and diverse community, Woolf's hybrid fiction offers an alternative approach to the imagined hinterland and its heritage, opposing the patriarchal, capitalist, and militaristic values deeply ingrained in society. In August 1939, when the downs were covered with barbed wire in preparation for an invasion, Woolf wrote to Smyth: "And now and then I walk off, miles away, into the downs, find a deserted farm wall, and lie among the thistles and the straw" (*L6* 352). Such refuge in the ruins of a building is a constant theme in Woolf's war letters in early 1940 when she was working on her last novel-play. Not earlier than in January 1941 and only after her second London house was destroyed in the Blitz, did Woolf try to embrace her radically changed living situation in a letter to Smyth: "How odd it is being a countrywoman after all these years of being Cockney! For almost the first time in my life I've not a bed in London" (*L6* 460). Though this letter is full of seemingly opposite visions of "England" – from London, symbolizing for Woolf "Chaucer, Shakespeare, Dickens" and her "only patriotism" (*L6* 460) to an image of a horse walking through the beech grove in Warwickshire – Woolf closes it with an invitation for the composer to deliver a lecture for the Women Institute in Rodmell, following her own talk about the Dreadnought Hoax, as well as those made by her niece Angelica Bell and Sackville-West. This gesture shows Woolf's growing engagement with the local community in urbanized and industrialized Sussex that no longer could be described as a purely "imagined" hinterland.

Notes

1 The author uses Virginia Woolf Standard Abbreviations (as indicated in the Works Cited list). Original spelling and punctuation have been retained in quotations.
2 The notation {~~word~~} is used for cancelled words.
3 See among others, Ravilious, Eric. *Cement Works No.2.* 1934, Sheffield Museums, Sheffield, UK.

Works Cited

"The Bloomsbury of the Country Side." *Westminster Gazette*, 29 Aug. 1927, p. 5. The British Library, British Newspaper Archive (hereafter BNA), UK.

Brenner, Neil. *Critique of Urbanization: Selected Essays*. Birkhäuser Verlag, 2016.

Burchardt, Jeremy. *Paradise Lost: Rural Idyll and Social Change Since 1800*. I.B. Tauris, 2002.

Carrington, Dora. *Carrington's Letters: Her Art, Her Loves, Her Friendships*. Ed. Anne Chisholm, e-book ed., Vintage, 2017.

Clarke, Stuart N. "Notes." In Virginia Woolf. *Street Haunting and Other Essays*, Ed. Clarke, e-book ed.. Vintage, 2014.

Cronon, William. *Nature's Metropolis: Chicago and the Great West*. Norton, 1991.

Gilbert, E.W. "The Growth of Brighton." *The Geographical Journal*, vol. 114, no. 1/3, 1949, pp. 30–52.

Hassan, John. *The Seaside, Health and the Environment in England and Wales Since 1800*. Routledge, 2016.

Hussey, Mark. *"I'd Make it Penal": The Rural Preservation Movement in Between the Acts*. Cecil Woolf Publishers, 2011.

Jones, Clara. "Virginia Woolf and 'The Villa Jones' (1931)." *Woolf Studies Annual*, vol. 22, 2016, pp. 75–95.

"Little Siberia of Sussex." *Sussex Express & County Herald*, 25 Aug. 1961, p. 6. BNA.

Lopokova, Lydia, and John Maynard Keynes. *Lydia and Maynard: Letters between Lydia Lopokova and John Maynard Keynes*. Eds. Polly Hill, and Richard Keynes. Andre Deutsch, 1989.

Neel, Phil A. *Hinterland: America's New Landscape of Class and Conflict*. Reaktion Books, 2018.

"Peacehaven: The Garden City by the Sea." *The Bystander*, 21 Sept. 1921, p. 41. BNA.

Scott, Bonnie Kime. *In the Hollow of the Wave: Virginia Woolf and Modernist Uses of Nature*. U of Virginia P, 2012.

Sparks, Elisa Kay. "Woolf on the Downs." *Virginia Woolf Miscellany*, no. 81, Spring 2012, pp. 20–22.

Sugg Ryan, Deborah. *Ideal Homes, 1918–39: Domestic Design and Suburban Modernism*. Manchester UP, 2018.

Survey of London. Vol. 31–32, edited by Francis Henry Wollaston Sheppard, County Council, 1963.

Tyson, Collin. *Sussex Industrial Heritage*. E-book ed., Amberley Publishing, 2018.

Wood, Alice. *Virginia Woolf's Late Cultural Criticism: The Genesis of* The Years, Three *Guineas and* Between the Acts. Bloomsbury Academic, 2013.

Woolf, Leonard. *An Autobiography*. Vol. 2. Oxford UP, 1980.

Woolf, Virginia. *The Years* (*Y*). 1937. Ed. Anna Snaith. Cambridge UP, 2012.

Woolf, Virginia. *Between the Acts* (*BA*). 1941. Ed. Mark Hussey. Cambridge UP, 2011.

Woolf, Virginia. *The Letters of Virginia Woolf*. Volumes 1–6 (*L1, L2, L3, L4, L5, L6*). Eds. Nigel Nicolson, and Joanne Trautmann, Harcourt Brace Jovanovich, 1975–80. 6 vols.

Woolf, Virginia. *The Diary of Virginia Woolf*. Vols. 3–5 (*D3, D4, D5*). Ed. Anne Olivier Bell. Penguin, 1982-83, 1985. 5 vols.

Woolf, Virginia. *The Essays of Virginia Woolf*. Vol. 4 (*E4*). Ed. Andrew McNeillie. Harcourt, 1994, Volume 5 (*E5*), edited by Stuart N. Clarke, Houghton Mifflin Harcourt, 2010; Volume 6 (*E6*), edited by Stuart N. Clarke, Hogarth Press, 2011. 6 vols.

Woolf, Virginia. "The Villa Jones: Transcription." Transcribed and edited by Clara Jones. *Woolf Studies Annual*, vol. 22, 2016, pp. 89–95.

Part IV

Hinterlands revisited and reimagined

12 Lower Silesian hinterlands

Revisiting and re-inhabiting the "recovered territories"

Ewa Kębłowska-Ławniczak

Introduction

The epistemology of urban studies has been characterized by a deeply ingrained interest in "methodological cityism" (Angelo and Wachsmuth 376–7) dominating the wide spectrum of engagement with the urban problematique – historical, geographical, political, methodological, cultural, and literary. The spatially bounded settlement type, often additionally anthropomorphized as in Peter Ackroyd's *London. The Biography* (2000) or in Norman Davies and Roger Moorhouse's *Macrocosm. Portrait of a Central European City* (2003), has been defined by a selection of features which includes largeness, density, heterogeneity, economic growth, and even subjectivity. Moreover, the city has been regarded in terms of its distinct political-economic, sociocultural, and symbolic functions, isolating the urban from the suburban as well as from the rural hinterlands and heartlands – all three located somewhere "outside" or "beyond". This reductive discourse with its hegemonic *dispositif* has been perpetuated, somewhat paradoxically, by the followers of Raymond Williams' seminal work, *The Country and the City* (1973), a trend that resulted in marginalization of the non-city and its inhabitants as culturally inferior, bland, amorphous, and therefore invisible.

With time, this binary-oriented demarcation of supposedly coherent realms – city vs. non-city – has proven problematic, notably due to rapid processes of up-building, degradation, military conflicts, political upheavals, and migration resulting in an increasing fuzziness of borderlands together with their growing complexity. The new "web of connections" demanded fresh visualization – "new cognitive maps of the ... unevenly woven urban fabric" (Brenner 218–220), a new grammar of spatial differentiations without an artificially demarcated "outside" (Brenner and Arboleda 270). The ensuing critique of the hitherto dominant spatial ideology revealed a shift towards "relational" approaches that resonate better with the concept of "extended urbanization" proposed by

DOI: 10.4324/9781032617732-17

Neil Brenner and Martin Arboleda (282). Accordingly, the non-city is not necessarily a horizontal emanation of the urban centre. On the contrary, it becomes a "fluidly mutating landscape" that embeds the urban by drawing it into "a vertical hierarchy of scales" (Brenner and Arboleda 269). Such a supraurban conceptualization enables a recognition of the "near" hinterlands *within* the urban and the urban within the distant hinterlands. This rearticulation of the urban, accompanied by a dis-integration of the traditional hinterland, leads to a reconfiguration of the latter and, as Neil Brenner and Christian Schmid indicate, marks the end of true "wilderness" (188). These relatively recent concepts encourage a new perception of Lower Silesia, whose hinterland involves both city and non-city, even though it can be also traced back to earlier concepts.

From spatial to relational and discursive concepts

The rearticulations put forward by recent urban studies have resulted in new visualizations of hinterland's hybridity and complexity. Critical urban theorists, sociologists, and geographers like Neil Brenner (220) and Kanishka Goonewardena (218, 220) have reflected on possible figurations of these new operationalized hinterlands, an increasingly abstract notion of an almost invisible landscape. In line with these relational concepts, hinterlands in literary and cultural figurations (Jameson 348–9) may become unstable sites of mediation (Titelstad 679) demanding new ways of writing. In a survey of transitional post-apartheid novels, Michael Titelstad explores five organizing tropes that include *transition, discrepancy, insinuation, ontology*, and *genre* (679), categories that engage in multiple forms of overlapping with "pathways of migrancy" (682). Tracing the new relations between hinterlands and inner-city, they trigger an endless process of rewriting as exemplified by Vladislavić's *The Restless Supermarket* and the fragmentariness that pervades his *Portrait with Keys: The City of Johannesburg Unlocked*. Landscape, in the old sense of a picture or scenery and a cognitive map, is no longer to be trusted. In *House of Day, House of Night* (2003), Olga Tokarczuk ponders the loss and recovery of a land partitioned and culturally invisible (meaning Lower Silesia), where the familiar notion of a man-made landscape becomes an illusion:

> Eyes are constructed to see nothing but still photographs from a living, moving film, and whatever they see they pin down and kill. When I look at something, I believe that what I'm seeing is fixed, but that's a false image of the world. The world is constantly in motion, always vibrating. It has no zero point that can be committed to memory and understood. Our eyes take pictures that are nothing but images, mere

outlines. The landscape is the greatest illusion of all, because there is nothing constant about it. You remember a landscape as if it were a picture. Your memory creates postcard images, but doesn't really comprehend the world at all. That's why a landscape is so affected by the mood of the person looking at it. (2003, 138)

To address the new cognitive complexity, Lisa Benton-Short and John Rennie Short propose approaching these landscape constellations as texts. In terms of *discourse*, they can be defined as frameworks in which ideas, words, concepts, and practices "take on a specific meaning … a set of widely held ideas that a society relies on to make sense of the world, a set of general beliefs about the nature of reality" (cited in Meister and Japp 6). Somewhat analogously, from a linguistic and semiotic perspective, Lionel Wee and Robbie B. H. Goh argue that the "new" hinterlands are better understood as multimodal palimpsestuous semiotic constructions, where "language interacts with other modalities such as visual images, nonverbal communication, and the infrastructure of the surrounding environment" (1). Such a semiotic constellation of hinterlands also involves memories, narratives, images, and affect (Wee and Goh 4–5) as an object-oriented verbal and nonverbal device, distinct from emotions whose understanding remains dependant on "centred subjectivity" (Terada 8). Assuming a correlation between emotions and anthropocentric urban concepts (and anthropomorphic urban representations), the recent writing on Lower Silesia the chapter addresses tends to avoid subject-oriented emotions, questions quasi Cartesian concepts (Marek Krajewski 2014:149 vs. 2013:302), and seeks inspiration in the gothic *noir* (Bator, Krajewski), the post-human and the ecocritical (Tokarczuk, Joanna Bator).

Concentrating on Lower Silesia, a Central European region, the chapter indirectly addresses its difficult history marked by a continual three-way struggle for control over its land, people, and destiny – a land whose palimpsestuous constellation (Demshuk 39, 41) the chapter views in terms of a hinterland rather than the borderland concept that dominates earlier studies. Bringing together ideas from urban and literary research, the chapter looks at a selection of mainly post-millennium novels offering pathways of mediation (Titelstad 679; Lefebvre 19, 29) between the land and its inhabitants, texts engaged in trying out new cognitive maps (Jameson 348). Within such a framework, Stefan Kipfer argues, criticism may be regarded as an endeavour to "revisit the content and form of literary texts in order to bring to life the lived realities that are refracted in literature" to offer insights into the relationship between "large scale historical forces" and "everyday routines" (294).

In her diary notes and reportage samples blending into short stories, Anna Kowalska immerses the reader in a detailed representation of post-war everyday life in the peripheral "recovered territories". In her writing, the "centre" is always far away in Lviv, Cracow, Warsaw, or even Rome. In the 1940s and 1950s, the recovered territories remained a cultural and political hinterland. The absence of texts addressing the non-existent relationship with Lower Silesia and the degree of dis-orientation experienced by the "arrivals" becomes a marker of aliena-tion, a condition shared by both the settlers and the indigenous population. It is only 40 years later that Karol Maliszewski, in *Dziennik pozorny* (Illusory journal) (1997), concludes that the centre is now "inside us" (23) as the land is awakening from slumber. The difficult process of unearthing and acknowledging the complex and often painful patterns of relationships in recent texts leads to the process of inhabiting (Ashcroft 171) or re-inhabiting the supposedly "recovered" but foreign land. Tracing connections between the newly establishing cognitive maps (rather than the official grand narratives) and individually per-formed storytelling, recent writing (Tokarczuk, Bator, Krajewski) shows how the variously displaced inhabitants begin to discover the cultural capital of the land in the process of their self-fashioning and how they develop their "ways of being" in place (Ashcroft 159, 161). While the South African writer and editor, Ivan Vladislavić, observes the peripa-tetic mode of being among the migrant scavengers entering post-apartheid Johannesburg, Karolina Kusznik (45) and Andrew Demshuk (57) reflect on the uprootedness of the post-war treasure hunters tra-versing the land of Lower Silesia, penetrating cellars and crypts in search of the "post-German".

Lower Silesia – transition

Andrew Demshuk argues that Polish, German, and Czech nationalisms fashioning their imagined communities and cultural landscapes produced narratives imposing anonymity on Silesia's "indigenous population" (42). A presumably analogous anonymity was imposed on the migrants who, having lost their homes in the East or in Central Poland, were persuaded to believe that the new land was their truly recovered motherland. The prevalent line of argument was inconsistent. Recognizing the pre-existence of a political, economic, and cultural system in Silesia, termed a *hinter-land*, the narratives insisted on its "'institutional vacuum' open to settle-ment" (Unangst 509). They referred to the migrants as "settlers" crossing frontiers into a land lacking history – an amalgam Eva Stachniak calls "necessary lies", a grand narrative signposted with the new street names celebrating the newcomers as colonists. Tomasz Kamusella's study,

Silesia and Central European Nationalisms (2007), is perhaps one of the first to "offer ... a fresh alternative" (Ingrao xv) to earlier national narratives by revealing the multilayered landscape of the polyglot society whose identity was defined by confession, class, language, and multiple environmental influences. The present discussion deals with a tiny fraction of the problematique and converges on two major shifts in Lower Silesia's history after 1945, namely the cultural landscape developing in the aftermath of the Second World War and the profound transformations following the collapse of the Berlin Wall.

The post-war map shows Poland shaped by the Potsdam Agreement from August 1945. *Kresy*, the pre-war Eastern borderlands, have been lost to the Soviet Union, while Silesia, Pomerania, and Masuria, now called the "recovered territories" or "recovered lands", have become part of the new Polish state to compensate for the loss of its lands in the East. While the German population was forced to leave and its property was defined as "abandoned",[1] the Polish people lost their property in *kresy*. As a result of the Agreement, there were two groups of displaced expellees. In many ways different, yet their individual experience was often similar – a fact acknowledged more openly by postmillennial fiction and non-fiction which shows on both sides of the border the vocabulary defining the displaced has been remarkably similar. While Harald Jähner (2019) refers to the expellees as "dehomed" or "Gesindel", i.e., rabble (45, 77), Eva Stachniak sees the Polish migrants as exiles from "Polish soil" to a land of transit and ruins (16). Anna Kowalska refers in her *Notatki wrocławskie* (Wrocław notes) to the migrants behaving as if they were just staying for a while in the new place but not inhabiting it (232). For a long time, the displaced nostalgically idealized the Eden left somewhere in the East. It was only around 1989 that the "land, frozen in time" and in the memory of the displaced population (Blackbourne 300) was no longer constrained by the collective memory sustained either by expellee organizations or by collective nostalgia. From the Polish side, 1989 became a breakthrough – a time for unlearning and revisions.

Post-war grand narratives

After the war, blending nationalism with communist ideology, grand narratives were compiled to "totalize meaning around a single foundation" (Kearney 51) with the aim of providing a sense of stability and counterbalancing the growing *mythophylia* of individual heritage nostalgia. The new roots were constructed around the medieval dynasty of the Piasts, whose minor branches established themselves in Silesia, a narrative that was easily embraced as few reflected more critically on "Polishness" in the Middle Ages and very few inspected the Latin and German inscriptions on tombstones. The "Polish-speaking stones", an often-repeated phrase, entered the public domain to provide a usable history. In her notes, Anna Kowalska refers to the Polish academics drawing maps of the once "Polish stronghold" (meaning Wrocław) and discovering "inscriptions" proving the "Polishness" of some nondescript inn while the "arrivals" engaged in overlaying the German past with new readable maps (225) sealing off the palimpsestuous past from the present. In the long run the gapped but "purely" Polish history of the region became a badly dressed wound,[2] reopening after the collapse of the Iron Curtain. The idea of purity involved also language. The German-speaking population was expelled and the local authorities banned the use of German in public places.[3] The policy of "purification" embraced more areas of language correctness, so that "wasserpolnish" and variants spoken by autochthons (indigenous inhabitants) defined the speakers as second-class citizens. Ongoing discussions on the status of Silesian as either a dialect or a regional language are continued as a heritage of times past and a desire for ethnic and cultural homogeneity vs. regional identity (Lower vs Upper Silesia). Wałbrzych (German Waldenburg) becomes a curious exception due to the inflow of French-speaking Polish immigrants from Brittany.

The systematic cleansing and production of new collective memory targeted monuments, for example, Aleksander Fredro (a comedy writer) supplanted Fredrick Wilhelm III. Not only monuments and politically charged landmarks, but also ordinary "signs of the city" (Kusznik 162, Stachniak 25), elements of "everyday life," were either painted over or removed. Kowalska's collection of post-war notes mentions no street names and makes only a handful of references to such obvious landmarks as The Oder River. Indeed, toponyms and homonyms were meticulously controlled – it meant a renaming of places and people creating a palimpsest to be rediscovered only after 1989. In *Gorzko, gorzko* (Bitter, bitter) by Joanna Bator, "Hitler Strasse" becomes "Lenin Street" to end up after 1989 with today's "Gen. Anders Street". It takes the character of Agnes (in *Gorzko*) – a hairdresser who stays in Waldenburg after the war – some time to pronounce her new name, "Agnieszka," correctly (245). Rosemarie (Alicja's mother) becomes Anna Lipiec (*Ciemno* 226 (Dark), Renaming saves some individuals from deportation – the old gardener in one of the notes discovers his grandfather's surname "Pękala" (Kowalska 255), which saves him the trouble of relocation. Cemeteries remembering the ethnically diverse population of Germans, Jews, Silesians, and Poles of the pre-war Lower Silesia disappear either due to negligence or to the regulations issued in the 1960s – 3,000 cemeteries were removed in Lower Silesia and over 30 in Wrocław (Breslau). In his nostalgic publication on Polish cemeteries (*Cmentarze*, 1996), Jacek Kolbuszewski barely mentions the ruined and erased necropoleis in the "regained territories".

For most of the arrivals in Lower Silesia, the ruins were simply mean-ingless rubble – no nostalgia and no question of memory – as opposed to the German migrants Harald Jähner describes as "brood[ing] in the wreckage of the cities like Dürer's Melancolia" (27), a cityscape reminiscent of James Thomson's "The City of Dreadful Night". Hence, Anna Richter, a migrant settled in Ełk (Lyck), in her diary entry from 1970 (quoted in Kusznik 55) praises the new apartment blocks that replaced the post-German unhomely, dilapidated housing.[4] The 11-store modern apartment block – nicknamed "Mrówkowiec" (anthill) – she eulogizes was built on the ruins of a once-elegant quarter in Wrocław (Breslau). Struggling to live under the umbrella of a homogenizing ideology – Stachniak's universe of lies – the new popu-lation remained perhaps comfortably unaware of Lower Silesia's history and cultural capital. An amalgam of the imaginary land of the Piasts, Gothic art, and Catholic baroque immersed in an all-embracing version of communist patriotism on the one hand, and an unacknowledged gap stretching between the Middle Ages and the present on the other formed a faulty, uncertain cognitive map. Stachniak writes about the intricate system of lies pervading the private and the public, the *Lebenslüge*, i.e., the lies that transform peo-ple's lives (106), they comfortably call "necessary" (9, 13, 36, 48, 106).

While the official narratives homogenized an imaginary that obliterated the region's heritage, the rising cultural capital, both the "classics" and the experimental artists of the new avant-garde, addressed neither the land's regional specificity nor its past. Several prominent creatives were en-couraged to resettle, notably in Wrocław. Among them were Jerzy Różewicz, the poet, playwright, and prose writer; Henryk Tomaszewski, founder of the Wrocław Mime Theatre (1959); and Jerzy Grotowski, who moved his activity from Opole to Wrocław to rename his world-famous company, Theatre Laboratory (1965). Both avant-garde theatre directors and theoreticians focused on universal works, topics, and experimenta-tion. Though *Apocalypsis cum Figuris* became a symbol of modern art, Grotowski was so far removed from current issues and contexts that the communist censorship found him not only cryptic, but also harmless. Różewicz, who addressed the traumatic war experience (vide *Card Index*), distanciated himself from the gapped collective memory, alienation, and disorientation experienced in the "recovered territories". In his geopoetics, from an autobiographical perspective of a *flâneur*, the poet saw the land as a labyrinthine collection of open, non-specific places (Browarny 74), a hinterland.

Hinterlands, hinterlands

After 1989 and, increasingly, in the post-millennium decades, there was a need for revisiting and re-visioning the post–World War II political scene.

The renewed interest in the recovered territories was marked by a spate of publications, both fiction and non-fiction. The novels of Bator, Tokarczuk, Krajewski, and Stachniak addressed a growing interest in the surrounding *terra nullus* whose ruins, all of a sudden, revealed semantic potential. Non-fiction included the discovery of a broad spectrum of life-writing and memoirs underpinning such publications as *Poniemieckie* (post-German) by Kusznik or multiple attempts at writing regional history, often initiated by local communities. Exceptionally interesting is the translation of an adapted pre-war journal by Marianne Wheelaghan. All of these publications contributed to a gradual discovery of Silesia's layered complexity.

Wheelaghan, Krajewski, Bator, and Stachniak foreground Lower Silesia as a hinterland explicitly and trace its status back to the German Reich with its constellation of forced labour camps, the buried past. In Marianne Wheelaghan's autofictional diary, which begins in 1932, *Niebieska walizka* (Blue suitcase), Antonia, a 24-year-old woman in 1944, is forced to work in a factory in Breslau. The entry from November 1944 refers to the endless flow of prisoners (labourers) in their garb and clogs plodding heavily along the same street she walks every day to Link-Hoffman (171). Labour camps also become a tangible motif in the background of Krajewski's novel, *Festung Breslau* (2006). The region's main function was to produce and supply what was needed for Berlin's political project. Stachniak, in her autofictional *Necessary Lies,* quotes from a fictionalized diary of Ursula (also German) referring to 1944 Breslau as a "hinterland" – once again a place of production and a source of supplies for the army, but otherwise insignificant and, according to Karl Hanke (the last Reichsfuhrer), to be turned into rubble without further regret:

> She saw him [Hanke] once more, in 1944, when she came to a Breslau clinic .... She was driven along the boulevards of the city. "We are safe here, working hard for the Reich," Hanke said, proudly, pointing to new factories attracted by the calm of the hinterland. But the refugees from the east were already swelling the streets. (150)

For the new authorities after the war, the resources and the geological maps of Lower Silesia were most important as the land was to be "assessed for deposits and drilled" (Stachniak 160). The professor who travels to Wrocław is hoping to arrive there before the looters to collect the abandoned "microscopes, scales, sets of encyclopaedias, typewriters, supplies of paper and ink ... rocks, fossils" that could enrich the museum collection (Stachniak 160). For entrepreneurs, Wrocław becomes a "Wild West" and "The land of opportunity" visited by "one-day pioneers" who come to loot and snatch whatever they can find – absurd collections of "pots, sewing machines, lamps, typewriters... ... , Jars with *Pfeffer, Salz, Zucker* on them, Rosenthal cups" (Stachniak 158–159).

Trauma and a world in fragments

The post-1989 writing opens the badly dressed wounds. The *centre* for the "arrivals" populating Bator's postmillennial novels is still elsewhere. All of them are suffering from inter/transgenerational trauma – the smell of burnt flesh (Pain 979–80) and meat haunts Grandmother Zofia from Central Poland, a character in *Piaskowa Góra* (Sandy mountain) (282, 304, 321, 322, 339). It is passed on to Dominika, the granddaughter born already in Wałbrzych (Waldenburg), a character further developed in *Chmurdalia* (Claudalia), the following volume of the saga. The smell associated with unspoken fear and evil (sometimes materializing, for instance in the ghostly figure of Maniek Gorgól) is followed by flashbacks to the traumatic events of World War II somewhere in Central Poland and in the distant East, becoming particularly prominent in the slowly un-covered life story of Grażynka Rozpuch – its fragments echoing the holocaust of the Jewish communities. Analogously, Zofia suffers from her memory of the family house being set on fire by hostile neighbours already after the war.

Traumatized and dispossessed, foundlings of various kinds proliferate in the orphaned "recovered territories" – parentless and uprooted: Rosemarie *alias* Anna Lipiec (in Bator's *Ciemno*) or Barbara Serce (Heart), in *Gorzko, gorzko*. The latter, a nameless orphan whose German-Gypsy origin we discover somewhat later, is adopted by a pair of "arrivals" who have lost their children in the Volhynia massacre. Barbara, as Berta Koch's daughter, has a dim recollection of languages she has heard – overlapping tectonic plates (Bator 2020, 180), a temporal entanglement that surfaces unexpectedly in childhood sing-song phrases of the mysterious *Wolfsstund Lyrics* – "Um Elf'e kommen die Wölfe"(Bator 2020, 644), a password granting access to her past. Orphaned once more, Barbara struggles to appropriate and inhabit a tiny attic apartment in Waldenburg, a potential place of healing. "Abandoned" by the former inhabitants, it is a place of "evacuation" (Pain 979), a haunted ruin opening up to different time layers – her own, her foster parents, and that of the former inhabitants. The dilapidated tenement house becomes a multi-layered entanglement of storylines and objects, where the underbelly of contemporary society and the suppressed pasts amalgamate. There is a sense of ambivalence in handling a myriad of "inherited" objects, the trash Barbara hoards obsessively, comparing the "German szajs" with the Polish-Chinese trash. The world in fragments, taken from different realities, blends in cheap post-German crap (Bator 2020, 14) no omniscient narrator can handle, curious collections inspected for their usability and meaning by detectives and multiplying focalizers (Bator 2020, 11).

Alicja Tabor, in *Ciemno, prawie noc* (Dark, almost night) by Bator, recalls the needles and fingernail clippings seeping through the cracks in the baseboards of her post-German house in Waldenburg. Alicja's sister teases her by saying that another German ghost is creeping from under the floor. The clasping of overlapping collective traumas and place adds to a frightfully painful geotraumatic sedimentation, and a sense of territorial anxiety. While "Tabor" is an anagram of Bator, "Alicja" invokes the famous *Alice in Wonderland* with its bizarre underground reality. Several years later, the young woman revisits her post-German house in the capacity of a journalist-detective to investigate the mysterious disappearance of children around Waldenburg, a *noir* motif blending with elements of the Gothic foregrounded in references to Gothic novels and romances, notably to *The Monk* by Matthiew Gregory Lewis, to the *Wuthering Heights* and *Jane Eyre*. The homecoming proves difficult. Displaced, drifting from one location to another or becoming world drifters, like Dominika (*Piaskowa góra*), performing diverse identities like Violetta, the female characters remain passers-by unable to put down roots. The Silesian saying has inhabitants compared to trees, bushes, and birds. Dominika from *Piaskowa góra*, like Alicja, returns as a bird of passage, her mother claims, a swallow perched on the window sill (Bator 2022, 392) only to leave – the title of the final chapter leading to *Chmurdalia* foregrounds yet another beginning. With few exceptions, the tiny setttlement in Tokarczuk's *Drive Your Plow Over the Bones of the Dead*, has no permanent inhabitants:

> Before the war our settlement was called Luftzug, meaning "current of air," and nowadays it's still called that unofficially, because we don't have an official name. All you can see on the map is a road and a few houses, no letters. It is always windy here, as waves of air come pouring across the mountains from west to east from the Czech Republic. In winter the wind becomes violent? and shrill, howling in the chimneys. (2018, 20)

Its name denotes a place of passage. When the human visitors leave, bats take up residence in the cellars (50), while deer and foxes roam the gardens and meadows.

The territorial anxiety thematized in the novels affects most of the settlers including small farmers, whose allocation of land could easily change the following year. The recollected sense of territorial instability was strengthened by uncertain land ownership partly eliminated by the recognition of the Oder-Neisse border as late as 1970, so that at least until then many would go on imagining either nostalgically or realistically their "true" life somewhere else. While in Bator's fiction the gothic, ghostly, and mysterious bring together past and present forms of patriarchal oppression, Tokarczuk concentrates more specifically on the fragile nature of hospitality and continuity where the German visitors, handling the possessive pronouns carefully, ensure the new inhabitants that the Frost family are no longer interested in "our house" (2003, 92) and show them places where houses "that no longer existed stood" (92). It encourages Marta to reflect on the disappearing worlds and makes her believe it is her duty to save them from decay. Indeed, the palimpsestuous nature of the Silesian landscape is most clearly formulated in Tokarczuk's writing:

> Every year the Germans come pouring out of coaches that park timidly on the hard shoulder, as if trying to be inconspicuous. They walk about in small groups or pairs, most often pairs, a man and a woman, as if looking for a spot to make love. They take photos of empty spaces, which many people find puzzling. Why don't they take pictures of the new bus stop. (91)

Collecting

After 1989, the new inhabitants becomes more openly aware of the invisible "subterranean world" thematized in fiction. The unaccommodated piles of "things," objects of tourist nostalgia for German visitors, begin to attract Polish collectors. Alicja's father acquires maps and obsessively searches for buried treasure (in *Ciemno*), a motif that also pervades Stachniak's *Necessary Lies*, where Anna thinks that "underneath the hazel bush the breadbox with family silver may still be buried" (190) concluding, however, that "It's better to let things be buried in the ground" (191). The search for the legendary train full of German gold and the discovery of a sealed basement filled with "real treasure" in 2022 (a more recent case, not an exception) only contribute to the growing mythophilia and taste for mystery[5] as a way of making sense of the unfamiliar multimodal palimpsest.

Objects of everyday usage, often taken for granted as family heritage, are unexpectedly identified as post-German. Sometimes a source of embarrassment (Kusznik 131, 12), they give rise to collections entering cultural and literary discourse. In 2009, Paweł Banaś, an art historian, a collector and a connoisseur, published a postcard album featuring views from the recovered territories. Entitled in the summary, *Befreundung mit den Westgebieten Polens,* the collection shared in the complex process of rediscovering the obliterated past with its invisible "natural landscapes" and attempting to "befriend" them (6). Ironically perhaps, collections tend to juxtapose often incompatible concepts of order – the order of the exhibit and the order of the collection (Mitchell 29). The collection promises to befriend but the exhibits are what Tokarczuk called "postcard images" (2003, 138). Collectors – post-disaster tourists and amateur historians – driven either by induced or real nostalgia (Kusznik 139) or by the affective intensity of the images (Daniel 20), tried to restore the disrupted sense of continuity by producing yet another thematized narrative. Collecting curios under various headings, the arrivals became more aware of the disappeared "subterranean world", the variously imagined sedimentation of things, memories, and lives that were not their own. Still, though gradually, the land ceased to be a *terra nullus*. Bator's (Wałbrzych) Waldenburg and Krajewski's Wrocław (Breslau) engage not only in archaeology, but in a world-building whose temporal and horizontal relations expand rhizomatically and unpredictably in multiple directions. Crossing the mountain range in the south they enter Prague (Bator 2013, 155–6), they reach beyond the western border to enter Bavaria and cross the Atlantic (*Chmurdalia*) in a globally spreading expansion of relations. In 2003, Michał Wisniewski, the red-haired pop-star launches his new album: *Keine Grenzen*, a refraction of the prevalent mood. The discovery of the invisible liberates and triggers bizarre cognitive pursuits and initiatives. In Bator's *Ciemno,* Jan Kołek's visions begin after he has been buried in a poverty mine for three days before rescuers dug him out, wondering what ghosts he had encountered underground – prisoners from Gross-Rosen or other vengeful figures. The biblical story of resurrection turns Kołek into a prophet and social leader.

Babel towers in Waldenburg – new landmarks?

Location on the map, toponyms, and landmarks in postmillenium fiction become specific and tangible. The Sandy Mountain (German *Sandberg*) in Waldenburg, which provides the title of Bator's novel, is a topographic feature which redefines the mining centre and grants identity to its new inhabitants. *Sandberg* becomes a counterpart of the once prominent landmark of the castle. It is on this sandy mound that the new apartment blocks were located and nicknamed Babel to give an idea of the "multicultural" crowd and to create an illusion of a bright future, comfort, and well-being that the "inhospitable" tenement houses in Nowy Zdrój failed to offer. The towering pyramid of tiny apartments was built on a mound of material for the glass industry and thus on a symbolically uncertain land unsuitable for construction. Their inhabitants, rootless like the buildings whose foundations would soon slide and whose walls would crack, are conceived by Bator as grains of sand easily blown away by the wind (Bator 2022, 29) – reduced to a labour force, physically ruined and ultimately swallowed by poverty mines. Human sacrifice is needed for a metropolis to rise both in Fritz Lang's 1927 film and in Krajewski's revival of the idea in *Moloch* (2020). Lower Silesia is to be drilled and its resources, including rubble, coal, ore, and construction materials, are to be supplied for the rebuilding of the distant centre – once Berlin, now Warsaw. Bricks from dismantled tenement houses, palaces, and ecclesiastical buildings, marble fittings as well as granite tombstones are all recycled and used for the reconstruction of the capital's buildings and the repair of its pavements (Kusznik 172, 80). Their cultural value is ignored. Warsaw's old town is invisibly but intimately related to Lower Silesia, which provided good quality bricks. While in Kowalska's notes, the Italian stonemasons "recover" the precious granite, there is no reference to their source being tombstones from the erased necropoleis. On the contrary, Bator's *Ciemno* searches obsessively for the nocturnal life going on underneath (2013, 347) so that Alicja is relieved to find an entrance into the subterranean in a pet store called "Rabbit's hole" (355). Eberhard Mock, in *Festung Breslau*, struggles in vain to project his Cartesian symmetries, transparency, and rational orderliness on the underground to become one monistic organism with the *ordo subterraneus* (Krajewski 2014, 149–50). Ultimately, the detective is forced to accept its existence as well as its incomprehensibility.

The term *territory* denotes a form of enclosure and certainty, signalling political and economic rights to the property of the land (Ingold 190), but in Lower Silesia it does not guarantee the legibility of places. If habitation is a way of being in a place, its construction involves a legible "pattern of relationships in which the place is located" (Ashford 159). For a long time, after the war, the Silesian hinterland remains a non-place, a place of passage, while Warsaw and the lost Eastern Borderlands function as the "real" Poland, whose "representation" is perpetuated in collective memory. The discussion in Stachniak's *Necessary Lies* on where Grandfather should be buried distinguishes between Wrocław, the land "Babcia"[6] did not "trust", and "Polish soil", the Powązki cemetery in Warsaw, a real place (137) where he can be buried. Many years later, in Bator's *Ciemno* the father's burial is performed the Eastern way by Albert Kukułka, a ritual left unexplained but necessary for reasons we are expected to know. Kukułka as master of the ceremony ensures a safe passage of his once good friend into the other world. As his name "cuckoo" signals, he is an "in between" born by one bird but brought up by another, a Gypsy child adopted by a German family during the war to be ultimately abandoned in the hinterland.

Cleansing and remapping

The new millennium has become witness to region-oriented publications – commercially successful fiction, non-fiction, and local history.[7]
They either marginalize or ignore the former homogenizing ethnocentric narratives, shifting their discourse towards postnational and
postmodern ways of re-telling to simultaneously address the past and
the present. In this new writing, the once-dominant narratives dissipate
to give way to individual testimonies and autofiction. New media
including e-book publications and internet communication enable
local communities to tell their own stories focusing on amateur historical, art historical, and community-oriented projects (e.g.,
Park Grabiszyński 51 in Wrocław) sometimes prioritizing environmental care for what the ecologically-conscious call "wild urban
nature". Rejecting the pan-European masterplans put forward by
city authorities, communities engage in local cognitive mapping
(Figure 12.1), insisting on their own projects. The maps create *loci* the
local walkers and users adopt as their own, *vide* "Andrzejki" or
"Jadzia's" avenue (Figure 12.2).

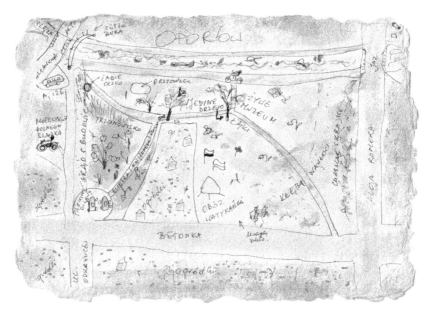

Figure 12.1 Newton's Meadow. Grabiszyński Park (fragment). Designed by Ewa
Zachara. Courtesy of Ewa Zachara.

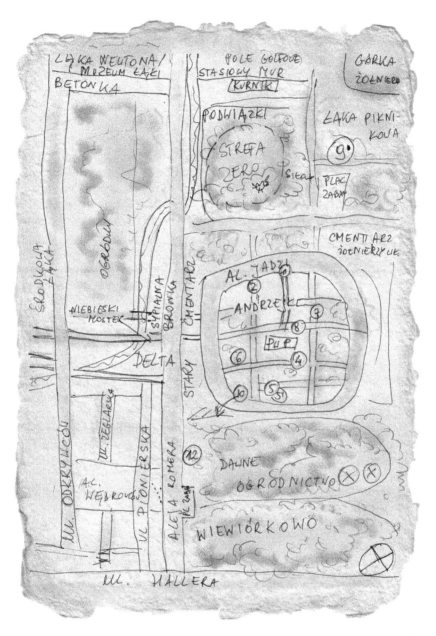

Figure 12.2 Former Cemeteries and Southern Outskirts (fragment). Designed by Ewa Zachara. Courtesy of Ewa Zachara.

Bator includes whole passages of local internet communication surfacing at night as yet another layer of the virtual subterranean and borderless web of relations. Finally, the almost biblical floods and heavy rains she invokes, inspired by the cathartic 1997 "Millenium flood," also liberate buried histories from their subterranean confinement, literally dismantling the official narratives. Both Jan Holoubek's films, *The Mire* (2018–2021), *Flood* (2022) and Bator's *Chmurdalia* invoke floods that drive out the rubbish and reveal the entanglement of both war and post-war and recent crime, institutional violence, private abuse, corruption, and what the gothic and horror would classify as a mystery – an impenetrable bog. In *Gorzko*, Barnaba's body, chopped up and put in jars by Barbara Heart, is discovered by the hungry musicians who invade her cellar in Waldenburg (Wałbrzych) – an episode resonating with the discovery of Hans Koch's pickled ears (Barbara's father slaughtered by her mother, Berta) buried in Sokołowsko (Görbersdorf). Violence and abuse (in gender rather than ethnocentric categories), symbolically sealed off, begin to surface. The flooded landscape, as multimodal palimpsest, liberates memories of suffering and emanates affective intensity which reaches out in various directions, crossing borders and time zones.[8] Similarly to Peter Ackroyd's idea of the repressed "'Catholic' strand (e.g., in *Hawksmoor* or in *The Three Brothers*) of English consciousness," the visionary suppressed by "protestant rationalism" (Coverley n.p.), Bator's novels release the "rational" protestant bodies from their subterranean prisons. Among a random collection of objects, the bodies of former inhabitants float side by side with the ghosts of Polish and German miners (*Chmurdalia* 400ff). The over-ground Waldenburg, whose patron is the Virgin Mary of Seven Sorrows (*Ciemno*), remains in the hands of false prophets (Łabędź and Kołek) driven by a conflation of religious fervour and nationalism though involved in down-to-earth business operations including the sale of relics, human organs, and human trafficking. Wałbrzych becomes a hinterland, but in a modern sense. The Virgin Mary, a mute image of pain and sorrow, ignored by the crowd who are driven by yet another imaginary ideology, signals unresolved social violence – current rather than past sources of geotrauma.

Entanglement

Both Bator and Krajewski combine themes and plots borrowed from detective fiction, gothic, and noir – a juxtaposition of ratiocination and the mysterious supernatural. Shuttling between the pre- and post-war realities, they enhance the awareness of Silesia as a palimpsest, an entanglement of lives, a simultaneous flow of events and things (Gorzko 12) in an expanding, porous constellation of places, where the over-ground and the subterranean, Friedland and Waldenburg (Gorzko 155–6) live *together* while languages, now in the plural, become overlapping tectonic plates

(Gorzko 181). Still, there are significant differences. Krajewski's writing resonates with the curiosity and imaginary nostalgia of the new collectors and tourists. The toponymy of Krajewski's Breslau is bilingual. The novels draw a precise map of the city with its German landmarks, so that the Partisan's Hill becomes Liebichshöhe. Polish equivalents appear in footnotes and glossaries as paratextual "subterranean" references. Homonyms bring together Silesian, German, and Polish names. The Eberhard Mock series seems to offer tourist guides for both visitors and new "Breslauers" who enjoy visiting the city which advertises itself as a hospitable "meeting place". Krajewski's popular novels give a habitation and a name to the materiality of the Silesian urban and non-urban, and help restore lost meaning to create a spirit of the place, which goes beyond linguistic presence (Till 2015: 301). Even though the series sponsors a tourist relationship of irresponsibility, it promotes a cohabitation of culturally diverse heritage and extends the right to the city to a cosmopolitan community. Foregrounding his strategies, Krajewski admits to a repetition of successful literary patterns like the *noir*, which guarantees a large audience. Withdrawing from nationalism, curbing patriarchal bias and misogyny, Eberhard Mock, the rationally minded detective overpowered by Erinyes, confesses that the occult ectoplasm as an affective intensity, i.e., what is beyond the frame of the landscape, does exist (in *Widma*, 302).

The need to address, re-search, and revise the defamiliarized homeland pervades the return journeys in Bator's *Ciemno*, where the unresolved and incomprehensible pain experienced in the past complicates recovery from a gnawing sense of loss. An investigative journalist, Alicja Tabor returns to Wałbrzych with the aim of exploring her own childhood, her mentally afflicted mother's past, her sister's suicide, and the cases of missing children. The missing child motif, a Nordic noir topos, redirects interest to landscape or, rather, to "the guilty landscape" (Hansen 279) as a place of habitation as opposed to the abstract, quantitative "land" or territory as "possession" (Ingold 190). The sense of "loss", compounded with a personal, self-referential nostalgia for homecoming, invites a "recherché". As opposed to the conceived space of Krajewski's cognitive maps, generating the perceived space of well-established spatial practices, the hinterland of Tabor's novels – *Ciemno* and *Gorzko* – cannot be easily confined by any representational idea of landscape genre but, as Les Roberts argues in reference to the noir in films, lends itself to a more contemplative gaze. The spectator's perception travels unconfined to any "representational idea of landscape as space that, of necessity, exists 'within' as a product of a 'frame'" (Roberts 6). If the frame as parergon indicates what is missing from ergon, Tabor's saga shows a longing for what never existed in the lives of either the pre- or the post-war female characters – Winnifreda,

206 Ewa Kębłowska-Ławniczak

Berta Koch, and Barbara Heart vs. Rosemarie, Eva, and Alicja Tabor, as well as those of the neglected and abused missing children. It is an unspeakable sense of absence that permeates the multimodal palimpsestuous landscape. It is the absence of care, protection, and parenthood that the "missing child genre" mobilizes (Wilson 2) to indicate an acute emotional deficit. Leaving behind the traumatic war experience with the hope of a homecoming as a prospect of recovery and restoration of wholeness, the novels refocus on "persistent acts of microaggresion" experienced by vulnerable women and children to define the overwhelming geotraumatic condition of the hinterlands as resulting from "insidious trauma" (Westengard 15–16). In such cases, nostalgia, or even *mythophilia,* do not serve a reconstitution of the lost "organic wholeness" imagined by Halberstam (2), but stage a homecoming that is, Malpas argues, "a coming home to what one has been and so also to what one is, and yet a coming home that is fundamentally uncanny – so that what one encounters is a ghostly spectral self" (171), the pervasively recurrent ectoplasm, whose existence Eberhard Mock is also forced to acknowledge.

Conclusions: from *terra nullus* to *unus mundus*

Accepting the perspective of the other, the ghostly, the inexplicable ectoplasm "personified" by amorphous matter, and a series of human and post-human characters including Dawid, Homar, the Cat-Ladies, and the Cat-Eaters haunting the *terra nullus* – a fairytale-like amalgam of the urban and the non-urban – involves not only a confrontation with unspoken past and present suffering, but an obligation "for producing a something – to-be-done" (Gordon xvi) to revitalize the otherwise uninhabitable, used and abused hinterland. Derek Walcott speaks about the need of special love to reassemble the fragments (27). Hence, it is Alicja Tabor, from Bator's *Ciemno*, who receives from the Cat-Ladies a special reward: Princess Daisy's pearl. The pearl comes from the charitable lady's famous necklace.[9] It is granted to the journalist in recognition for her engagement in the recovery of the lost, abused children and, indirectly, a revitalization of the dis-eased land. Kalina from *Gorzko* settles in Görbersdorf (Sokołowsko), where she inhabits an old post-German house and lets the house inhabit her. Homecoming and inhabiting involve the risk of stripping boundaries/barriers and an acceptance of porous borders, a dangerous form of exposure, where anthropocentric concepts and language with their Cartesian underpinnings must be suspended to acknowledge the subjectivity to the other. Krajewski's Cartesian detective, Eberhard Mock, must abandon his anthropocentric, patriarchal concepts and language to access the subterranean mysteries of Wrocław as more than a tourist attraction. Wildlife and civilization, the wolf and the dog, co-inhabit Görbersdorf. The old German *wolfstunde* lyric helping children to learn the hours, which Barbara Heart uses as a secret password, may precipitate the twilight of the gods (*Götterdämmerung*) and a new beginning (Lopez 210). In the novels of Tokarczuk – *House of Day, House of Night*, and *Drive Your Plow Over the Bones of the Dead* – as well as in Bator's *Gorzko*, subjectivity is extended to the non-human. The non-anthroponormative language in Tokarczuk's writing (Sławkowa 76) brings together the human and the non-human, bestows nature with human faculties, and recognizes the ennobling effect of granting animal faculties to man. Reinterpreted wilderness becomes a new category entering community projects, an interlace of urbanity and wild life – *unus mundus*.

Notes

1 Decree from May 8, 1946, defined the post-German property as abandoned.
2 Appadurai points to the necessary "system of semiotic recognition and communication" a nation-state develops in the form of flags, stamps, and protocols (25) – a spectacular manifestation of the grand narrative.
3 The general assumption was that the remaining German population would leave Poland within five years (Kacprzak 230).
4 Richter Anna, Diary P531-202, Archives of the Institute of Western Affairs, Poznań.
5 Paweł Gołębiowski, "Skarb z Wałbrzycha – przedwojenne artefacty odnalezione w zamurowanej przez 80 lat piwnicy," *Gazeta Wrocławska* December 16, 2022. https://gazetawroclawska.pl/skarb-z-walbrzycha-przedwojenne-artefakty-odnaleziono-w-zamurowanej-przez-80-lat-piwnicy-nowe-zdjecia/ar/c7-17084063
6 "Babcia" meaning "Grandma".
7 E.g., Marek Czapliński, *Z dziejów Oporowa*[the history of Opperau], 2002. The book was commissioned by the local council. The writing was started by amateurs, but the manuscript had to be rewritten and completed by prof. Czapliński, a historian.
8 Berta Koch's mother bears the name of Winnifred, a Celtic saintly woman who falls prey to patriarchal oppression and dies early.
9 Daisy von Pless has been mythologized in the post-millennium decades. The princess won a competition with Pope John Paul II and became a school patron in Waldenburg/Wałbrzych.

Works Cited

Angelo, Hilary, and David Wachsmuth. "Urbanizing Urban Political Ecology: A Critique of Methodological Cityism." *Implosions/Explosions: Towards a Study of Planetary Urbanism*. Ed. Neil Brenner. Berlin: jovis Verlag GmbH, 2014, pp. 372–385.
Ashcroft, Bill. *Post-Colonial Transformation*. Taylor and Francis Group, 2001.

Banaś, Paweł. *Oswajanie ziem odzyskanych. Dolny Śląsk na pocztówkach pierwszej Powojennej dekady.* Korporacja Polonia, 2009.

Bator, Joanna. *Ciemno, prawie noc.* Foksal, 2013

Bator, Joanna. *Gorzko, Gorzko.* Wydawnictwo Znak, 2020.

Bator, Joanna. *Piaskowa Góra.* 2009. Wydawnictwo Znak, 2022.

Bator, Joanna. *Chmurdalia.* 2010. Wydawnictwo Znak, 2022a.

Blackbourne, David. *The Conquest of Nature: Water, Landscape, and the Making of Modern Germany.* (2006). Pimlico, 2007.

Brenner, Neil, and Martin Arboleda. "Coda: Critical Urban Theory, Reloaded?" *Critique of Urbanization: Selected Essays.* Ed. Neil Brenner. Bauverlag, 2017, pp. 268–289.

Brenner, Neil, and Christian Schmid. "Planetary Urbanization." *Critique of Urbanization: Selected Essays.* Ed. Neil Brenner. Bauverlag, 2017, pp. 186–191.

Brenner, Neil. "The Hinterland, Urbanized?" *Critique of Urbanization: Selected Essays.* Ed. Neil Brenner. Bauverlag, 2017, pp. 212–223.

Browarny. *Historie odzyskane. Literackie dziedzictwo Wrocławia i Dolnego Śląska.* Wydawnictwo Uniwersytetu Wrocławskiego, 2019.

Coverley, Marlin. *Psychogeography.* Oldcastle Books, 2012.

Daniel, Adam. *Affective Intensities and Evolving Horror Forms: From Found Footage to Virtual Reality.* Edinburgh University Press, 2020.

Demshuk, Andrew. "Reinscribing *Schlesien* as Śląsk. Memory and Mythology in a Postwar German-Polish Borderland." *History and Memory*, vol. 24, no. 1, 2012, pp. 39–86. 10.2979/histmemo.24.1.39

Goonewardena, Kanishka. "The Country and the City in the Urban Revolution." *Implosions/Explosions: Towards a Study of Planetary Urbanism.* Ed. Neil Brenner. Berlin: jovis Verlag GmbH, 2014, pp. 218–231.

Gordon, Avery F. *Ghostly Matters. Haunting and the Sociological Imagination.* University of Minnesota Press, 1997.

Halberstam, Jack. *Skin Shows: Gothic Horror and the Technology of Monsters.* Duke UniversityPress, 1995.

Hansen, Kim Toft. "From Nordic Noir to Euro Noir: Nordic Noir Influencing EuropeanSerial SVoD Drama." *Nordic Noir, Adaptation, Appropriation.* Eds. Linda Badley, Andrew Nestingen and Jaakko Seppälä. Palgrave, pp. 274–294.

Ingold, Tim. *The Perception of the Environment: Essays in Livelihood, Dwelling and Skill.* Routledge, 2000.

Ingrao, Charles. "Foreword." *Silesia and Central European Nationalisms: The Emergence of Nationaland Ethnic Groups in Prussian Silesia and Austrian Silesia, 1848–1978.* by Tomasz Kamusella. Perdue UP, 2007, pp. xv–xvi.

Jähner, Harald. *Aftermath. Life in the Fallout of the Third Reich 1945–1955.* (2019). WH Allen, 2021.

Jameson, Fredric. "Cognitive Mapping." *Marxism and the Interpretation of Culture.* Eds. Cary Nelson and Lawrence Grossberg. University of Illinois Press, 1988, pp. 347–357.

Kacprzak, Paweł. "Polityka władz polskich wobec ludności niemieckiej w okresie funkcjonowania Ministerstwa Ziem Odzyskanych." *Czasopismo Prawno-Historyczne*, vol. LXII, no. 2, pp. 215–235.

Kipfer, Stefan. "Worldwide Urbanization and Neocolonial Fractures: Insights from the Literary World." *Implosions/Explosions: Towards a Study of Planetary Urbanism*. Ed. Neil Brenner. Berlin: jovis Verlag GmbH, 2014, pp. 288–305.

Kowalska, Anna. "Notatki wrocławskie." *Opowiadania wrocławskie*. Państwowy Instytut Wydawniczy, 1955, 221–314.

Krajewski, Marek. *Widma w mieście Breslau*. Wydawnictwo Znak, 2013.

Krajewski, Marek. *Festung Breslau*. Wydawnictwo Znak, 2014.

Kusznik, Karolina. *Poniemieckie*. Wydawnictwo Czarne, 2019.

Lefebvre, Henri. *Rabelais*. Les Editeurs Français Réunis, 1955.

Maliszewski, Karol. *Dziennik pozorny*. Abakart, 1997.

Malpas, Jeff. *Heidegger and the Thinking of Place. Explorations in the Topology of Being*. The MIT Press, 2012.

Meister, Mark, and Phyllis M. Japp. "Introduction: A Rationale for Studying Environmental Rhetoric and Popular Culture." *Enviropop: Studies in Environmental Rhetoric and Popular Culture*. Eds. Mark Meister, and Phyllis M. Japp, Praeger, 2002, pp. 1–12.

Mitchell, Timothy. *Colonising Egypt*. (1988). University of California Press, 1991.

Pain, Rachel. "Geotrauma: Violence, place and repossession." *Progress in Human Geography*, vol. 45, no. 5, 2021, pp. 927–989.

Roberts, Les. "Landscapes in the frame: exploring the hinterlands of the British procedural drama." *New Review of Film and Television Studies*, 2016, pp. 1–23.

Schmid, Christian. "Planetary Urbanization." *Critique of Urbanization: Selected Essays*. Ed. Neil Brenner, Bauverlag, 2017, pp. 186–191.

Sławkowa, Ewa. "*Unus mundus*. Człowiek i natura w języku prozy Olgi Tokarczuk." *Poradnik Językowy*, vol. 3, 2021, pp. 73–84.

Stachniak, Eva. *Necessary Lies*. Simon&Pierre, 2000.

Terada, Rei. *Feeling in Theory. Emotion after the "Death of the Subject*. Harvard UP, 2001.

Till, Karen E., and Anna-Kaisa Kuusisto-Arponen. "Towards Responsible Geographies of Memory: Complexities of Place and the Ethics of Remembering." *Erdkunde*, vol.69, no. 4, pp. 291–306.

Titelstad, Michael. "Writing the City After Apartheid." *The Cambridge History of South African Literature*. Eds. David Attwell and Derek Attridge. CUP, 2011, pp. 676–694

Tokarczuk, Olga. *House of Day, House of Night*. (1998). Translated by Antonia Lloyd-Jones. Northwestern University Press, 2003.

Tokarczuk, Olga. *Drive Your Plow Over the Bones of the Dead*. 2009. Translated by Antonia Lloyd-Jones. Penguin, 2018.

Unangst, Matthew. "Hinterland: The Political History of a Geographic Category from Scramble for Africa to Afro-Asian Solidarity." *Journal of Global History*, vol. 17, no. 3, 2022, pp. 496–514.

Walcott, Derek. "The Antilles: Fragments of Epic Memory"(Nobel lecture). *New Republic*, 28 December 1992, pp. 26–32.

Wee, Lionel, and Robbie B.H. Goh. *Language, Space, and Cultural Play*: *Theorizing Affect in the Semiotic Landscape*. Cambridge UP, 2020.

Westengard, Laura. *Gothic Queer Culture. Marginalized Communities* and the *Ghosts* of *Insidious Trauma*. University of Nebrasca Press, 2019.

Wheelaghan, Marianne. *Niebieska walizka. Pożegnanie z Breslau*. 2010. Translated by Marcin Melon. Canon Silesiae, 2021.

Wilson, Emma. *Cinema's Missing Children*. Wallflower Press, 2003.

13 "There was nothing"

Return journeys and the creation of (multi)directional postmemories in twenty-first-century anglophone novels

Mona Becker

The National Socialist persecution and extermination of the European Jews saw not only more than 6 million murdered and a whole way of life irretrievably lost, but entire villages depopulated and millions displaced. After the fall of the so-called Iron Curtain, survivors and descendants seized the opportunity to return to those sites of former belonging and destruction.

In this essay, I discuss the correlation between the depiction of such return journeys, the creation of what Marianne Hirsch has termed *post-memory*, and notions of complicity in three novels written at the turn of the century. Rachel Seiffert's debut *The Dark Room* (2001) examines issues of perpetrator memory and complicity, moving from 1940s Berlin through war-torn German landscapes to a postgenerational German's search for the traces of his grandfather's crimes in 1990s Belarus. In Lisa Appignanesi's novel *The Memory Man* (2004), Shoah survivor and memory researcher Bruno Lind goes on a cross-European road trip chasing his own fragmented and suppressed memories of World War II with his adopted African American daughter and two Polish travel companions of the "generation after". While Appignanesi's novel moves from the "present tense" of the early 2000s to the various "past tenses" of Bruno's recollections, Jonathan Safran Foer's *Everything Is Illuminated* (2003), fictionalizes the "nothing" the author encountered on his own return journey to Ukraine in the late 1990s, seeks to repopulate and reclaim lost places and memories with an act of creative recall that spans centuries.

Emma Doolan defines "hinterland" "as a conceptual space imbued with connotations of imperial possession, othering, and marginality" via the literal definition given by the *Oxford Dictionaries Online* of hinterland as "a term meaning literally the 'land behind' or a region 'lying beyond what is visible or known'" (175). All three novels

DOI: 10.4324/9781032617732-18

discussed here position the places of their respective returns as "dark, submerged" (Hoffman 203) sites of an unknown and unknowable past – hinterlands in both the literal and figurative use of the term proffered by Doolan. The term *hinterland* with its connotations of marginality and "unknowability" is, therefore, useful when working with the already-established relationship between memory and place. Drawing on Marianne Hirsch's concept of postmemory and Michael Rothberg's multidirectional memory, I investigate how these three novels present and fill the "nothing" of their various hinterlands through the collaborative sharing of memories. I will begin with a brief overview of the main concepts of this essay, linking the hinterland with memory via Eva Hoffman's "era of returns". I will then reflect on three aspects of the return journeys presented in the novels: beginning with the notion of "marginality", I will consider the return journey as a move from a (perceived) centre to its (equally perceived) periphery, focusing on Seiffert's *The Dark Room*. I will then examine the sense of absence or "nothingness" found at the site of the return, particularly haunting in *Everything Is Illuminated*. In the final section, I will consider the links between questions of implications and the construction of (post) memory as a collaborative effort, as presented especially in *The Memory Man*.

Hinterlands, memory, and the "era of returns"

The postgenerational experience is dominated by inherited narratives of trauma (Hirsch 2012, 3–5). As the effects of trauma are not limited to the individual or generation who experienced them, as Marianne Hirsch points out, postmemory describes a connection with the traumatic experiences of others, but, as she elaborates, one that is "not actually mediated by recall, but by imaginative investment, projection, and creation" (2019, 172). Postmemory therefore, according to Hirsch, expands and complicates the categories of communicative and cultural memory as defined by Aleida and Jan Assmann, allowing especially for the impact of the rupture, destruction, and erasure of "carriers of memory" that accompanied the National Socialist genocide:

> Postmemorial work, [...] strives to *reactivate* and *re-embody* more distant political and cultural memorial structures by reinvesting them with resonant individual and familial forms of mediation and aesthetic expression. In these ways, less directly affected participants can become engaged in the generation of postmemory that can persist even after all participants and even their familial descendants are gone. (Hirsch 2012, 33)

Postmemory's capacity for creative investment and its awareness of the experiences of others also resonate with Michael Rothberg's concept of multidirectional memory. Posing the question of how it is possible to remember responsibly in a globalized world, Rothberg envisions a collective memory that is not competitive, but "subject to ongoing negotiation, cross-referencing, and borrowing" (2009, 3). For him, such multidirectional memory also includes a willingness to engage with one's own potential implication as "[m]ultidirectional memory describes the way collective memories emerge in dialogue with each other and with the conditions of the present; such dialogue can create solidarity even as it reveals implication" (2019, 20).

The construction of memories of any kind is closely linked to the concept of place. Sarah De Nardi points out that "[p]lace is certainly one way that remembrance is attached to the visible, tangible world", even though "the situating of memory in a meaningful space, does not necessarily lead to an objective or streamlined way of remembering" (18). Eva Hoffman describes the desire to return to such a "meaningful space" for purposes of remembrance expressed in the surge of "return journeys" by survivors of the Shoah or their descendants after the end of the Cold War:

> With the era of memory, the era of returns. The lifting of the Iron Curtain has made it possible to enter Eastern Europe with new ease, and ever since, people who have not set foot in countries of their origin for decades have been coming back in numbers to see, to remember, to test their fantasized images of 'the Old Country' or to confirm their prejudices. Children of survivors and others as well make their 'returns' to lands they have never seen and that have remained, in postwar Jewish imagination, a dark, submerged Atlantis. (203)

While she makes a strong connection between what she calls the era of memory and the era of returns, her description resonates equally strongly with the definitions of hinterland given by Emma Dolan: the return journey takes the travellers to "lands they have never seen", that have been laying "behind" the so-called Iron Curtain. For the travellers, the places they seek out are also never entirely in the present; they are "dark" and "submerged", their meaning and significance entangled with an often unknowable and irrevocably lost past. The destinations of those "return journeys" could therefore be described as fantasized hinterlands of the past. As such, with its potential for creative recall, it is not surprising that the return journey has gathered a "literature of its own", as Hoffman also points out (203–204).

The three novels I wish to discuss today all utilize return journeys in their creation of postmemories of National Socialist genocidal violence.

Rachel Seiffert's debut novel *The Dark Room* traces the development of collective memory of the Shoah in Germany through the trope of photography which features in each of the distinct three stories making up the novel. It is the only one of the three novels that is explicitly concerned with perpetrator memory. Jonathan Safran Foer's debut *Everything is Illuminated* has become exemplary of the literature of the return, as Aarons and Berger point out: "Foer's novel is part of the return narrative structure characteristic of third-generation Holocaust representation" (139). It is based on Foer's own journey to unearth his family's roots in Ukraine, depicting the joint journey of discovery by a fictionalized author and his Ukrainian guides. Finally, Lisa Appignanesi's novel *The Memory Man* examines the formation of memory and how it can be shared with others. Survivor and memory researcher Bruno Lind goes on an impromptu road trip to southeast Poland with his adopted African-American daughter and two Polish second-generation travel companions. Appignanesi's novel is not only the only novel discussed here that is not a debut but also the only one with a first-generational protagonist who once knew the place he now returns to.

In all three texts, the postmemorial project hinges on the return journey to the novels' various hinterlands as a collaborative effort that also "facilitate[s] awareness of implication in the present as well as the past" (Rothberg 2019, 20). In all three novels, a return journey takes the protagonists to rural and isolated places. In these "dark, submerged" hinterlands, memory is located underground and hidden, having been erased from and seemingly forgotten on the surface.

From "Centre" to "Periphery": *The Dark Room*

In all three of these novels, the protagonists are taken on a journey to a hinterland in the literal meaning of "the land behind", in the case of these novels, the land behind the former Iron Curtain. Those hinterlands can be both places of past belonging and sites of atrocity, as in the case of the Jewish protagonists in Foer's and Appignanesi's novels, who travel to contemporary Ukraine and Poland, respectively, to revisit the places of their families' past, or present sites of implication in past crimes, as in *The Dark Room*'s Belarus. In all three novels, the move to the "land behind" also reflects on notions of urbanized, knowledgeable centre and rural, ignorant periphery, and their interdependence. Within the context of the end of the Cold War, the novels therefore also reflect on global political changes following the collapse of the bilateral world order.

In *Everything is Illuminated*, the "hero", fictional author Jonathan Safran Foer, travels from the United States to Ukraine to find the shtetl Trachimbrod where his grandfather had escaped from a German mass execution during World War II. He is accompanied on his trip by Alex and his grandfather, whose family business, the travel agency Heritage Touring, caters to "Jewish people, like the hero, who have cravings to leave that ennobled country America and visit humble towns in Poland and Ukraine" (Foer 3). Alex repeatedly comments in this manner on the discrepancy between "that ennobled country America" and the "humble towns" of his home country, initially positioning Ukraine as a peripheral hinterland to the new global superpower. But his comments also destabilize such notions of centre and periphery, as Alex repeatedly compares his home Odessa to places in the USA and himself feels extremely out of place in the Ukrainian countryside, because, as he notes

> I had never talked to people like that, poor farming people, and similar to most people from Odessa, I speak a fusion of Russian and Ukrainian, and they spoke only Ukrainian, and … people who speak only Ukrainian sometimes hate people who speak a fusion of Russian and Ukrainian, because very often people who speak a fusion of Russian and Ukrainian come from the cities and think they are superior to people who speak only Ukrainian, who often come from the fields. (Foer 112)

These observations serve to further complicate and diversify otherwise simplifying notions of a unified and universal global hinterland.

In *The Memory Man*, Bruno Lind, who lives in London, attends a conference on memory in Vienna, where he grew up, before embarking on a journey to the Polish countryside where he survived the war years. One of his Polish travel companions, Irina, repeatedly expresses unease with the 'Western' gaze on and perception of her home country, reflecting on the "Eastern European" chip on her shoulder. In Appignanesi's novel, it is a defining feature of the peripheral hinterland that it is both "the land behind" as well as an unknown and unknowable region. The main character himself contemplates this qualitative difference between his daily commute in London and "real journeys" like the one he is about to undertake: "It had been an age since he had spent more than a necessary hour on a train. And those weren't real journeys. The one before him was" (Appignanesi 57). As in *Everything is Illuminated*, Bruno's journey is "real" not only because of the distance he travels from "centre" to "periphery", but because of the scope of the task he encounters in this "land beyond": the unearthing of memory.

In *The Dark Room*, the move from "centre" to "periphery" occurs on a number of levels. First, in the way the novel is structured into three, seemingly disconnected stories. It moves from the 1940s, in which bystander Helmut witnesses the rise and fall of National Socialism in the

German capital via a hectic journey through war-torn Germany from rural Bavaria to Hamburg taken by Lore and her siblings after the arrest of their National Socialist parents to contemporary history teacher Micha, who travels from Frankfurt to rural Belarus in an attempt to unearth his grandfather's actions during the war.

The arc from 1940s Berlin to a rural Belarussian village in the late 1990s is not only a spatial and temporal one from the centre of the National Socialist power to the remaining traces of its genocidal violence on the fringes of its reach but also details the development and transfer of German collective memory: in the first story, Helmut takes pictures of a deportation in Berlin which he later destroys because they "convey none of the chaos and cruelty" (Seiffert 40), which moved him to document the scene. While he still deems the photograph an unworthy witness, the second story opens with Lore, who "stocks the stove from the piles on the table and watches Mutti sorting through the photo album" (Seiffert 75–76) in order to identify and destroy those family pictures already considered incriminating. On her ensuing journey, Lore encounters photographs of concentration camp victims, but she struggles to read these pictures, thinking they must be fakes.

Micha, in the final part, has no such issues when encountering historical photography, he is highly apt at placing it. But as a result of the development outlined in the previous stories, he is unable to reconcile the memory and image of his loving grandfather from his grandmother's carefully curated family albums with the missing picture of his grandfather as an SS officer noting that while he can claim and identify the grandfather, his "Opa" from the photographs, *"[t]here are no pictures of him holding a gun to someone's head, but I am sure he did that, and pulled the trigger, too"* (Seiffert 370–371). In order to close this gap, Micha eventually travels from Frankfurt to the Belarussian countryside where his grandfather had been stationed. This slightly different kind of return journey sees Micha thus also return, albeit not to a place of former belonging, but to the site of former crimes he finds himself still implicated in. He is eventually directed to a local man, Kolesnik, who is willing to discuss the occupation with him. During their conversations, it is revealed that Kolesnik not only "remember[s] the Germans" (Seiffert 276), but that he has been a collaborator who can finally confirm to Micha what he has been suspecting about his grandfather: "He killed people. I am sorry, Michael. He killed Jews and Belarussian people" (Seiffert 362). Even though Micha had access to his grandmother's family albums and historical archives and records in Frankfurt, he needs to hear the confirmation of his grandfather's crimes in the – for him – precarious and peripheral space where they took place, although even Kolesnik cannot give the ultimate validation that Micha craves – he "knows" of Micha's grandfather's crimes, but he, too, did not see him commit them (Seiffert 362).

While the return journey thus enables insights and access to memory, it does not grant certainty. The hinterlands to which the protagonists return in these novels are uncooperative and unrecognizable landscapes that withhold secure, absolute knowledge of the past.

Landscapes of nothing: *Everything is Illuminated*

The second definition of hinterland describes it as "laying beyond what is visible or known", and in all three novels, it is the "land" in those hinterlands and landscapes that contains memory seemingly lost on the surface. All three novels thus include landscapes that are the covered up and forgotten sites of past terror and, in the case of the Jewish return journeys, also of past belonging, which need to be "unearthed" to be made "visible or known".

After the collaborator's death in *The Dark Room*, Micha returns to Belarus once more. Kolesnik's widow, Elena, with whom Micha cannot communicate because neither speaks the other's language, takes him to a clearing in a forest where she mimes shooting, revealing the clearing to be the site of a mass execution. This former execution site is unmarked with no visible traces remaining, and while the widow appears to try to perform an act of grieving there, Micha quickly flees the scene, spooked by this "clearing that is also a grave" (Seiffert 386). While Elena's intentions with her re-enactment of both execution and mourning remain unclear, Micha finds himself unable to participate or even stay with her as he "[c]an't stand here on this soft ground, on this grass and moss" (Seiffert 387). There is no grand recognition or reconciliation; the site remains unmarked and whatever Elena knows about the crimes committed there cannot be shared with Micha. After he escapes from the clearing, she takes him to the train station, where she speaks at length to him through the window of his train, but he fails to understand her: "The few words he might have recognized are smothered by her tears. She speaks and speaks, gripping Micha's hands, knowing he doesn't understand" (Seiffert 387–388). When the train leaves, Micha "knows why she [...] took him there", but that knowledge is a "terrible thought catching up with him" (Seiffert 388), almost more of a self-realization rather than communicated shared knowledge. What the "land" in this particular hinterland knows about the past remains ambivalent and invisible – at least to the visitor.

While in *The Dark Room*, locals like Elena and Kolesnik appear to attempt to communicate their memories and knowledge to their visitor to some extent, in both *The Memory Man* and *Everything is Illuminated*, the past world has doubly disappeared, to use an observation by

Audrey Bardizbanian (46). In *The Memory Man*, Bruno does find the site
of his childhood home where he had witnessed the murder of his mother
and sister in 1942, but only with great difficulty, as "[n]o one they had
asked had been able to help either. It was as if the landscape itself
had shifted, taking with it distance and a sense of measure. So he didn't
know where to begin. [...] He no longer even knew why it had come into
his head that he needed to find the house" (Appignanesi 167). When they
finally find it, he struggles to recognize the house, until his memory is
triggered by "a gnarled old apple tree that had been half-hidden"
(Appignanesi 173), which is where he buried his family in unmarked
graves. Bruno originally opposes his daughter's idea to have their graves
marked now, objecting "[i]n this wilderness? Where no one was kind to
them?" (Appignanesi 188), but she nonetheless makes the current occupants of the house promise to erect a stone on the site of the graves.
However, the protagonists leave the place and do not return to it again,
so this marker is never revisited by the narrative.

In *Everything is Illuminated*, the village Trachimbrod has not only been
completely destroyed by the Germans, its name removed from maps, but
the existence of the town seems to have been erased from local memory,
too. Alex, the narrator of the journey part of the novel, notes that "[i]t was
seeming as if we were in the wrong country or the wrong century, or as
if Trachimbrod had disappeared, and so had the memory of it" (Foer 115).

There are, however, remains and traces to be found of the town and its
inhabitants. A sole survivor keeps clothes laying in her yard, "in abnormal
arrangements, and they appeared like the clothes of unvisible dead
people" (Foer 116). She preserves the memory and keepsakes of the shtetl
in carefully labelled boxes in her house "in case" someone comes looking
for them. But, as she points out, the many "men's clothes and women's
clothes and clothes for children and even babies" (Foer 116) that she keeps
are only a small sample: "The ground is still filled with rings, and money,
and pictures, and Jewish things. I was only to find a few of them, but they
fill the earth" (Foer 152). While those remains and traces in the ground
indicate a past richness of life, belongings, and documents, on the surface,
where Trachimbrod used to be, nothing can be found. Even though the site
of the former village is marked by a monument placed in the middle of the
field where the village used to be, the narrator is insistent in his description
of the emptiness as all-encompassing:

There was nothing. When I utter "nothing" I do not mean there was
nothing except for two houses, and some wood on the ground, and
pieces of glass, and children's toys, and photographs. When I utter that
there was nothing, what I intend is that there was not any of these
things, or any other things. (Foer 184)

This "nothing" is a direct result of the rapturing and erasure described by Marianne Hirsch and *Everything is Illuminated*, more so than the other texts discussed, "strives to *reactivate* and – *re-embody* more distant political and cultural memorial structures by reinfesting them with resonant individual and familial forms of mediation and aesthetic expression" (*Generation* 33). Inventing a rich and colourful past for the "hero" and his family in the Trachimbrod sections of the novel, *Everything is Illuminated* compensates for this "nothing" through the use of narrative devices. While these sections, beginning in the early eighteenth century, are fragmented and juxtaposed with the sombre realization of the journey chapters that the travellers will find "nothing" – no clarity and no answers – they imagine a layered genealogy dating back to the "hero's" forbearers, one of whom has his own statue in the village, self-reflectingly modelled "after the faces of his male descendants" (Foer 140). A number of traditions are described as specific to the village and closely linked with the "hero's" genealogy: Trachimday celebrates the mysterious discovery of the author's several-times great-grandmother Brod as a newborn in the river of the same name with which the novel opens; this is in turn juxtaposed with the devastating passage describing his grandfather's daughter drowning in the same river at the moment of her birth as the result of a German air raid at the very end of the text (Foer 272–273).

In par with Judaism's more permitting attitudes towards sex and procreation, these fantasized and fantastical traditions usually centre on occasions celebrating love and sex, marriage and birth, a defiant insistence on life in face of the mind-numbing absence encountered in the novel's contemporary narrative. The assertion that this place, this village, and its inhabitants, has, indeed, once existed, even travels through time and space: "*There's definitely something out there*", Neil Armstrong observes during the moon landing in 1969 as he gazes "over the lunar horizon at the tiny village of Trachimbrod" while the author's grandmother and mother weep in front of their TV set (Foer 99). Despite the complete "nothing" of the site Trachimbrod, the villagers' fierce love for life once made them visible from space:

> Trachimday is the only time all year when the tiny village of Trachimbrod can be seen from space, when enough copulative voltage is generated to sex the Polish-Ukrainian skies electric. *We're* here, the glow of 1804 will say in one and a half centuries. *We're here, and we're alive.* (Foer 96)

The lost multitude reimagined to ascertain the life and distinct culture of the village is also reflected in the multitude of different literary devices and narrative voices that the novel employs, as I will detail in the following section.

Memory is a road trip: *The Memory Man*

In all three novels, the postmemorial project is a collaborative one, making tenuous multidirectional links to other histories of violence, allowing for a possibility of reconciliation as one result of the return journey.

In *Everything is Illuminated*, the creation of postmemory is realized as a shared writing project by the fictional author, Jonathan, who writes these sections of the author's family and the town dating back to the 1700s, and the first-person narrator Alex, who describes the search for the village in 1997. Alex's letters to the author are a third strand that interrupts, comments on, and occasionally corrects the other two. In addition to those three distinct strands, the sections on Trachimbrod's history also quote from books and even drama written by inhabitants of the village, while Alex's sections often include translations or double content that has been already introduced in a different context in another section. Alex's letters interfering with the narratives of the other two strands and authorial interjects in the historical narrative, especially toward the end of the novel, further highlight the dialogical nature of this construction of memory. Alex explicitly names the collaborative aspects of their writing: "We are talking together now, Jonathan, together and not apart. We are with each other, working on the same story [...]" (Foer 214). In line with Michael Rothberg's assertion that "such dialogue can create solidarity even as it reveals implication" (2019, 20), Alex does not only shed much of his initial preconceptions and inhibitions in his continued dialogue with the fictional author. More importantly, their journey is eventually shown to be a joint return. Their "talking together" eventually illuminates Alex's own family history, as his grandfather's own roots in this specific hinterland and his implication in the murder of his Jewish friend, Herschel, are slowly revealed over the course of the novel.

In *The Dark Room*, the three distinct parts also exemplify how memories are created and erased collectively, cumulating in Micha's story. His postmemory can only be established in dialogue with the Belarussian collaborator. His section also investigates how cultural memory can be maintained in an increasingly multicultural Germany at the dawn of a new millennium, for example in Micha's discussions with his Turkish-German girlfriend Mina:

- *I can't be the only one. There must be others in that hall every year with grandfathers like mine.*

- Not everyone. Some of your students are Turkish, aren't they? Greek? Iranian?
- *OK, then I'm talking about the ones with German parents, grand-parents.*
- But they *didn't* do it, Michael. They really didn't. The children, the students. Even the very purest of the pure German ones. (Seiffert 289)

Mina appears to argue from an assumed outsider position with regard to the history of the country she lives in, which is not questioned by either Micha or the narrative. Mina's claimed outsider position is far from uncontested; in *The Implicated Subject,* Rothberg for example discusses Zafer Şenocak's "dilemma" faced by immigrants such as the Turkish so-called "guest workers" and their descendants with regards to legacies of implication and their "responsibility to acknowledge history" (2019, 18). But it is not only this question about how to position oneself towards a history not quite one's own (yet) that complicates Mina's position, but also her self-articulated ignorance with regard to her ability to be able to understand what it feels like to live with *"grandfathers like"* Micha's and their legacy. After all, there are other histories of violence the character could draw on to comprehend this struggle with one's legacy, not least the Armenian genocide that remains notably absent in their discussions. While Micha's single-mindedness in his endeavours to find out the "truth" about the degree of his grandfather's involvement in genocide occasionally threatens to eclipse the fate of the actual victims, this introduction of a character who could, but pointedly does not, offer the introduction of a multidirectional reflection on the German legacy stands out, to say the least. Micha even attempts to continue this separation with the next generation: as if to spare his baby daughter his own, more complicated position of implication, Micha seems to try to sever her connection with his family's past. When they think of names for their newborn, Micha insists on her being named only after Mina's Turkish grandmother and refuses to visit his own with the baby (Seiffert 370). Despite this initial attempt to exclude the future generation from their history of implication, the novel eventually closes with Micha taking little Dilan to see her German great-grandmother in a tentatively reconciliatory gesture towards both the legacy of the past and the responsibilities of the future.

In *The Memory Man*, memory only works through collaboration. Bruno Lind, even though he is a Shoah survivor and thus a direct witness, needs triggers to help him remember his own past. When looking for the family home where his mother and sister had been buried, he is thrown off by changes in the landscape, by differences in the architecture. It is the tree under which he buried his murdered mother and sister, and which is still being used as a swing as it was then by his little sister, which triggers his memory. Above all, his ability to recollect relies on physical triggers. At the beginning of the novel, when walking through Vienna, it is his body that takes him to his old street – "[m]emory triggered by his legs along ancient pathways to the cerebellum" (Appignanesi 11). As he stares up at the façade of his old home, he is overcome by a memory from his childhood that sets in motion the entire chain of events leading to his embarking on his journey. And at the end of the novel, it is the body of a past lover – Irena's mother, herself suffering from Alzheimer's – that triggers his memory of the last war years and his relationship with a Polish woman that had been overshadowed by his hatred of Polish collaboration during the war:

> "I'm not sure what I recognized first. That drawing. Or maybe it was her voice. Husky, yet somehow precise. Or the gestures. Those large hands with their small neat motion. You know," he looked at them all with an air of wonder, "I really think I'd all but forgotten that period. Or not remembered it. I needed the trigger. The stimulus of those hands and the murmur". (Appignanesi 234)

While Irena's mother herself is unable to remember the past, her body – her voice, her hands – provides the triggers that Bruno needs to access that which is "lying beyond what is visible or known", in this case, his own, repressed memories. In addition to those physical triggers, he is reliant on the efforts of the second generation – his daughter, Amelia, and their Polish travel companions, Irena and Aleksander – to be able to access his memories.

But the second generation, facilitating the encounters that trigger Bruno's memory, is also dependent on him to make sense of their own condition, in particular the two Polish characters, who describe their formative years to have been formed by silence about the war. Irena, looking for her biological father after her mother, the Alzheimer patient, cannot share any light on his identity anymore, needs Bruno to fill in the blanks: "It was all so strange. The way memory was so crucial to who one was, the very foundation on which identity was built, yet that crucial bit of one's identity [...] was something memory couldn't deal with" (230). Despite the singular *Memory Man* of its title, in Appignanesi's novel memory needs to be shared to be able to access the past.

This act of collaboration is also multidirectional. The presence of Bruno's adopted daughter Amelia already indicates an acknowledgement of different histories of violence and the complicated role of collective memory in an increasingly globalized world. In the novel, as in Rothberg's thoughts on the nature of collective memory, these are initially set up as being in competition with each other, but easily – maybe too smoothly –

reconciled, for example, in a scene in which Aleksander uses the phrase "slave labour" to describe his father's experiences in a German ammunitions factory:

> He stumbled and stammered as the word "slave" tumbled from his lips. He had the air of a man who had somehow condemned himself.

> Amelia laughed. "That's ok. I'm prepared to learn about other people's histories of slavery. Nice not to be alone". (Appignanesi 143)

But at the heart of the novel lies the difficult relationship between Jewish and Polish suffering during the war – Bruno's trip is partially inspired by his anger and hatred of Polish complicity, directed at Aleksander, whom he believes to be related to an anti-Semitic Polish partisan he had encountered during the war. The different narrative strands are eventually reconciled when Bruno turns out to be the biological father Irena is looking for and the misremembered or repressed memories of Bruno's former Polish lover are revealed under the layers of his anger:

> His personal memory had functioned in the spirit of what collective memory had made of the time – Poles and Jews mired in hatreds, when the killing machine which made murderers and victims of them all had in the first instance been put in place by a Nazi regime that despised them both. (248)

While the relationship between Jewish and Polish suffering during the war is, in many ways, at the centre of *The Memory Man*'s conflicts, the figure of the collaborator – or of those somehow implicated in German genocidal violence – is scrutinized in all three novels, to the extent that it almost eclipses the German perpetrator. In *The Memory Man*, Bruno's memories of Aleksander's uncle, the partisan, have been changed by time and impacted by "the spirit of what collective memory had made" of it; in the reconciliation at the end of the novel, Aleksander is paired off with Bruno's daughter and Bruno's anger is appeased. However, in his recollections, as the character realizes towards the end of the novel, this anger and its consequences are mostly directed at Polish characters who collaborated with the German perpetrators – the farmers who betrayed his mother and sister to the Germans, the partisan who sends Bruno on a dangerous mission after finding out he is Jewish – rather than the perpetrators. In *Everything is Illuminated*, the Germans raiding the village constitute a demonic, incomprehensible presence, while it is Alex's grandfather, forced to reveal his Jewish best friend's identity under extreme duress, whose sense of implication and responsibility is examined. Even though Micha sets out to investigate his grandfather's crimes in *The Dark Room*, his emotional reaction is directed at Kolesnik, the collaborator: he "will never get used to it; that Kolesnik likes him" (Seiffert 364) and reconciles with his grandmother instead. He refuses to have his photo taken with Kolesnik, yet takes Dilan to his grandmother's apartment in which his section began with them looking at family pictures, including the ones with his feature young Micha and his grandfather together.

Conclusion: multidirectional postmemories?

All three novels under discussion use return journeys to confront the hinterlands of a traumatic and violent past. On these journeys, the protagonists encounter seemingly empty landscapes. Their meaning, and the memory of belonging and atrocity that these places contain, must be uncovered and recreated through collaboration and the sharing of memories. Through this process, the postgenerational identity is also formed in dialogue with the various "hinterlands" at the core of the return journey.

In their construction of postmemory, the novels all explore notions of complicity and implication, and make tentative, multidirectional links to other histories of violence. Especially *Everything Is Illuminated* and *The Dark Room* use formal experimentation to tackle the traumatic lack of knowledge, demonstrating how writing can "emerge a possible way of working through the traumatic legacy of the Shoah, a therapeutic encounter, so to speak, which enables one to live in the present, project into the future, and not forget the past" (Aarons and Berger 116).

In all texts, the confrontation with a violent past, the journey to an unknown or half-forgotten hinterland, and the focus on collaboration on the one hand and on complicity on the other hand brings with it a possibility of reconciliation. How such "dialogue can create solidarity even as it reveals implication" (2019, 20), to quote Rothberg again, is most clearly expressed at the end of *Everything is Illuminated*. After their return to Odessa, Alex's grandfather commits suicide, as he cannot bear the memory of his own implication, but he leaves a note, addressing the fictional author, in which he expresses the hopes for a more peaceful life he has for his grandsons:

> I would give everything for them to live without violence. Peace. That is all that I ever want for them. Not money and not even love. It is still possible. I know that now and it is the cause of so much happiness in me. They must begin again. (Foer 275)

Works Cited

Appignanesi, Lisa. *The Memory Man*. Acardia Books, 2008.

Bardizbanian, Audrey. "From Silence to Testimony: Performing Trauma and Postmemory in Jonathan Safran Foer's *Everything Is Illuminated*." *Holocaust Studies*, vol. 25, no. 1–2, 2019, pp. 43–58., doi:10.1080/17504902.2018.1472875.

De Nardi, Sarah. *Visualising Place, Memory and the Imagined*. Routledge, 2019, doi:10.4324/9781315167879.

Doolan, Emma. "Hinterland Gothic: Subtropical Excess in the Literature of South East Queensland." *ETropic*, vol. 18, no. 1, 2019, pp. 174–191, doi:10.25120/etropic.18.1.2019.3679.

Foer, Jonathan Safran. *Everything is Illuminated*. Harper Perennial, 2005.

Hirsch, Marianne. "Connective Arts of Postmemory." *Analecta Política*, vol. 9, no. 16, 2019, pp. 171–176, doi:10.18566/apolit.v9n16.a09.

Hirsch, Marianne. *The Generation of Postmemory: Writing and Visual Culture after the Holocaust*. Columbia University Press, 2012.

Hoffman, Eva. *After Such Knowledge: A Mediation on the Aftermath of the Holocaust*. Vintage 2005.

Rothberg, Michael. *Multidirectional Memory: Remembering the Holocaust in the Age of Decolonization*. Stanford University Press, 2009.

Rothberg, Michael. *The Implicated Subject: Beyond Victims and Perpetrators*. Stanford University Press, 2019.

Seiffert, Rachel. *The Dark Room*. Vintage, 2002.

14 Ukrainians in Canadian hinterlands

Young adult historical fiction on the World War I internment

Mateusz Świetlicki

Since the late nineteenth century, nature has been an essential element of Canadian national identity and Anglo-Canadian children's literature. In her influential collection *Survival* (1972), Margaret Atwood writes that Canadian depictions of nature and landscapes can be found "almost everywhere" (49). Atwood highlights that in most of these images, nature is hostile or unreal, and has to be controlled and tamed. However, in many texts focalized by Eastern European immigrants looking for a new beginning, the seemingly wild and uninhabited Canadian landscapes function as symbols of hope. For example, the prairies of Manitoba, Alberta, and Saskatchewan in most Ukrainian Canadian children's historical books set at the turn of the twentieth century emerge as spaces where the immigrants from the Austro-Hungarian provinces of Galicia and Bukovyna can finally escape poverty and exploitation. Although the landscapes play the role of a simulacrum of the old country, by conquering the wilderness, Ukrainians can prove their usefulness for their new state (cf. Świetlicki 31). As Elizabeth Galway notes, the association of Canada with its wastelands was connected to "a vision of a nation that is on a steady and successful civilising mission" and contributed to the conviction that the country has "to be settled and developed in order to secure national economic security and independence" (146). The belief that the wilderness should be tamed played an essential role during and after the First World War. That is why General William Dillon Otter and Parks Commissioner James Bernard Harkin decided to build new roads and facilities in Canada's hinterlands. This, however, was done with the use of "enemy aliens", predominantly Ukrainians, seen as an inferior "surplus to the national need", who were interned in 24 labour camps after the implementation of the 1914 War Measures Act (cf. Semchuk 1–11; Luciuk[1]). While the war ended in 1918, the last camp, Kapuskasing in Northern Ontario, was closed two years later.

DOI: 10.4324/9781032617732-19

Ukrainian Canadian historians have been publishing about the internment since the late 1970s, but until the mid-2000s it was of marginal status in the Canadian First World War mnemonic discourse. This situation started to change with the official implementation of Bill C-331 Internment of Persons of the Ukrainian Origin Recognition Act in 2005. In this document, which was proposed by Inky Mark – a Chinese Canadian MP from Manitoba – the Parliament finally apologized for the imprisonment of Ukrainians. The recognition of the internment was followed by commemorative practices, and the appearance of multiple books, including those for children and young adults (Świetlicki 72–101). This chapter showcases the various ways in which three Canadian texts aimed at young readers – Marsha Forchuk Skrypuch's *Dance of the Banished* (2014), Kassandra Luciuk and Nicole Marie Burton's *Enemy Alien: A True Story of Life Behind Barbed Wire* (2020), and Pam Clark's *Kalyna* (2016)[2] – depict the hinterlands of the camps in Kapuskasing, Ontario, and Castle Mountain, Alberta. After introducing my understanding of the hinterlands in the following paragraphs, I next demonstrate the place of the internment in the Canadian and Ukrainian Canadian mnemonic discourses and children's literature. Then, in close readings of the three aforementioned books, I investigate the disparities in the descriptions of Canadian landscapes. I show that while Clark and Skrypuch portray conquering nature as a sacrifice that the immigrants have to pay to eventually be accepted as Canadians, in Luciuk and Burton's graphic novel the hinterlands of the camp emerge as symbols of disappointment and loss of faith in Canada as the promised land.

Depending on the implication, the hinterland can refer to various physical and symbolic spaces. This notion has been used in multiple ways in the context of Canada. First, despite being the second-biggest country in the world, Canada is often seen as a hinterland of the United States, a "frozen land of ice and snow" (Galway 147), as 48% of its territory is inhabited by 1% of its population. Sometimes all provinces other than Ontario and Quebec, known as the country's heartland, are called hinterlands (Ray, Lamarche, Beaudin 297). Other times only the northern provinces – Yukon, Northwest Territories, and Nunavutare – are referred to as hinterlands (Weller 213–230). The hinterland is also used to define non-urban areas. For example, Roberta Balstad Miller refers to counties as hinterlands of cities (6). Moreover, as Emma Doolan notes, the hinterland can be described "as a conceptual space imbued with connotations of imperial possession, othering, and marginality" (Doolan 174).

In this chapter, I understand the hinterland in two ways. First, as a distant space where the First World War internment operations took place. Second, metaphorically, as a silenced – thus marginal – part of collective memory. The hinterlands of the camps – both physical and metaphorical – represent colonial and political violence directed against both immigrants and Canada's First Nations.[3] In my close reading of three books published more than a decade after the implementation of Act C-331, I demonstrate that for many years repressed and forgotten, the internment remained in the metaphorical hinterlands of memory. However, gradually, the camps' spaces have become important *lieux de mémoire*.[4] Notably, as I point out in my study, these landscapes/memories are heterotopic. After all, the traditional territories of the First Nations' were taken away by the government, then forcefully tamed and conquered by the imprisoned enemy aliens, primarily Ukrainians, and finally (re)claimed by Canadians. Importantly, "the suppression of the Cree ... and the projection of settler fears on them in 1885, provide a historical context for the creation of the War Measures Act, a registration certificate system, and the internment camps during the First World War" (Semchuk xxxvii). During the next World War, the War Measures Act was once again used, this time against Japanese Canadians and Italian Canadians (Luciuk 1988, 7; 2001, 4).[5]

First World War internment

While literature for young people can increase readers' understanding and appreciation of landscapes and the environment, historical fiction also introduces them to the changes happening to these places and their populations. Moreover, present-day texts set in the past can bring attention to little-known predicaments of marginalized social groups. Representing the previously unheard voices – including those of the victims of the internment camps – and keeping their memory alive have been one of the most important roles of Canadian literature in the last few decades. For decades, the history of the interment remained on the margins of Canadian and Ukrainian Canadian cultural memory. In *The Stories Were Not Told*, a volume featuring interviews with the families of the internees, documents, and present-day photographs of the hinterlands where the camps were once located, Sandra Semchuk asks: "Was the silence necessary for internees to continue a relationship with this nation rather than be further alienated?" (Semchuk xlvi). As many of the internees later recalled, they continued living in fear of possible imprisonment, especially during the Great Depression and the Second World War, when ethnic minorities were once again considered suspicious. This sentiment is reflected in Clark's *Kalyna*, when in the early 1930s, the titular character hears: "Ukrainians don't speak of this time because the older generation still lives in fear of the barbed fence" (Clark 247). Moreover, the experience of the internment of poor farmers was initially of little interest to the educated Ukrainian immigrants who came to Canada in the 1950s to escape communism.

However, the situation began to change in the late 1970s with the appearance of studies by Ukrainian Canadian intellectuals, who would spend decades bringing attention to the costs of the War Measures Act. As historian Lubomyr L. Luciuk notes, 8,579 people were imprisoned as "enemy aliens" between 1914 and 1920 (2001, 6). Notably, most of them were not prisoners of war but civilian men of Ukrainian origin who had come to Canada from Galicia and Bukovyna after being promised a homestead for $10.[6] In Spirit Lake, Quebec, and Vernon, British Columbia men were joined by women and children. The internees were forced to cut down trees and build houses, roads, hotels, and golf courts. Some rioted, tried to escape, went on hunger strikes, or committed suicide (Luciuk 1988, 20). More than 80,000 "enemy aliens" who were not interned were issued identity documents and forced to report to the North West Mounted Police or special administrators. Those who did not carry the documents "could be subjected to arrest, fine, even imprisonment", writes Luciuk (2001, 6). Moreover, some people were interned "only because they did not speak English very well and thus 'could not explain [their] nationality'" (Luciuk 2001, 30). Ukrainians were considered Austro-Hungarian subjects, but in some contemporary accounts and documents, they were referred to as Ukrainians, which suggests that the official knew that most of the "Austrians" were Slavs (Luciuk 2001, 30). Even though the war ended in 1918, some camps operated until 1920. This was possible because "'enemy aliens' were made out to be 'dangerous foreigners' or 'Bolsheviki' after the 1917 revolution and subsequent coup d'etat in the former Tsarist Empire" (Luciuk 2001, 48). While the War Measures Act targeted primarily immigrants who were not naturalized subjects, the War Time Elections Act, which was introduced in 1917 by Robert Borden's Conservatives, deprived British subjects naturalized after 1902 of voting rights (Swyripa 2000, 357). Thus, most immigrants were directly or indirectly victimized by the acts.

After the implementation of Bill C-331 (Internment of Persons of Ukrainian Origin Recognition Act)[7] by Canada's House of Commons and Senate in 2005 and the subsequent formation of the Endowment Council of the Canadian First World War Internment Recognition Fund in 2008, the interment of Ukrainian Canadians became a vital element of the country's memory politics. This resulted in the appearance of both new academic texts and children's and young adult books set in the hinterlands of Spirit Lake, Quebec (Skrypuch 2007; Brien), Castle Mountain, Banff National Park, Alberta (Huser; Clark), and Kapuskasing, Northern Ontario (Skrypuch 2014; Luciuk and Burton) (cf. Świetlicki 72–101).[8]

Becoming Canadian by taming the hinterlands.
Kapuskasing, Ontario

Marsha Forchuk Skrypuch was the first Ukrainian-Canadian author who wrote a children's book about the First World War internment. This picturebook, titled *Silver Threads*, was illustrated by Michael Martchenko and appeared in 1996. Writing *Silver Threads*, Skrypuch was inspired by the story of the internment of her grandfather in Jasper, Alberta. Four years after the introduction of Bill C-331, she returned to the topic in *Prisoners in the Promised Land*, a novel published in the popular "Dear Canada" series, and its companion short story "An Unexpected Visitor". Both texts are focalized by Anya, a girl interned with her family in Spirit Lake, Quebec. Although in these books Skrypuch focuses predominantly on Ukrainian Canadians, the protagonists of the 2015 critically acclaimed and award-winning YA novel *Dance of the Banished*[9] – her latest one set during the First World War – are Alevi Kurd teenagers from Anatolia in the Ottoman Empire. After escaping to Canada, Ali, his brother, and 98 other Alevi men are "imprisoned in a vast cold wilderness in a place called Kapuskasing Internment Camp" (Skrypuch 2014, 62). Thus, Ali, the main character, is interned together with Ukrainians in the same hinterlands of Kapuskasing, Ontario. Ali's fiancée, Zeynep, who is left behind and witnesses the atrocities committed by the Ottoman Army,[10] eventually joins the man in Canada. Notably, *Dance of the Banished* showcases not only the consequences the War Measures Act had on the imprisoned immigrants – Alevis and Ukrainians – but also the destruction of the landscapes of Kapuskasing, traditionally occupied by the Cree.

Although a Ukrainian docs not focalize *Dance of the Banished,* the chronotope of the camp is that of Kapuskasing, where most of the internees are immigrants from Galicia and Bukovyna. Thus, it is the same physical space as the one described in Luciuk and Burton's graphic novel I examine next. Moreover, Skrypuch points to the similarities between the legal status of Alevis and Ukrainians in Canada, as both come from the hinterlands of empires and are not recognized as separate peoples by the imperial powers.[11] This is clarified by Ali, who states: "I tried to explain that I am an Alevi and no friend of the Turks who control the Ottoman Empire, but they don't understand. To them, I'm from Turkey, and therefore a Turk" (Skrypuch "Banished" 62). Such description positions him as parallel to Ukrainians from Austro-Hungary who, despite being Slavic and usually not speaking German, are called inferior Austrians; therefore, their separate identity is denied.

While Skrypuch frequently refers to Kapuskasing as a "wilderness", in *Dance of the Banished,* the landscape emerges as grandiose (cf. Skrypuch 2014, 66, 102, 103, 119, 132, 137, 195). The use of this word to describe the hinterlands is common in Canadian literature and culture, where "the image of Canada as a land of rugged wilderness prevailed and continues to dominate to this day" (Galway 145). The camp is located far away from Brantford, Ontario, where Ali lived before being interned. To get to the hinterlands, the prisoners have to take a "train through cities and towns", and "[w]hen the cities and towns thinned out, the train kept on going through a land of snow and trees and rocks" (Skrypuch 2014, 62). The landscape appears hostile and treacherous. Because it is wild and untamed, most non-Indigenous people cannot survive there: "We're in the middle of the wilderness. An escapee would either freeze to death or be killed by a bear of wolf" (Skrypuch 2014, 103).

Canadian soldiers in *Dance with the Banished* do not respect nature and seem to have no limits when cutting down trees. Unlike them, Ali sees their splendour and "savore[s] the majesty of this universe", the snow with "spark[s] like jewels in the sun", and the trees "robed in glittering white" (Skrypuch 2014, 106).[12] Notably, it is the untouched beauty of the landscape that helps Ali to identify with Canada and start having hope that a good life there is possible: "If I had come to this place as a free man instead of a prisoner, I could grow to love it ... Maybe we could find wilderness like this that isn't yet destroyed by greedy men" (Skrypuch 2014, 106). However, in order to become Canadian, Ali has to make a sacrifice and detach himself from nature.

Because Ali emerges as a character possessing a special relationship with the land, he personifies the hinterlands. This positions him closer to First Nations and more distant from Anglo-Canadians who, as Atwood notes, "do not trust Nature, they are always suspecting some dirty trick" (Atwood 49). After cutting down most of the trees in the camp, Ali compares the view to "one huge, ugly wound on the earth" (Skrypuch 2014, 104). While for the soldiers this is a sign of success, Ali recognizes the wound as "soul breaking", because for him it is a sign of "destruction" (Skrypuch 2014, 105). The woods are further anthropomorphized when Ali compares "the scent of resin" with that of "blood on battlefields" (Skrypuch 2014, 105).

The landscapes in *Dance of the Banished* are symbolically wounded also because the Cree,[13] their original inhabitants, whom Ali identifies with, are banished.[14] After bonding with Nadie, a young Cree woman who sells furs to the soldiers, Ali notices that "[their] cultures were vastly different yet [they] had so much in common" (Skrypuch 2014, 131). Nadie introduces Ali to Cree culture and the history of the hinterlands. While the landscape seems untamed, Nadie says that "[t]he entire forest is [her] home", and she knows the river like her "own heart" (Skrypuch 2014, 128, 126). When Ali and Nadie go to the opposite shore of the river, the man sees that it looks similar to the camp's landscape before the destruction. As he recalls, "[t]his was a part of the forest that we hadn't been sent to cut down. Yet" (Skrypuch 2014, 127). The last word suggests that Ali is aware that there is no stop to the planned destruction of the lands.

Despite the similarities between the Alevis and the Cree, Ali understands that he cannot appropriate their way of life and that there are also significant differences between their cultures, especially regarding their attitudes towards wildlife.[15] Ali recognizes his own implication in the process of destroying the lands of the First Nations, but he also remembers that it is his only way to fulfil the dream of becoming Canadian and reuniting with Zeynep. When Ali defends Nadie from an aggressive internee, he is punished with "isolation on Prison Island, which is in the middle of the river", and seems to be the same place where the internees are sent in Luciuk and Burton's graphic novel (Skrypuch 2014, 103; Luciuk and Burton 31). Nadie offers to save the protagonist from the camp when he is in solitary confinement. Although at first he agrees, eventually, Ali decides to return to Prison Island and serve his time in Kapuskasing, which he – like his Ukrainian friend, Bohdan – sees as his only way to become Canadian and be reunited with Zeynep: "As an escapee, I would never be allowed to be a Canadian citizen" (Skrypuch 2014, 138). When Ali eventually leaves the camp, he is allowed to return to Bradford with Zeynep and is told to consider the internment as his "sacrifice to Canada's war effort" (Skrypuch 2014, 197). However, the sacrifice of enemy aliens becomes forgotten after the camp closes in 1920.

Another book set in Kapuskasing is Kassandra Luciuk and Nicole Marie Burton's graphic novel *Enemy Alien: A True Story of Life Behind Barbed Wire* (2020), based on an anonymous journal of an internee written in 1945. The book's protagonist, John Boychuk, is a 22-year-old Ukrainian man who is arrested in Toronto, interned in Kapuskasing, and later taken to Sydney, Nova Scotia, where he is forced to work in stone mining. In *Enemy Alien,* it is Burton's illustration of a map that further highlights the distance between the cities and the hinterlands of the camp (Luciuk and Burton 6). Next to the textual layer, the illustrations position Kapuskasing as a wilderness filled with trees, which are eventually cut down and replaced with barracks. Notably, the title of the graphic novel and the colours used for its cover – light shades of green and brown – reference Lubomyr Y. Luciuk's influential *In Fear of the Barbed Wire.* All other illustrations in *Enemy Alien* feature various shades of grey. This may be attributed to the high publishing costs of colourful illustrations, but the lack of any colours other than white, black, and grey also symbolizes the protagonist's difficulty in finding any beauty in the hinterlands.

In both *Enemy Alien* and *Dance of the Banished*, enemy aliens are used to conquer nature by clearing the woods and helping to build a town in the distant hinterlands of Northern Ontario. However, unlike Ali in Skrypuch's novel, Boychuk does not question the sense of cutting down trees. Yet he recognizes the fact that "all of [the internees] were buried alive in [their] own way" (Luciuk and Burton 46). Thus, in one of Burton's illustrations, the modest graves of the internees start replacing the trees (Luciuk and Burton 23). After all, wood is necessary to build quarters and continue the civilizing mission of Canada. Boychuk recalls that "[t]he work was brutal and exploitative" and contributed to the death of 32 people (Luciuk and Burton 8). In a few months, the internees are forced to build "11 barracks, a hospital, three barracks for the soldiers, a modern building for the officers, and a barn" (Luciuk and Burton 20). Notably, *Enemy Alien* mentions the arrival of "100 Turks ... from Toronto", who must have been Alevis, because ethnic Turks were not interned in Kapuskasing (Luciuk and Burton 10). Initially, the men refuse to work, but are forced to undress and are beaten by the soldiers. While this form of abuse is absent from *Dance of the Banished*, the mention of the "Turks" suggests that both books portray the same hinterlands.

The last few pages of *Enemy Alien* show Boychuk's return to Kapuskasing in the summer of 1945. He wants to see the "wasteland" he helped to make "fertile" and pay a visit to a cemetery where his former colleagues are buried (Luciuk and Burton 74). Kapuskasing no longer looks like a wilderness, and no one currently living there seems to remember the camp. "This is Western democracy ... This is the reality of Canada for 'enemy aliens' like me", says Boychuk (Luciuk and Burton 76). When Boychuk, now an elegant man in a suit, visits the graveyard, he meets a police officer who tells him: "I've lived here a long time and I've never seen anyone come to this cemetery" (Luciuk and Burton 77). Looking at the abandoned old wooden crosses, Boychuk says: "[h]ere the men who cleared the forests lay forgotten by the world as if they were made by another God" (Luciuk and Burton 78). The last illustration depicts the protagonist walking on a bridge built between the mountains, looking at a town with big factories and many buildings, and promising to move the internment from the hinterlands of Canadian history to its centre.

Hinterlands of memory. Castle Mountain, Alberta

The theme of making a sacrifice to become accepted in Anglo-Canada and bringing awareness to the history of the internment are central in Pam Clark's crossover novel *Kalyna*.[16] The book is divided into four parts titled after the elements – water, earth, fire, and air. The first three tell the story of a young Ukrainian couple, Katja and Wasyl Federchuk, who immigrate to Canada from Galicia in the early 1910s.[17] As Katja notes:

"[h]er country had always been in transition, the very name Ukraine meant borderland, with the boundaries of her beloved country fluid and ephemeral" (Clark 8). What never changed, though, was the fact that Ukrainian peasants were exploited by their landlords. Katja and Wasyl leave "the idyllic Galician countryside, its prairies grasses swaying marigold yellow and canary green" for a homestead in the Edna-Star block settlement near Edmonton, Alberta. Although in Canada "[t]he air smelled fresher", the landscape of the prairie is depicted as a simulacrum of Ukraine, a "promise of a new life in a land that could have been a picture postcard of Drobomil" (Clark 27, 38; cf. Świetlicki 31). During the next three years, the couple clear the land, build a house, and become active members of the local community, which seems like an improved version of Galicia. Most importantly, here Ukrainians own the land. Katja's life changes when Wasyl is arrested for not carrying his identity papers and is interned in Castle Mountain in the Banff National Park, Alberta. Katja has to take care of the farm and the couple's two children, Olek and Pavla. She is helped by friends and neighbours, including Edward Smith, a sympathetic English doctor. While initially the man takes care of Katja and her children, he rapes the young woman and leaves Edna-Star for Edmonton.[18] Katja gets pregnant with Smith's child and gives birth to a daughter named Kalyna, whom Wasyl raises as his own. The last part of the book, titled air, is focalized by the eponymous Kalyna, the couple's teenage daughter, who is introduced as a beginning student of law in Edmonton. After finding out about Wasyl's First World War imprisonment and that he was not her biological father, Kalyna decides to dedicate her career to bringing attention to the internment and fighting for an official apology from the government. Thus, in the last part of the book, Clark shows the slow process of bringing back the internment from the hinterlands of memory to the mainstream and points to the importance of reconciliation.

Wasyl is interned in Castle Mountain, Alberta, in the hinterlands of Banff National Park, and then briefly in the Cave and Basin hot springs. The Banff camp was established in 1915 and existed until 1917. The internees there were forced to tame the uninhabited hinterlands and turn them into recreational spaces. They cleared the land, cut trails, and built golf courts, ski jumps, and the luxurious Banff Springs Hotel (cf. Kordan and Melnycky 6–23). Due to the weather conditions, the prisoners, who lived in tents, had to move to Cave and Basin for the wintertime temporarily, but in the spring, they returned to Castle Mountain. The conditions in the camp were poor, and abuse was common; some internees tried to escape, and others committed suicide (cf. Kordan 127–128).

Wasyl saves the memory of the camp in the letters he writes to Katja. However, as both he and his wife know, all correspondence is censored.

Thus, he focuses on the good things, such as the hot springs in Cave and Basin, in which the prisoners can bathe: *"The hot water feels like heaven in these cold temperatures. We now sleep in barracks with a stove in the middle"* (Clark 158; emphasis in original). Nevertheless, he manages to incorporate mentions of the hardships and dangers connected to the work, such as an explosion that kills one of the internees. Therefore, Clark's novel reflects the condition of the internees, who are constantly guarded, live in tents, and lose feeling in their toes because of the harsh weather. Moreover, their blankets are moth-bitten, their clothes are dirty and ripped, and they are "[h]ungry as dogs, rationed on fermented cabbage and rolled oats in place of meat" (Clark 136–137). However, Wasyl decides to become a model prisoner and prove he is worthy of being in Canada. Unlike his fellow internees, who either try to escape or riot, Wasyl just "watched and learned and waited" (Clark 135). The man believes that all it takes to go back home is "to keep silent" and "work hard" (Clark 137). Wasyl knows that the prisoners "must never lose faith", which is the only thing they have (Clark 137). Thus, unsurprisingly, the man becomes "a quiet leader among the men, a most determined worker" and gains the respect of the Anglo-Canadian soldiers, especially Private Davis, who eventually tells him: "You're a good man, Wasyl Federchuk; a good, honest man ... Another place, another time, I think we would have been friends" (Clark 2016, 214).

The hinterlands of Banff are heterotopic spaces where the Canadian hotel guests and enemy aliens have no direct connections. What is a luxurious resort for the former is a prison for the latter. When the internees are transferred from the distant Castle Mountain to Cave and Basin to build new facilities for the wealthy guests of the spring, they become surrounded by tourists, which makes Wasyl feel *"like a caged animal in a zoo on view"* (Clark 194; emphasis in original). The heterotopic character of the Rocky Mountain National Park is best showcased in the contrasting ways in which Wasyl and Edward Smith see it. After raping Wasyl's wife, the English doctor goes to the spring for a holiday because "he had heard of the revitalizing health benefits of the natural hot springs" (Clark 187). On his way to the national park, the man comes across "men lined up like cattle" with "eyes soulless" and realizes they are prisoners from Castle Mountain (Clark 188). Smith sees the enemy aliens "waiting outside of the end car [who] were like ghosts that only he could see and smell and hear ... their spirits already broken" (Clark 188). However, instead of facing them, Smith tries to look back because "[i]t was too much to look these men in the eyes" (Clark 188). What he does not know, though, is that the internees are also headed to Cave and Basin and that Wasyl is among them.

While in his letters Wasyl writes about the camp predominantly as a prison, Smith focuses on the beauty of the hinterlands: "valleys of wildflowers, Indian Paintbrush dotting the grasses, still green from the snowy melt" (Clark 188). The hotel "rose majestically in the valley of the Rocky Mountains, its copper-plated spired reaching to the heavens", and the elegant people he sees in the nearby streets convince him that "[i]t all felt perfect" (Clark 189). The beautiful landscapes fill Smith with "a sense of renewal, a chance to begin again", and the beautiful hotel makes him appreciate Canada's developmental achievements (Clark 190). However, the view of the men who are forcefully used to accomplish this progress, temporarily destroys his idyllic view of the park. The faces of enemy aliens "line with grime, some wincing with pain as they lifted boulders onto a platform" and provoke Smith to think about "the paradox of their harsh circumstances and the creation of something that would last a lifetime" (Clark 191). Among the internees, whose "faces were downtrodden", Smith notices Wasyl, the only one who "kept looking up, up at the sky, at the trees and mountains as if revelling in their splendour, glancing up at the hotel too" (Clark 191). Although Smith does not recognize Katja's husband, he waves back at him and "fe[els] conspicuous, like a spy who had just been caught" (Clarks 192). However, instead of reflecting on the fate of the internees and the way they are used by the government, Smith just "retreated to the bathroom to run a hot bath and ready himself for dinner in the hotel dining room" (Clark 191–192). Thus, he represses his complicity.

The last part of Clark's novel focuses on the process of moving the internment from the hinterlands of collective memory to its centre by the subsequent generations of Ukrainian Canadians. The eponymous Kalyna represents the symbolical rape of the enemy aliens committed by the Canadian government. Notably, her name, Ukrainian for *viburnum opulus*, which symbolizes land, blood, roots, and beauty in Slavic folklore, implies the strength and resilience of Ukrainian Canadians. Although she was raised by Katja and Wasyl in Edna-Star, Kalyna does not feel a strong connection to the land. On the contrary, she wants to leave the prairie and go to university. Thus, the girl shares the qualities of her biological parents: she is independent and strong-willed like her Ukrainian mother and intelligent like her English father.[19] While Kalyna is "[i]nde-pendent, confident, and successful", she does not reject her humble roots (Clark 224). On the contrary, she dedicates her life and career to bringing justice to men like her adoptive father.

Clark demonstrates that the memory of the internment remained repressed for decades, and the next generations of Ukrainian Canadian intellectuals had to fight to have it recognized by the government. Until Wasyl died, no one in his family and village talked about the internment and he always "professed his love for this country which gave him freedom" even after "his freedom had been taken away" (Clark 245). Even following Wasyl's death, Kalyna's older brother, Olek, hesitates to share his own memories of the First World War with the protagonist. The process of moving the interment from the hinterlands of memory starts when Kalyna moves to Edmonton and Katja gives her daughter a growing quilt where she hides Wasyl's release documents in a square with a red maple leaf. The leaf, which since 1965 has been on the Canadian flag, seems to further point to the future of Canada, a country no longer closely tied to Britain, one where acknowledging and commemorating past atrocities, such as the internment, is possible. However, in the late 1930s, with another war looming in the air, this is still unthinkable.

Kalyna decides to make a change, and becomes an activist and a lawyer specializing in human rights[20] and "Aboriginal Nations' resolution", but is constantly encouraged to understand the government and wait patiently for the right moment to bring attention to the internment (Clark 267). The situation starts to shift after her mother's death in 1956, long after the Great Depression and the Second World War, in which some of Kalyna's Ukrainian Canadian friends and neighbours died fighting for Canada. Only then the woman meets Private Davis, who corresponded with her in 1939 but then enlisted and lost his sight. The blind man gives Kalyna his old journal, in which he documented what was happening in the camp. What is worth noting is that since most official documents were deliberately destroyed in the 1950s, by giving Kalyna the journal, Davis wants to make sure that the memory of the camps is maintained. Although Davis tries to excuse himself when he tells Kalyna that the internees *and* the soldiers "were all forced to be there and made the best of it", by handing in the journal he acknowledges his complicity (Clark 274).[21] Unfortunately, the real process of redress and reconciliation happened almost 50 years after Kalyna's meeting with Davis.

Conclusion

For more than a century, Canada's ethereal and unique landscapes have been the main factor distancing the country from Britain and the USA. As Galway notes, "the environment was seen to have a spirit of its own and was pictured as a vast territory full of mystery, adventure and symbolic meaning" (17). However, in other contexts it was "viewed in pragmatic terms and seen as full of possibilities for economic development and exploitation" (Galway 17). The representations of the physical and metaphorical hinterlands of the Canadian First World War internment camps in the three texts examined in this chapter demonstrate both sides of Canada's environment. In *Dance of the Banished,* the traditional lands of the Cree are beautiful and wild, yet they are gradually destroyed in the name of progress. Although Clark and Skrypuch showcase that taming nature was a necessary sacrifice for immigrants who wanted to become accepted members of Canadian society, *Kalyna* and *Enemy Alien* suggest that this sacrifice – and exploitation – remained largely forgotten for decades. Similar to other books about the internment, the three texts investigated in this chapter attempt to move the topic of the predicament of First World War enemy aliens from the margins of Canadian mnemonic discourse to its heartland. The growth of the visibility of this topic in literature and the commemorative practices suggest that the history of the internment will not be lost in the hinterlands of Canadian history.

Notes

1 For maps showing the location of the camps, see Luciuk and Kordan (1988, 20). An interactive map is available online (cf. "Digital Interactive Map". *Canadian First World War Internment Recognition Fund*. https://www.internmentcanada.ca/map.cfm Accessed: September 8, 2022).

2 While Skrypuch is one of Canada's most popular authors of middle-grade historical fiction, *Dance of the Banished* is a YA novel. Clark's *Kalyna* was marketed as both YA an mainstream literature. Luciuk and Burton's graphic novel is a crossover text that can be enjoyed by both adults and adolescents (cf. Świetlicki 72–101).

3 Interestingly, the word *Ukraine* is believed to come from the Church Slavonic language, where it meant "border lands". Hence, it can be argued that the name of the country suggests its status as a hinterland located between Western Europe and Russia. In this context, it is worth noting that the Ukrainian diaspora in Canada has played an important role in showcasing the distinctiveness of not only Ukrainian Canadian history and culture but also that of Ukraine, thus moving them from the metaphorical hinterlands to the mainstream of the Canadian mnemonic discourse.

4 Here I am referring to the concept of *lieux de mémoire* (sites of memory) introduced by Pierre Nora (1989, 7–24). I understand a site of memory as a place of a historical significance in collective memory.

5 For more about the Japanese internment in Canadian literature, see Davis (2012, 57–76).

6 For more about the history of Ukrainian immigration to Canada, see Luciuk and Kordan; Świetlicki "Next-Generation".

7 Notably, when MP Inky Mark tabled Bill C-331 in 2001, it was rejected (Luciuk and Kordan 2001, 126).

8 The internment operations had been a part of the school curricula in some Canadian provinces even before they were officially recognized by the government and the first children's book devoted to this topic, *Silver Threads* by Marsha Forchuk Skrypuch and Michael Martchenko, was published in 1996 (Luciuk 2001, iv; Świetlicki 72–101).

9 The book was praised by professional reviewers and won many awards, including the 2015 Geoffrey Bilson Award for Historical Fiction for

Young People Winner. It was also selected as one of the best books of 2015 by the International Youth Library in Munich and the USBBY.

10 *Dance of the Banished* is Skrypuch's sixth book set during the Armenian Genocide.

11 As Skrypuch admitted in an email, initially she believed that some of the internees were Turkish and was not familiar with the history of Alevis. However, she soon discovered that the internees were not ethnic Turks but Alevi Kurds from the Ottoman Empire.

12 Interestingly, in Skrypuch's earlier book, *Prisoners of the Promised Land,* it is Anya, a Ukrainian girl, who notices the splendour of the hinterlands of Spirit Lake where she is interned.

13 Notably, Skrypuch is the only author examined in this chapter who includes First Nation characters in her books about the internment. This is of particular importance since "[f]or the most part, North American children's literature has excluded Indigenous authors, peoples and themes from its contents" (Korteweg, Gonzalez, Guillet 334). Moreover, many books tend to romanti- cize First Nations and their ceremonies (cf. Korteweg, Gonzalez, Guillet 334–335). While Skrypuch points to the similarities between the Cree and the internees, her portrayal is respectful and deprived of romanizations and oversimplifications.

14 Upon entering the woods, Ali becomes "overwhelmed with the sense of how insignificant we humans are" and feels "at one with the universe" (Skrypuch 2014, 64–65). Moreover, the old spruce trees "with impossibly tall narrow trunks that sway gracefully in the wind as they reach up to touch the sky" remind him of the landscapes of Anatolia (Skrypuch 2014, 64–65). Although Ali knows that "[t]his forest is a holy place" (Skrypuch "Banished" 64), the imprisoned men are forced to cut down trees, which is against the beliefs of the Alevis. For Ali cutting down trees – thus con- quering and taming the hinterlands – is blasphemous, and he feels as if he were "committing a sin" (Skrypuch 2014, 66). As he notes, "All wildlife is sacred to us – the trees, the deer, the rabbits, even the smallest rodents. To kill wildlife is to steal from God" (Skrypuch 2014, 64). The soldiers ridicule Ali's beliefs, and while he befriends a fellow Ukrainian prisoner, the only person who truly understands him is Nadie, a Cree woman. Notably, Ali realizes that by forcing the men to "kill trees", the soldiers tell them to build their own "prison camp in the northern wilderness on the bank of a mighty river called the Kapuskasing", which, as his closest Ukrainian friend Bohdan tells him, stands for "bend in the river" in Cree (Skrypuch 2014, 56, 102).

15 When Ali goes to Nadie's house and sees animal furs and bones, he thinks: "I was surrounded by corpses" (Skrypuch 2014, 129). However, Nadie informs him: "We are one with nature … We take what we need to survive, but no more. And we do not waste" (Skrypuch 2014, 130).

16 More recently, this theme has appeared in Glen Huser's children's novel *Firebird*.

17 Clark mistakenly identifies Galicia as part of what she calls "mother Russia".

18 Unlike in Skrypuch's *Dance of the Banished*, there are no Indigenous People in *Kalyna*, and the only mention of Canada's First Nations is when the internees are forced to dress up in "deer-skin fringed jacket[s]" and participate in "Indian Days", which, according to the soldiers, "represent the best of the Wild West" (Clark 203).

19 While Smith supported Katja financially throughout the years, the man never apologized for his actions, which echoes the government's attitude.
20 Initially, Kalyna wants to become "the first Ukrainian female lawyer to be admitted to the Alberta Bar" and "use her education to further the rights of women in government"; however, upon learning about the First World War predicament of Ukrainian Canadians, she decides to focus her attention on the internment (Clark 225). Although Kalyna is passionate about the history of female enfranchisement in Canada, Clark never mentions the War Election Act that disfranchised Ukrainian Canadians (Clark 225). This aspect of Ukrainian Canadian history remains on the margins of the mnemonic discourse. Surprisingly, Clark also does not mention the WWII internment of Japanese Canadians and Italian Canadians, which brought further attention to the WWI of Ukrainian Canadians.
21 A similar sentiment is expressed in one of Wasyl's letters in which he states: "*[p]eople are inherently kind, they are good, they only get led astray*" (Clark 168; emphasis in original).

Works Cited

Atwood, Margaret. *Survival*. Anansi Toronto, 1972.

Brien, Sylvie. *Spirit Lake*. Paris: Gallimard Jeunesse, 2008.

Clark, Pam. *Kalyna*. Stonehouse Publishing, [2003] 2016. E-book.

Davis, Laura K. "Joy Kogawa's *Obasan*: Canadian Multiculturalism and Japanese-Canadian Internment." *British Journal of Canadian Studies*, vol. 25, no. 1, 2012, pp. 57–76.

Doolan, Emma. "Hinterland Gothic: Subtropical Excess in the Literature of South East Queensland". *eTropic – Special Issue: Tropical* Gothic, vol. 18, no. 1, 2019, pp. 174–191.

Galway, Elizabeth A. *From Nursery Rhymes to Nationhood: Children's Literature and the Construction of Canadian Identity*. Routledge, 2008.

Huser, Glen. *Firebird*. Ronsdale, 2020.

Kordan, Bohdan S., and Peter Melnycky (eds.). *In the Shadow of the Rockies: Diary of the Castle Mountain Internment Camp, 1915–1917*. Edmonton: Canadian Institute of Ukrainian Studies Press, 1991.

Kordan, Bohdan S. *Enemy Aliens, Prisoners of War: Internment in Canada during the Great War*. McGill-Queen's University Press, 2002.

Korteweg, Lis, Ismel Gonzalez, and Jojo Guillet. "The Stories Are the People and the Land: Three Educators Respond to Environmental Teachings in Indigenous Children's Literature." *Environmental Education Research*, vol. 16, np. 3–4, 2010, pp. 331–350.

Luciuk, Kassandra and Natalie Marie Burton. *Enemy Alien: A Graphic History of Internment in Canada During the First World War*. Toronto: Between the Lines, 2020.

Luciuk, Lubomyr Y., and Bohdan S. Kordan. *Creating a Landscape: A Geography of Ukrainians in Canada*. University of Toronto Press, 1988.

Luciuk, Lubomyr Y., and Bohdan S. Kordan. *In Fear of the Barbed Wire Fence: Canada's First National Internment Operations and the Ukrainian Canadians, 1914–1920*. Kashtan Press, 2001.

Miller, Roberta Balstad. *City and Hinterland*. Greenwood Press, 1979.

Nora, Pierre. "Between Memory and History: Les Lieux de Mémoire." Trans. Marc Roudebush. "Representations", vol. 26, Spring 1989, pp. 7–24.

Ray, D. Michael, R. H. Lamarche, and Maurice Beaudin. "Economic Growth and Restructuring in Canada's Heartland and Hinterland: From Shift-share to Multifactor Partitioning." *The Canadian Geographer/Le Géographe Canadien*, vol. 56, no. 3, 2012, pp. 296–317.

Semchuk, Sandra. *The Stories Were Not Told: Canada's First World War Internment Camps*. University of Alberta Press, 2018.

Skrypuch, Marsha Forchuk. *Silver Threads*. Illustrated by Michael Martchenko. Toronto: VIKING (Penguin Books Canada), 1996.

Skrypuch, Marsha Forchuk. *Prisoners in the Promised Land. The Ukrainian Internment Diary of Anya Soloniuk*. Scholastic Canada, 2007.

Skrypuch, Marsha Forchuk. *Dance of the Banished*. Pajama Press, 2014.

Świetlicki, Mateusz. *Next-Generation Memory and Ukrainian Canadian Children's Historical Fiction: The Seeds of Memory*. Routledge, 2023.

Swyripa, Frances. "The Politics of Redress: The Contemporary Ukrainian-Canadian Campaign." *Enemies Within: Italian and Other Internees in Canada and Abroad*. Ed. Angelo Principle. University of Toronto Press, 2000, pp. 355–378.

Weller, Geoffrey R. "Health Care in the Northern Hinterlands: Canada, Scandinavia, and the United States." *Scandinavian Studies*, vol. 61, no. 2, Spring 1989, pp. 213–230.

15 Internal hinterland

Post-racial geography in Paul Beatty's *The Sellout*

Sascha Pöhlmann

One of the effects of the apparently geographic metaphor of the hinterland is to construct a deceptively neat spatial hierarchy that demarcates foreground and background. Historically, this may have once applied to the precise reference of the term in commercial geography that distinguished a seaport from its inland environment, and yet the term has been quickly, and by now thoroughly, detached from this narrow denotation, so that now its original usage is virtually lost among all the connotations the term has evoked in its usage over time. For one thing, the spatial image no longer holds, as seaports are no longer the centres of civilization they once were (in a certain perspective on "civilization," of course), and the linear view from water onto a port and the area behind it no longer applies. Instead, a hinterland now may well *surround* the centre that defines it and which it also defines, and it cannot be assigned to one particular background that could be confronted as such. This makes its boundaries even more fluid than they always were, and so the hinterland cannot be sufficiently externalized to set it apart from an internal core that takes precedence over it. One might describe this as a conceptual state of permanent siege in which the centre must fend off the assault of its surroundings to remain central: it must perpetually assert and exert its normative hegemony to maintain it. This need is connected to the temporal connotation of the hinterland that supplements the spatial metaphor: compared to the centre, this is a space that is lagging behind the times whose norms are set elsewhere. At this point, at the latest, the metaphor becomes what it will be treated as in the following: a cultural one.

In this essay, which is written from the perspective of U.S. American literary and cultural studies, I want to elucidate the cultural metaphor of the hinterland in reference to another that works in similar ways: "flyover", as in "flyover country". In doing so, I blend two related but not identical discourses, as flyover is one way of talking about hinterlands just as hinterlands are one way of talking about flyover, and both draw on an

DOI: 10.4324/9781032617732-20

urban/rural binary and transcend it at the same time. As the more specific term that has distinct roots in the United States, "flyover" describes a particular imagination of cultural polarization that constructs hierarchies of relevance and neglect for the purpose of either struggling for recognition or hegemony. This relative precision, I hope, can help contain the relative fuzziness of the hinterland concept and add to its critical value. At the same time, I want to evoke the more general notion of the hinterland to detach flyover from its original American specificity so that it can be abstracted and applied to inter- and transnational phenomena.

I will make this theoretical point in reference to a practical example by discussing a novel that is uniquely exemplary in this regard: Paul Beatty's *The Sellout* (2015). I argue that this novel delivers its satirical critique of an allegedly post-racial USA by combining a geographical and cultural imagination of a hinterland that is swallowed (and not marginalized) by the urban space of Los Angeles. Since this eradication occurs within an alleged cultural centre of the United States, it challenges the macroscopic fantasies of the flyover imagination and of the hinterland while feeding on their tropes of marginalization and hegemony. As such, it draws attention to the neglectful aspects of the very discourses that are often used to question precisely such neglect. With its focus on race and ethnicity, *The Sellout* especially draws attention to what is otherwise ignored in a purportedly territorial imagination that glosses over such markers of identity and difference. As Raymond Williams has it, an overly reductive discourse of contrasting town and country serves to "promote superficial comparisons and to prevent real ones" (1983, 54), and the same often applies to the reductive discourses of hinterlands and flyover country. This makes their imagination as dangerous as it is useful, as it can be a means of valid critique and also a means of preventing it. I explore these questions in two steps in the following: first I theorize a flyover imagination as a certain mode of constructing cultural hierarchies, and then I show how *The Sellout* both draws on and subverts this mode as it constructs an internal hinterland.

Hinterland and flyover

The first compelling reason to connect the hinterland and flyover metaphors is that both seem to say something about geography when they are really talking about culture. "Hinterland" has the more distinctly geographical roots of the two, as George Chisholm introduced it to the field in 1903 in the fourth edition of his *Handbook of Commercial Geography* and defined it as "the land which lies behind a seaport or a seaboard, and supplies the bulk of the exports, and in which are distributed the bulk of the imports of that seaport or seaboard" (54). As Matthew Unangst shows in a recent article, the economic term took on a political meaning not soon after, and what "began as a concept to describe a physical relationship in space" eventually became "a justification for imperial expansion as western states claimed nearly the entire globe" (19). Once describing a relatively balanced economic relation, the term is now distinctly hierarchical and always closely related to power and representation with a variety of cultural implications: "Hinterlands are at the edge of the places where history takes place, the port cities, oceans, or empires that integrate the hinterland into bigger historical narratives, their inhabitants the recipients of change but without the agency to create their own histories" (Unangst 4).

This parallels what Anthony Harkins describes as an "evolving conception of a nation divided in cultural far more than geographic or economic terms between 'places that matter' and 'places that don't'" (102), only that he is not talking about hinterland but flyover country. This term may be used as a synonym for the U.S.-American Midwest and adjacent regions or more generally as a label for anything between the East and West Coast, and especially between the metropolitan areas of New York City and Los Angeles.[1] Like "hinterland", the concept of "flyover country" is rooted in modes of transport, only that it is no longer seaports and the transport of goods that matter. Instead, the latter term is directly connected to the transport of people, to the "development of high altitude and nonstop jet air travel and the construction of a vast interstate highway system [that] dramatically increased the speed and ease of crossing the country in ways that were largely disassociated from geography and lived culture" (Harkins 101). It is also connected to corresponding media representations and infrastructures that established New York City and Los Angeles as cultural centres dominating what is between them to the point where it seems like space rather than a multiplicity of places. This notion of flyover has distinct roots in the USA, but it may be adapted to other places as well. In fact, I would argue that the concept *only* becomes a useful analytic tool when it is detached from its original meaning so that it is no longer a vague and misleading synonym for the Midwest but rather a marker of a certain kind of cultural differentiation—when it no longer describes a certain regionalism but serves to analyze regionalism as such. The same is true of "hinterland", which has already undergone such an abstract expansion as a concept and can be a model for a similar process with regard to "flyover".[2]

The movement from the concrete to the abstract helps define the larger cultural significance of the flyover imagination outlined in this essay. This concrete foundation is Meghan O'Gieblyn's essay collection *Interior States* (2018), and especially her "Dispatch from Flyover Country". Using flyover semantics, the language of being passed over, she describes "the sound of transit, of things passing through" (5), and the impression "that whatever promise the future holds, its fruits may very well pass by, on their way to somewhere else" (7), but most importantly this: "a sense that the rest of the world is moving while you remain still" (6). The most concise phrase to describe that sense is actually to be found in the blurb of *Interior States* that declares the book is about "the challenges of living in the Midwest when culture is felt to be elsewhere." This, then, is the main meaning of "flyover": the feeling that culture is elsewhere. "Culture" here refers to a narrow sense of an elitist high culture and its hegemonic aesthetic standards, but also to a way of life in the sense of everyday practices and customs.[3] Both relate to hierarchies, neglect, and even domination, but there is a notable difference in quality: while people may well accept that what counts as valuable aesthetic culture is (re)produced elsewhere, they will certainly not accept as readily the suggestion that they do not *have* a culture in the second sense, as it implies that their way of life is *wrong*, and that they are not aesthetically but *morally* at fault – and this is where we enter the discursive arena of culture wars.[4]

The feeling that culture happens elsewhere is more than a personal or psychological phenomenon, and it corresponds to Unangst's definition of the hinterland as a place whose inhabitants are "the recipients of change but without the agency to create their own histories" (4). In O'Gieblyn's account, this sense is distinctly tied to the Midwest, and yet it is much more universal than that, not least because she herself considers the Midwest "a somewhat slippery notion" (4) that does not provide sufficient stability for a purely regional framework or even local pride. Therefore, this way of describing cultural hierarchies – imagined, real, or both – transcends geographical regional differences, and it also transcends binaries of city/country and indeed the U.S.-American context from which it springs. Harkins even makes this transregionalism a core point of his approach to the flyover discourse and its act of demarcation. He shows that the notion of flyover country actually eschews the geographical concern it purports to have as it *eradicates* regional differences instead of reaffirming them: it "envisions the nation divided into only two vast and seemingly polar opposite meta-regions defined almost exclusively in cultural terms" (99).

This crucial concept of the oppositional cultural meta-regions lends itself to abstraction, especially as it is already detached from any concrete place, even though it pretends otherwise. Instead of simply perpetuating this eradication, though, a critical take on such cultural meta-regional imaginations may draw attention to what is being glossed over and neglected within the very discourse that claims to challenge established hierarchies, while at the same time acknowledging their ability to still do just that. Most importantly, it can be abstracted from the national framework from which it arose, in two different ways: first, flyover discourses may transcend such national limits and occur inter- or transnationally (perhaps expressed most concisely in such rhetorically dubious metaregional divisions as that between "developed countries" and the rest); second, flyover discourses may also exist in other contexts that may or may not be defined in national terms (for example, East and West Germany after "reunification" in 1990 are often constructed in metaregional cultural terms with corresponding imaginations of dominance and neglect, in journalistic texts and elsewhere).[5]

This relevance of the national as a reference point – even as it is overcome or challenged – takes us to another, crucial aspect of flyover discourse that is less pronounced but still tacitly present in the hinterland metaphor: the tension between recognition and hegemony. On the one hand, flyover discourse may be used to genuinely expose and challenge processes of marginalization and domination, and it can be a way of demanding recognition by a cultural mainstream that would otherwise deny it. This is particularly effective with regard to class and the economic exploitation of certain parts of America for the benefit of others, which is also where flyover discourse most clearly connects to the concept of the hinterland.[6] In this sense, such discourses participate in a more general struggle for recognition, to adapt Axel Honneth's term: the expression that "the other person is supposed to possess social 'validity'" (Honneth 2001, 115).[7]

Yet this may also become a struggle for hegemony when a part of the whole is not merely fighting to be recognized as such but actually strives to *become* the dominant, representative part that gets to represent the whole. I call this a synecdochal contest, as it follows a pars-pro-toto logic that posits one part to be particularly representative, authentic, or normative with regard to the culture as a whole (and it perpetuates the fiction that there is such a thing as "the culture as a whole"). In the national terms that often frame flyover discourse, this means that some parts are presented as more genuinely American than others, with the suggestion their version of Americanness should be the dominant one, whether it is that of the "Heartland" or of the "coastal cultural centers." In this binary logic, both sides actually make their hegemonic claims by basically *agreeing* on the same thing: New York City and Los Angeles should be normative because they are *not* normal; the rest of the country should be normative because it *is* normal.[8] Here, the close relation of flyover discourse to the rhetoric and ideology populism becomes apparent, whose "core claim" is that "only some of the people are really the people" (Müller 21), and both discourses intersect in their normative, generalizing claims.

The final point to make in this brief theoretical sketch relates to who exactly is making such claims, and how. This marks a difference between the flyover and hinterland concepts, but it also indicates that what is operative in one discourse may well be operative in the other. Harkins shows that the term *flyover country* "was largely introduced to the general public by midwestern news and media reporters and critics, always emphasizing its derisive intentions" (106), and so it describes a double othering. It is "a stereotype of other people's stereotypes" (Ben Zimmer qtd. in Bullard).[9] "Flyover country" imagines others imagining ourselves, and it constructs both us and them in the process (and the imagined and real poles of ourselves do not necessarily match but always exist in a complicated and shifting relation to each other). This process invents and cultivates meta-regions along with their hierarchy: describing one's own place as "flyover country" gives it more substance than the other place has, which is cast as vague, homogeneous, and indeed passed over in turn. It is the *elsewhere* of the definition above, but no more specific than that, and when it does take on a particular reference, it remains synecdochical and generalizing: "Los Angeles" is as much a simplification as "the Midwest" when it comes to glossing over and reducing the diversity of these places. The fiction of flyover country is also a fiction of the elites that allegedly refer to it as such, and both are interrelated fictions of sufficient homogeneity.

The term *hinterland* does not exhibit a similar duality, and it did not enter the language via a dual imagination the way that "flyover" did. Undoubtedly, it is often used in a straightforwardly derogatory way – for example in H. L. Mencken's 1922 essay "Totentanz", in which he imagines an independent New York City that is "licensed to prey upon the hinterland but unharassed by its Crô-Magnon prejudices and delusions" (90). Yet "hinterland" may still be used in parallel to "flyover" to describe oneself through the projected imagination of others. For example, Melissa Faliveno uses the term in her essay collection *Tomboyland* when she defines the Midwest, like O'Gieblyn, as a fuzzy space of uncertainty that allows for the blurring of categories instead of harboring a neglected but authentic American identity:

> When I think of the Midwest, a place whose boundaries and borders are contentious, a place given so many names—from the Great Plains to the Great Lakes states to the Upper Midwest—I think of a place that transcends boundaries, that defies definition, a body that holds within it a multitude of identities. When I think of my Midwest—the heartland, the hinterland, a place of farmland and factories, of forests and rivers and lakes—I think of it as Tomboyland. (52)

Faliveno uses the tropes of flyover and hinterland to speak of ambiguous gender identities and sexualities beyond heteronormativity, turning their neglect by others into a metaphor of operating under the radar of their hegemonic discourses, relatively free to explore alternatives to them: "Maybe it's the job of those of us who live in that liminal space, who live beyond what is already defined, to determine what might exist in the unnamed places between" (57). To be sure, Faliveno does not simply romanticize the Midwest as a liberal space here. Instead, she thoroughly complicates the tropes of "metronormativity" that reveal "the rural to be the devalued term in the urban/rural binary governing the spatialisation of modern U.S. sexual identities" (Halberstam 37).[10] She describes the Midwest as a place that allows her to "live the butchest version of myself" (65) while at the same time "[k]ids in my hometown used the word [queer] as a weapon, and a lot of people still do" (59). But in general, she uses an imagination of neglect in her struggle for recognition, and she uses the geographic semantics of flyover and hinterland to address cultural issues of normative identity.

These metaphors, then, are modes of talking about gender and class through a spatial imagination that makes complicated processes more accessible and communicable. At the same time, these modes risk over-simplification or distraction, and their meta-regional extrapolations may well gloss over fault lines instead of drawing attention to them. The imagination of cultural meta-regions that vie for national hegemony or recognition may serve as a way of pointing out structures of inequality, but it may also simply eradicate other relevant differences within these meta-regions. This is most evident with regard to issues of race and eth-nicity: the synecdochical contest between flyover country and the coastal centres is basically a fight between white people for cultural hegemony in the United States, only that its geographic framing suggests otherwise and allows the contestants to pretend that this is not about race. Texts such as Ayad Akhtar's mock-memoir novel *Homeland Elegies* deliberately reinsert ethnicity into this often whitewashed picture, as can be seen in his confrontation as a Pakistani Muslim American with a white state trooper in which he claims to have been born in Wisconsin (and not Staten Island) because it "felt like a stronger move in this negotiation around the impression forming inside him" (92). And yet, more often than not in American fiction, both flyover and hinterland remain ways of talking *around* race and ethnicity instead of talking *about* them, although both are appropriate metaphors of doing just that by way of an imagination of cultural hierarchy, dominance, neglect, and resistance.

The exception confirming this rule rather than invalidating it is the novel I will analyze in the following. *The Sellout* is so fundamentally built on spatial imagery that it can legitimately be described as a geographical allegory: like the flyover and hinterland metaphors, it speaks the language of geography to say something about culture. In particular, it satirizes an

America that would love to think of itself as post-racial, especially at the beginning of the Obama presidency, and it does so by spatializing what is being repressed rather than overcome in this fantasy. Race and ethnicity are at the heart of this satire, but class and other markers of identity and distinction certainly intersect with these.[11] It is a flyover fiction that situates the hinterland not at the margins, where it can be safely controlled and kept at an appropriate distance, but within one of the hegemonic places that allegedly exert strong normative power over American culture as a whole. Here, the hinterland is right *in* Los Angeles, and its marginalization is an *internal* process of distinction that is part of urbanity itself and not the result of its distinction from rurality. By creating this internal hinterland, *The Sellout* shows that hegemonic culture may happen and be defined elsewhere, but that its discursive normativity is not enough to fully determine reality, so that its power is revealed to be as fragile as it is oppressive.

The Sellout and its internal hinterland

The Sellout opens with the Black narrator-protagonist at the Supreme Court, hearing arguments in the case "*Me v. the United States*" (21),[12] as "Me" is both his surname and an apt symbol of his individual resistance. He is on trial for violating the Thirteenth and Fourteenth Amendment "by owning a slave" (*TS* 23) and reintroducing segregation in a "six-month campaign of localized apartheid" (*TS* 233). This outrageous proposition already indicates that *The Sellout* is not pulling any punches in confronting an American society that keeps trying to convince itself that it has moved beyond race, and which "preaches racial equality while dismissing whole communities of color as socially dead" (Wolfson 641).[13] As Me puts it: "It's illegal to yell 'Fire!' in a crowded theater, right? ... Well, I've whispered 'Racism' in a post-racial world" (*TS* 262). He is a "social pyromaniac" (*TS* 195), but he is only setting fire to what is smoldering already while everyone else pretends not to see the glow. The novel is about this transgression, about offending sensibilities that serve to maintain the status quo instead of changing anything: while America is "preening in the mirror", it manages to keep itself "from actually looking in the mirror and remembering where the bodies are buried" (*TS* 87), and Me is practically digging them up again.

This multifaceted denial is represented mainly in geographical terms in the novel, and this does relate to the flyover imaginary discussed above, only not in the straightforward sense one might expect. *The Sellout* neither stages a struggle for cultural recognition by a marginalized group nor depicts a struggle for cultural hegemony among parts that all claim to be more authentic and representative than any other.[14] Instead, the novel stages a deliberate, painful return of the repressed[15] as it focuses on the precarious but powerful hegemonic mechanisms that literally *make* history and culture: what is pulled back from the margins here is something nobody can reasonably romanticize into a cultural norm, yet at the same time its marginalization *prevents* an engagement with its factual, persistent normativity of the "Caucasian panopticon" (*TS* 209) in American society. In other words, by positing that race has been *passed*, American culture is *passing over* how relevant race remains. This not only perpetuates the "social death" of people of color in a racist society but actually doubles down on it, as its removal from discourse prevents its discursive engagement while its symbolic and material practices remain unchanged. Me's reinstitution of slavery (in a very limited, individual, and complicated way with regard to the character of Hominy Jenkins) and segregation is not an attempt to restore a system of oppression and make it the national cultural norm again. Instead, it is a symbolic reminder that the logic and structure of slavery and segregation still persevere in a culture that congratulates itself on having to progress beyond them. In doing so, as district judge Nguyen points out, Me is drawing attention to

> a fundamental flaw in how we as Americans claim we see equality. "I don't care if you're black, white, brown, yellow, red, green, or purple." We've all said it. Posited as proof of our nonprejudicial ways, but if you painted any one of us purple or green, we'd be mad as hell. And that's what he's doing. He's painting everybody over, painting this community purple and green, and seeing who still believes in equality. (*TS* 265–66)

While American culture at large is trying to move toward a discursive framework in which racial injustice and oppression may only be talked about in terms of their historical transcendence and not of their contemporary persistence, Me keeps it from achieving this questionable goal: "You know how when you play Chutes and Ladders and you're almost at the finish line, but you spin a six and land on that long, really curvy red slide that takes you from square sixty-seven all the way back to number twenty-four? … I'm that long red slide" (*TS* 17).

The Sellout comments on this conflict by establishing a crucial contrast with regard to moving on from the past and present into the future:

> Daddy never believed in closure. He said it was a false psychological concept. Something invented by therapists to assuage white Western guilt. In all his years of study and practice, he'd never heard a patient of color talk of needing "closure." They needed revenge. They needed distance. Forgiveness and a good lawyer maybe, but never closure. He said people mistake suicide, murder, lap band surgery, interracial

marriage, and overtipping for closure, when in reality what they've achieved is erasure. (*TS* 261)

The novel symbolically condenses this difference into a place as its plot revolves around what is explicitly described as "Dickens's erasure" (*TS* 59) and not its closure. Dickens is "a ghetto community on the southern outskirts of Los Angeles" (*TS* 27) that is part of the metropolitan area and at the same time rural. "A not-so-proud descendant of the Kentucky Mees, one of the first black families to settle in southwest Los Angeles" (*TS* 21), Me actually "grew up on a farm in the inner city" (*TS* 27) and continues to work the land there:

> Founded in 1868, Dickens, like most California towns except for Irvine, which was established as a breeding ground for stupid, fat, ugly, white Republicans and the chihuahuas and East Asian refugees who love them, started out as an agrarian community. The city's original charter stipulated that "Dickens shall remain free of Chinamen, Spanish of all shades, dialects, and hats, Frenchmen, redheads, city slickers, and unskilled Jews." However, the founders, in their somewhat limited wisdom, also provided that the five hundred acres bordering the canal be forever zoned for something referred to as "residential agriculture," and thus my neighborhood, a ten-square-block section of Dickens unofficially known as the Farms was born. (*TS* 27–28)

This hybrid place complicates the stereotypical binary of city and country, just as it complicates the neat binary of the flyover imagination that considers Los Angeles to be one homogeneous, privileged place with an immense cultural relevance for American national culture as a whole. Its hybridity also debunks Christopher Baker's suggestion that Me being "a farmer in the middle of one of America's largest urban cores ... symbolize[s] the idea of race in America, ... with the Black community feeling out of place or othered in a majority White country" (128–29), as such neat allegorical distinctions are disturbed rather than established here (and not least the existence of a "Black community," which I will return to later). Cameron Leader-Picone's more precise argument is a convincing one, though, and it relates to the flyover binary:

> The implicit contrast here between "farm" and "inner city" elucidates a cultural imaginary in which not only is the rural marked as white, but the exclusive right of whites to self-ownership is presumed. The inner city that Beatty invokes is the province of cultural stereotypes of black gangsterism and poverty, stereotypes that contrast with farm imagery used to construct the image of a white American heartland. (70)

Dickens symbolically challenges these various simplifications by drawing attention to the pars-pro-toto fictions that are at work in the imagination of urbanity[16] as much as in that of flyover meta-regions, as it is a part of Los Angeles that apparently has no bearing on its purported cultural relevance as a whole. The novel thus transposes the stereotypical flyover axis of Los Angeles, New York City, and everything in between onto L.A. itself as it carves out a disregarded place within a place that normally does the disregarding.

Thus this disregard becomes self-reflexive as a way of externalizing and ejecting something that cannot be managed internally, especially as "L.A. is a mind-numbingly racially segregated city" (*TS* 204) that some even call "the most racist city in the world" (*TS* 129). Me's attempt to reintroduce segregation to a Dickens school is stalled by his realization that there is nothing to reintroduce, really: "How do you racially segregate an already segregated school?" (*TS* 168). Yet the city cannot admit any of this to itself, and therefore it actively tries to diminish the relevance of Dickens to the point of diminishing Dickens itself right out of existence. In flyover terms, the rest of the city wants to move but Dickens is remaining still, not because it is stubbornly conservative but because it is simply passed by. Dickens once was "the most infamous ghetto in Los Angeles County" (*TS* 52), and the "statistics related to Dickens" always basically remain the same: "Everything that was always up—unemployment, poverty, lawlessness, infant mortality—was up. Everything that's always down— graduation rates, literacy, life expectancy—was even further down" (*TS* 94). Dickens is a blemish on a place that otherwise lays claim to (or is ascribed) normative cultural significance, and as such it is a blemish on America itself – not because it is rural among an urban setting, but because it is *racial* in a post-racial fantasy.

The town is directly opposed to "White America" in a schematic Me draws up (*TS* 99), but the racial contrast isn't made in terms of white and Black but in terms of white and non-white. This dichotomy corresponds to Me's assertion that, historically, "everyone in Dickens, regardless of race, was black" (*TS* 164), suggesting that this was how a white hegemonic gaze constructed race and that its normativity didn't care about any finer distinctions. It still may not care all that much more, but now the parameters of race have at least become slightly more complicated. For example, there are "middle-class black out-of-towners and academics" that keep coming to Dickens to theorize about "an indigent black community that, if they'd just taken their racial blinders off for one second, they'd realize was no longer black but predominantly Latino" (*TS* 93), and when Me puts up a flyer in search of his missing hometown, he describes it as "Mostly Black and Brown. Some Samoan" (*TS* 108). Thus, Dickens is not so much symbolic of Black America as of race in America, a geographic manifestation of differentiation instead of any particular difference that results from it.

As a manifestation of race itself, Dickens was a problem not just for the people who lived under its conditions but also for those who created them, yet instead of solving this problem, it was simply ignored, denied recognition, and erased:

> You won't find Dickens, California, on the map, because about five years after my father died, and a year after I graduated college, it, too, perished. There was no loud send-off. ... It was quietly removed like those towns that vanished from maps of the Soviet Union during the Cold War, atomic accident by atomic accident. But the city of Dickens's disappearance was no accident. It was part of a blatant conspiracy by the surrounding, increasingly affluent, two-car-garage communities to keep their property values up and blood pressures down .... One clear South Central morning, we awoke to find that the city hadn't been renamed but the signs that said WELCOME TO THE CITY OF DICKENS were gone. There was never an official announcement, an article in the paper, or a feature on the evening news. No one cared. (*TS* 57–58)

This erasure is symbolic and has material consequences: institutions are dismantled, public records are changed, signs are taken down, boundaries erased. If the decision to do so was even made by someone, that source has not found its way to Dickens. Because "[n]o one cared" enough to even comment on this erasure, Dickens simply disintegrated by being integrated into the surrounding places so they could maintain their values (in both senses of the term). Me argues that, "in America, 'integration' can be a cover-up" (*TS* 167), and this applies to this particular integration as well.

This discursive dismantling further supports the allegorical reading of Dickens as a geographic manifestation of something conceptual: Me asks, "What are cities really, besides signs and arbitrary boundaries?" (*TS* 87), and the same defining parameters apply to race as well. As a fundamentally unreal concept with no material, essential foundation, race comes about through signs and arbitrary boundaries, through discursive practices of imagination, demarcation, and definition, although its consequences are certainly real and result in oppression, violence, and death. Similarly, Dickens is created, erased, and reestablished due to this arbitrary quality of cities, and yet its continued existence suggests that discourse cannot shape material reality in a straightforward way. The novel dismisses the idealism of the representational argument that erasing race from culture results in a post-racial culture by showing how Dickens persists in its reality despite its eradication from the map. Just because something was discursively *created* doesn't mean that it can be overcome discursively; putting up signs and drawing boundaries has real effects, but these effects don't go away once you remove the signs and eradicate the boundaries.

The Sellout drives home this anti-idealist point by having the inhabitants remain even as the city has vanished. Dickens's symbolic erasure is at odds with the fact that people still call it their home, as much as they might despise it. Me states that it "hurt knowing that Dickens had been exiled to the netherworld of invisible L.A. communities" (*TS* 89), and so he embarks on a campaign to put it back on the map, literally and figuratively, by engaging in the same symbolic practices that erased Dickens earlier. He draws "a crooked outline of my hometown as best as I could remember it" on the map that otherwise shows merely "a nameless peach-colored section of gridiron streets bordered by freeways on each side" (*TS* 89). Then he first puts up homemade freeway signs that mark the exit to Dickens and then paints a boundary line around the vanished city in an effort that quickly turns from individual to communal: "Sometimes, after retiring for the day, I'd return the next morning, only to find that someone else had taken up where I'd left off. Extended my line with a line of their own, often in a different color" (*TS* 107). When his "intervention of *counter-mapping*" (Dal Checco 157)[17] is completed, the line *works*, which suggests the power of symbolic demarcation beyond a naïve idealism:

> Sometimes I'd chance across an elderly member of the community standing in the middle of the street, unable to cross the single white line. Puzzled looks on their faces from asking themselves why they felt so strongly about the Dickens side of the line as opposed to the other side. When there was just as much uncurbed dog shit over there as here. When the grass, what little of it there was, sure in the fuck wasn't any greener. When the niggers were just as trifling, but for some reason they felt like they belonged on this side. And why was that? When it was just a line. (*TS* 108–09)

The constructed nature of the line is evident to all, but this does not diminish its power of demarcation and definition. On the contrary, the line is so powerful *because* it is arbitrary and irrational. Me says he likes "the line's artifice" (*TS* 109), and given how "squiggly" (*TS* 107) it is, he means its craftedness rather than the quality of the craft.

Me also likes the line for "[t]he implication of solidarity and community it represented" (*TS* 109), but this does not suggest that it represents the self-assertion of a pre-existing group or its plea for recognition. The line *constitutes* the group much more than it circum-scribes it, which is highly relevant when it comes to the novel's notion of "Black community." Me makes a point in dismissing this as a fantasy that is no more than an awkward racial marker that suggests a coherence that does not exist per se, and at the same time he uses a single, unlikely exception to show that it is still possible – the donut store: "In 7.81 square miles of vaunted black community, the 850 square feet of Dum Dum Donuts was the only place in the 'community' where one could experience the Latin root of the word, where a citizen could revel in common togetherness" (*TS* 46). Yet this very local and very limited togetherness, at least for Me, never translates to a larger sense of iden-tity, and even his artificial line cannot (and should not) provide the community it creates with a coherence that is any deeper than its arbitrary construction would allow.

Me illustrates this most concisely when commenting on how he once witnessed a Black stand-up comedian ejecting a white couple from his show by telling them "'This shit ain't for you! Understand? Now get the fuck out! This is our thing!'" (*TS* 287): "I wish I'd stood up to the man and asked him a question: 'So what exactly is *our thing*?'" (*TS* 288). Here, negative differentiation does not result in positive identification: the comedian affirms Black identity through distinction from white identity, but *only* so, and he fails to invest it with any positive, self-sufficient qualities that would exist independently of such oppositions. This puts Me's own acts of demarcation in perspective: instead of affirming any given ethnic identity, he creates identities by creating distinctions in the first place, and he never has to define what their thing is as long as it's suggested that others have their own thing. A practicing deconstructionist, Me knows that value is created only in negative distinction but never in positive terms, and that both sides of any opposition crucially depend on each other. "[E]ven in these times of racial equality," people respond to "someone whiter than us, richer than us, blacker than us, Chineser than us, better than us, whatever than us" (*TS* 208) rather than whiteness, Blackness, whateverness, because these relative terms do not mean anything by themselves.

Thus, the reconstruction of Dickens is not simply that of a Black community that is lifted again from a white mainstream. Dickens is not restored as a positive model in any sense of the term at all. Instead, it arises as one of L.A.'s many "racism vortexes. Spots where visitors experience deep feelings of melancholy and ethnic worthlessness" (*TS* 129). The resurgence of Dickens is that of a thorn in the side of America that hasn't been pulled out or absorbed but, in a combination of Langston Hughes's phrase and Colson Whitehead's metaphor in *Apex Hides the Hurt*, "festers like a sore" underneath all the band-aids that have been put on it to

cover it up (426). This is not the neglect that results from cultural hierarchies; it is the neglect that results from a particular kind of cultural
supremacy whose latest strategy of maintaining the status quo is to pretend it has already passed beyond it, and that there was never a contest to
begin with.

Dickens is, ultimately, a place that *cannot* be passed over, though not
for lack of trying, as becomes evident when Jon McJones, "a black conservative who'd recently added the 'Mc' to his slave name" in a thinly
veiled attempt to promote "his latest book, *Mick, Please: The Black Irish
Journey from Ghetto to Gaelic*" (*TS* 215), is promptly reprimanded for his
denigration of Dickens by King Cuz:

> But I must take exception to your implication that Dickens is a city;
> when it's clearly a locale, nothing more than an American shantytown.
> A post-black, post-racial, post-soul flashback, if you will, to a time of
> romanticized black ignorance ...
>
> Hey, look, fool, save that post-soul, post-black bullshit for somebody
> who gives a fuck, 'cause all I know is that I'm pre-black. Dickens born
> and raised. Homo sapiens OG Crip from the god-damn primordial
> giddy-up, nigger. (*TS* 220)[18]

Dickens is the geographical manifestation of this rejection of the post-
racial narrative, its stubborn placeness a reminder that the mobility that is
at the heart of such a fantasy is a corrosive lie that actually works against
what it seeks: it cannot be passed by or flown over, just as one cannot
simply move on. Me makes exactly this point: "That's the problem with
history, we like to think it's a book—that we can turn the page and move
the fuck on. But history isn't the paper it's printed on. It's memory, and
memory is time, emotions, and song. History is the things that stay with
you" (*TS* 115).

By "brushing the dirt off an artifact that had never really been buried"
(*TS* 223), Me refuses to let America turn the page, and this is why
he so passionately opposes the post-racial endeavors of "the semifamous"
(*TS* 93) Black intellectual Foy Cheshire to rewrite American history:

> That's the difference between most oppressed peoples of the world and
> American blacks. They vow never to forget, and we want everything
> expunged from our record, sealed and filed away for eternity. We want
> someone like Foy Cheshire to present our case to the world with a set of
> instructions that the jury will disregard centuries of ridicule and
> stereotype and pretend the woebegone niggers in front of you are
> starting from scratch. (*TS* 98)

Cheshire struggles for racial equality through cultural revisionism and especially through rewriting American literature, for example in creating "the character of Tom Soarer [who] will galvanise a nation to whitewash that fence!" (*TS* 217), as if racism in the present could be overcome by pretending it had never existed historically. Cheshire is as subtle in his derivative fiction as he is in his real life: in the climactic scene of the novel, he literally whitewashes himself by emptying a bucket of paint over his head and putting a gun to it (*TS* 259), as if doubly eradicating his own Blackness were the logical conclusion of his post-racial revisionist logic.

Cheshire does not carry out his suicidal plan, and the novel moves elsewhere as Me confronts the Supreme Court, but he returns in the final scene that symbolically captures his post-racial fantasy and Me's opposition. Me finds Cheshire waving an American flag on "the day after the black dude was inaugurated," saying "that he felt like the country, the United States of America, had finally paid off its debts" (*TS* 289). The national symbolism is relevant here and provides another link to the flyover imagination: By symbolically turning race into a concrete place that doesn't matter to America any longer, Cheshire's post-racial discourse embraces the ultimate meta-regional fantasy of the nation, whose unity is such that there is not even an opposing meta-region to challenge its ideological hegemony – and thus Me can only disrupt this pretense to unity from within by uncovering its internal hinterland again.

Finally, though, the novel also transcends this national fantasy by placing Dickens in a global context. This is most evident in Me's hilarious attempt to find a sister city for Dickens once it is sufficiently established again, enlisting the services of an agency in the process. The whole scene is a comical parade of flyover stereotypes, of places that have become symbolic non-places that cannot or can barely sustain human lives, and it establishes a connection between marginalized places beyond the national context. The agent tells him not only that Dickens is only compatible with Ciudad Juarez, Chernobyl, and Kinshasa, but also that all three have rejected Dickens because they consider it too violent, too polluted, and not too poor but "too black" (*TS* 147). Remarkably, these transnational parallels also extend historically, as Me points out when Foy threatens him with a gun and he waits for the police to arrive:

The sirens were half a town away. Even when the county was flush with property tax revenue on overvalued homes, Dickens never received its fair share of civil services. And now, with the cutbacks and graft, the response time is measured in eons, the same switchboard operators who took the calls from the Holocaust, Rwanda, Wounded Knee, and Pompeii still at their posts. (*TS* 259)

As Hominy puts it, "no one gives a fuck about the hood until they give a fuck" (230), and this applies to many more contexts than the hood in question here. Dickens is part of a geography and history of places that have been and are passed over, of places and events that don't matter – or at least don't matter until they do. These and numerous other references leave no doubt that *The Sellout* is not merely concerned with race in America but genuinely "a post-racial world" (262), and that the specifics of neglect and oppression relate to a much larger context of inequality and injustice. It sets up one particular internal hinterland to show that there are plenty more, and it drags them from the background into the foreground to create a different map on the world in which it is not just the centres that get to define whatever may lie between or behind them.

Notes

1　Harkins' essay is the best critical assessment of the history and meaning of the concept.
2　See Neel for an example of this abstraction that intersects with US-American flyover country (without ever using that term). Neel analyses "the distinctly American landscape of crisis and class" while arguing that "the geographies detailed here are essentially international, since the crisis itself is a world crisis" (20). Neel's study usefully distinguishes between a "far" and a "near" hinterland: the former "is more traditionally 'rural,' though now the 'rural' is largely a space for disaster industries, government aid, and large-scale industrial extraction, production, and initial processing of primary products" (17–18); the latter "encompasses the foothills descending from the summit of the megacity. It is largely 'suburban' in character, though this is something of a misnomer given the term's connotation of middle-class white prosperity" (18). The "internal hinterland" I discuss here can be seen as a further symbolic extension of this distinction.
3　See Williams' classic essay "Culture is Ordinary" for more on this basic distinction, p. 3.
4　Dana Loesch's *Flyover Nation: You Can't Run a Country You've Never Been To* is a useful example in this regard because it is so transparent and blunt. With binary simplicity and in an act of construction that masks as description, Loesch pits "coastal snobs" (2) against "Flyover" with a capital F, "the real America" (7) that is "miles away from the freakish image coastal elites have concocted over Flyover" (4).
5　Steffen Mau's 2021 essay in *DER SPIEGEL* reaffirms this division while also questioning its usefulness.
6　See Kendzior.
7　Honneth's extensive exploration of recognition – in publications from *The Struggle for Recognition* (1994) to *Recognition: A Chapter in the History of European Ideas* (2018) – occurs mainly in philosophical, political, social, and moral terms, but this does not mean that he never acknowledged the cultural side of recognition at all; for example, his 2001 essay "Recognition or Redistribution?" does just that.

8 This normativity of the normal is famously captured in the famous Middletown study conducted by sociologists Robert and Helen Lynd in 1924 and 25. Using Muncie, Indiana as a model for the American normal, "Middletown reflects ideological notions of what constitutes 'averageness' or 'the typical' in both the United States and the Midwest" (Ochonicky 59).

9 See Bullard for a short overview of the history of this dual construction.

10 See Herring for an in-depth discussion of how this particular manifestation of simplistic rural/urban binaries is subverted.

11 Steven Delmagori discusses how the novel "wrestles with the dialectic of racism and class inequality in a neoliberal climate" (417), and he argues that, while "vigorously critiquing privilege itself, the novel also illuminates and critiques the limits to the concept of privilege" (419).

12 *The Sellout* will be cited as *TS* in subsequent references.

13 Roberta Wolfson's analysis of the novel in terms of this social death, and more generally with regard to its critique of the "necropolitics of black exceptionalism" (621), resonates further with the flyover themes of neglect, marginalization, dismissal, and denial of recognition established here.

14 In fact, Cameron Leader-Picone is right in claiming that "the ultimate targets of [Beatty's] satire [are] discourses of authenticity" (66), which is another reason why the novel lends itself to a reading in terms of the flyover imagination.

15 This phrase suggests that one might as well analyze the processes of marginalization and hegemony in psychoanalytic terms, but this would add only another, unnecessary figurative layer onto the geographic allegories that the novel actually employs. Furthermore, the novel itself satirizes this very discourse in the ambiguous figure of Me's father, "the esteemed African-American psychologist F. K. Me" (275), and Me adds that "Freudian hermeneutics doesn't apply to Dickens ... since everybody's fucking each other over" (73).

16 Julia Wiedemann convincingly reads Dickens in the context of silent suburbs that resonates with the concept of hinterland: "they have no history and they are not worth mentioning" (271). Along the same lines, she argues that "Dickens is not a place where history was made, but rather one where individual and collective memories merge" (261).

17 Monia Del Checco explores various facets of Me's "alternative cartography" (158) in her spatial reading of the novel.

18 See both Dal Checco and Leader-Picone for readings of the novel in relation to post-blackness.

Works Cited

Akhtar, Ayad. *Homeland Elegies*. Tinder Press, 2020.

Baker, Christopher. "You Are What You Eat: Connecting Food with Identity in Paul Beatty's *The Sellout*." *The Explicator*, vol. 77, no. 3–4, 2019, pp. 128–131, DOI: 10.1080/00144940.2019.1668341.

Beatty, Paul. *The Sellout*. 2015. Oneworld, 2017.

Bullard, Gabe. "The Surprising Origin of the Phrase 'Flyover Country.'" *National Geographic*, 14 March 2016, https://www.nationalgeographic.com/history/article/160314-flyover-country-origin-language-midwest

Chisholm, George. *Handbook of Commercial Geography*, 4th revised ed., Longmans, 1903.

Delmagori, Steven. "Super Deluxe Whiteness: Privilege Critique in Paul Beatty's *The Sellout*." *Symploke*, vol. 26, no. 1–2, 2018, pp. 417–425.

Faliveno, Melissa. *Tomboyland*. Topple Books, 2020.

Halberstam, Judith. *In a Queer Time and Place: Transgender Bodies, Subcultural Lives*. New York UP, 2005.

Harkins, Anthony. "The Midwest and the Evolution of 'Flyover Country.'" *Middle West Review*, vol. 3, no. 1, Fall 2016, pp. 97–121, DOI: 10.1353/mwr.2016.0016.

Herring, Scott. *Another Country: Queer Anti-Urbanism*. NYU Press, 2010.

Honneth, Axel. "Invisibility: On the Epistemology of 'Recognition.'" *Aristotelian Society Supplementary Volume*, vol. 75, no. 1, 1 July 2001, pp. 111–126, DOI: 10.1111/1467-8349.00081.

Honneth, Axel. *Recognition: A Chapter in the History of European Ideas*. Cambridge UP, 2020.

Honneth, Axel. *The Struggle for Recognition: The Moral Grammar of Social Conflicts*. Translated by Joel Anderson. The MIT Press, 1995.

Hughes, Langston. "Harlem." *The Collected Poems of Langston Hughes*. Eds. Arnold Rampersad and David Roessel, Vintage, 1994, p. 426.

Kendzior, Sarah. *The View from Flyover Country: Dispatches from the Forgotten America*. 2015. Flatiron Books, 2018.

Leader-Picone, Cameron. "Whispering Racism in a Postracial World: Slavery and Post-Blackness in Paul Beatty's *The Sellout*." *Slavery and the Post-Black Imagination*. Eds. Bertram D. Ashe, and Ilka Saal. U of Washington P, 2020, pp. 65–82.

Loesch, Dana. *Flyover Nation: You Can't Run a Country You've Never Been to*. Sentinel, 2016.

Mau, Steffen. "Warum sind gerade Ostdeutsche so krawallig?" *DER SPIEGEL*, 21 May 2021, https://www.spiegel.de/kultur/debattenkultur-warum-sind-gerade-ostdeutsche-so-krawallig-a-03ef7b88-0002-0001-0000-000177604486.

Mencken, H.L. "Totentanz." *Prejudices: Fourth, Fifth, and Sixth Series*. The Library of America, 2010, pp. 84–91.

Müller, Jan-Werner. *What is Populism?* 2016. Penguin, 2017.

Neel, Phil A. *Hinterland: America's New Landscape of Class and Conflict*. Reaktion Books, 2018.

O'Gieblyn, Meghan. "Dispatch from Flyover Country." *Interior States*, Penguin, 2018, pp. 3–18.

Ochonicky, Adam R. *The American Midwest in Film and Literature: Nostalgia, Violence, and Regionalism*. Indiana UP, 2020.

Unangst, Matthew. "Hinterland: The Political History of a Geographic Category from the Scramble for Africa to Afro-Asian Solidarity." *Journal of Global History*, 2021, pp. 1–19, DOI: 10.1017/S1740022821000401

Whitehead, Colson. *Apex Hides the Hurt*. Doubleday, 2006.

Wiedemann, Julia. "Re-Designing the Suburb as a Memorial of Racism." *Remembering Places: Perspectives from Scholarship and the* Arts. Eds. Richard Nate and Julia Wiedemann. Königshausen & Neumann, 2019, pp. 261–274.

Williams, Raymond. "Culture is Ordinary." 1958. *Raymond Williams on Culture & Society: Essential Writings*. Ed. Jim McGuigan. Sage Publications, 2014, pp. 1–18.

Williams, Raymond. *The City and the Country*. Oxford UP, 1983.

Wolfson, Roberta. "Race Leaders, Race Traitors, and the Necropolitics of Black Exceptionalism in Paul Beatty's Fiction." *American Literature*, vol. 91, no. 3, September 2019, pp. 619–647, DOI: 10.1215/00029831-7722152.

Index